1/7

4/17

P9-DNN-630

5 0 5 0 8 2 0 0 6 8 8 9 4 4

ADVANCE PRAISE FOR
BOSS BITCH

"Women are underrepresented among entrepreneurs. *Boss Bitch* is a great guide to help us close that gap."

—Daniel Lubetzky, CEO and founder of KIND Snacks

"*Boss Bitch* is a fun and engaging read to help build your brand and rock your career."

—Tony Hsieh, CEO of Zappos

"Whether you're wanting to branch out on your own start-up or just get ahead in your current job, Nicole knows just how to develop those skills to get you where you want to be. She's a perfect role model for young women learning to be their own boss (bitch)."

—Brit Morin, founder of Brit + Co.

"What I love about Nicole is that you don't need a dictionary to understand her advice. It's crystal clear, straight up, and spot-on."

—Alyssa Milano, founder of Touch by Alyssa Milano

"Nicole delivers expert business advice straight up, no chaser, in a tone that's as lively as it is likable."

—Neil Blumenthal and Dave Gilboa, founders of Warby Parker

"Nicole is the money expert with sensible advice to help you be the CEO of your own life."

—Fred DeLuca, founder of Subway

"Mandatory reading for every young professional woman who wants to take control of her financial destiny."

—Mindy Grossman, CEO of HSN

"Stressing over money can harm your overall health. Let Nicole be the doctor for your financial health, and you will feel better in more ways than you'd think."

—Dr. Oz

"Nicole's advice is a swift kick in the pants to the young, ambitious, upstart women out there who want control over their lives, debts, and careers."

—Wendy Williams

"Lapin's unfiltered, energetic advice speaks to anyone taking aim at their own career destiny."

—Mike Perlis, president and CEO of Forbes Media

"Nicole brings to life in a highly readable way the real pitfalls and solutions of financial life in a more complex world."

—Nigel Travis, CEO of Dunkin' Donuts

"I wish I'd had Nicole's book when I was starting my business. She makes business feel accessible but does it in a sassy, humorous way. It's a must-have for any budding entrepreneur."

—Kristi Yamaguchi, founder of tsu.ya

"Nicole Lapin is back, this time to show you how to be the baddest boss in town. *Boss Bitch* is the no-holds-barred guide to taking your career to the highest level."

—Aliza Licht, author of *Leave Your Mark*

BOSS BITCH

ALSO BY NICOLE LAPIN

*Rich Bitch: A Simple 12-Step Plan for Getting Your
Financial Life Together . . . Finally*

BOSS BITCH

A Simple 12-Step Plan
to Take Charge of Your Career

NICOLE LAPIN

CROWN
BUSINESS
NEW YORK

Library of Congress Cataloging-in-Publication Data
Names: Lapin, Nicole, author.
Title: Boss bitch : a simple 12-step plan to take charge of your career / Nicole Lapin.
Description: First edition. | New York : Crown Business, 2017.
Identifiers: LCCN 2016032418 | ISBN 9780451495860 (hardback)
Subjects: LCSH: Women—Vocational guidance. | Career development. | Women
executives. | Businesswomen. | Entrepreneurship. | Executive ability. | BISAC:
BUSINESS & ECONOMICS / Entrepreneurship. | SELF-HELP / Personal
Growth / Success.
Classification: LCC HF5382.6 .L37 2017 | DDC 658.4/09082—dc23 LC record
available at https://lccn.loc.gov/2016032418

ISBN 978-0-451-49586-0
Ebook ISBN 978-0-451-49586-0

PRINTED IN THE UNITED STATES OF AMERICA

Book design by Anna Thompson
Jacket design by Tal Goretsky
Jacket photographs by Winnie Au

10 9 8 7 6 5 4 3 2 1

First Edition

To my former self,

who would be proud of me now.

And for all my Boss Bitches—

the women who understand that

you don't have to be either to be both.

CONTENTS

SECTION 3: BEING THE BOSS OF YOUR OWN BUSINESS

My life didn't please me, so I created my life.

—COCO CHANEL

BOSS BITCH

CHOOSE YOUR OWN CAREER ADVENTURE

There's a Boss Bitch Inside All of Us

S o you wanna be a boss. You *feel* like a boss, right? You might even post boss quotes on social media. Like, you've always known you have that boss-lady thing in your blood, but now you're finally ready to do something about it?! Well, awesome. You've picked up the book that will help you do just that.

You don't need dozens or hundreds of employees to be a boss. Hell, you don't even need one. You just need to tap into your inner Boss Bitch. We all have one inside of us.

A Boss Bitch is the she-ro of her own story. She is the heroine who doesn't need saving because she has her own shit handled. I became a Boss Bitch by embracing being a "boss" in all aspects of the word: first as the boss of my own life and career, then as the boss at work, and ultimately as the boss of my own company. I'm a Boss Bitch because I made my life happen—and so can you.†

---

† You might notice that I tend to refer to people generally by "her" and "she" throughout the book. Don't get me wrong, I'd love for the dudes to read this, but with a title like *Boss Bitch*, I'm going to go ahead and assume that most of you readers out there are ladies. So while, of course, all the advice in this

Before we get started, I want to make one thing very clear: being a Boss Bitch is a good thing. In fact, it's a *great* thing. A Boss Bitch takes ownership of her life, knowing that she's the only one in charge of her future. She is confident in her power to create a successful life on her terms.

I've been called both a boss and a bitch (and variations of those words) throughout my career in a derogatory way. But I never understood how my ambitions deserved even the slightest insult. I mean, if killing it at work means I'm a bitch, then great, I'm a bitch and I'm owning it! If being on top of my business means I'm bossy, then great, I'll own that, too. Being a badass in your career is something that should be praised, not put down. So I'm taking back any dumb, offensive, or negative connotations those words have had in the past and, instead, using them in a positive way. From here on out, I'm going to call you my fellow Boss Bitches out of tribe solidarity and camaraderie. I wear it as a badge of honor, and by the time you finish reading this book, you will, too.

As you may remember from reading *Rich Bitch*, I'm super honest. I also swear . . . a lot. I'm here to tell you everything I've learned about business in the exact same tone as I'd use with any of my girlfriends. I'm not a fan of the fake holier-than-thou voice that some so-called experts take, so I'm not going to use that. I'm also not going to add any sweetener to this story. I'll tell you about all the times life gave me lemons. I'll show you how I squeezed the shit out of them and made some bomb lemonade. And then I'll teach you how I sold that lemonade for a juicy little profit.

Success in business is a hot topic. There are a ton of rah-rah books out there by very successful people who tell you how *they* did it. Well, I'm here to tell you how *you* can do it. Don't get me wrong, who *doesn't* love a good success story?! I'll share some, too, but only if they are relatable to your career. The stories I'm more interested in telling are the real-deal ones: the struggles and the ugly secrets that others might edit out. I don't edit *anything* out. Why? Because those hot-mess stories are a hell of a

---

book is not gender specific, I've opted to go the female personal pronoun route as the girls' girl I am and in honor of you, my fellow Boss Bitches.

lot more common than the ones of breakout success—and far more in-structive.

Consider me your cheerleader and this your playbook for the career game you'll *actually* play. I won big in my career not because I was lucky or special but because I defined what *winning* meant. And that's how you are going to win your career game. As a matter of fact, you are guaranteed to win, because you are going to decide what winning means to *you*.

From now on, you're going to decide *everything*, including how to read this book. It's broken down into twelve steps divided into three sections. You can tackle it like those "Choose Your Own Adventure" books you read as a kid. If you're itching to start a business, jump to **Section 3: Being the Boss of Your Own Business,** where you'll learn all the nuts and bolts to go from idea to thriving company: everything from how to set it up with the best structure, to raising money and growing your team, to selling that baby for a pretty profit. If you're cool working for someone else but want to be more of a rock star at your job, head over to **Section 2: Being the Boss at Work.** Or if you're unsure of the career path you want to take, start at the beginning with **Section 1: Being the Boss of You.**

You can read *Boss Bitch* however you want; it's *your* book. All I ask is that you go easy on yourself. You don't need to tackle it all today, and the steps that take you where you ultimately want to go aren't always linear. You might, for instance, have started your own business but are so caught up in the stress and chaos of running it that you lose yourself. That's okay; go back to Section 1 to remember why you started your own thing in the first place. Or maybe you run a successful business but have been flirt-ing with going back to working for someone else: head back to Section 2. There are plenty of women who start a business, then leave to run the business of their household, then go back to working for someone else later in life. Maybe you've already experienced several of these stages in some combination. There's no one-size-fits-all path for your career. And, I promise, it can and will often be messy. Once you *think* you have it all figured out, shit, as they say, happens.

But when it does (and it will), you'll be in control. It's time to take charge of your life and your career. It's time to be a Boss Bitch.

SECTION

1

BEING THE BOSS
OF YOU

OWNING THE BOSS MENTALITY

Be a Boss Anywhere You Are

I didn't create a multibillion-dollar company. I'm not the founder of some groundbreaking tech invention. I haven't been on the cover of any business magazines or in society pages. I consider myself a pretty ordinary girl who's just figured out how to do some pretty extraordinary stuff in my career, making more money on my own than I ever thought I would.

The truth is, I wasn't dealt the greatest hand in life. Quite the contrary. My father died of a drug overdose when I was 11, and my family was far from stable (but I'll save that for my memoir). There were days growing up when I didn't have a proper meal, much less a silver spoon, to put in my mouth. When I was starting out in my career, I didn't have fancy connections or a big financial safety net. I simply played my hand the best I could, beat the odds, and succeeded in ways that my childhood self would never have imagined.

Along the way I fell flat on my ass . . . a lot. That is, until I learned that the only difference between stumbling blocks and stepping-stones is how you use them. In the first step of "Being the Boss of You," I'll show you how to feel like a boss no matter where you are.

STOP STUMBLING AND START STEPPING

I started working pretty early, by traditional standards, with the goal of being a network news anchor. In my late teens (yes, teens), I bounced from Sioux Falls, South Dakota, to Lexington, Kentucky, hustling hard for any local news gig I could get.

At 18, I thought I was ready to be on air in a "big market." So I harassed a broadcasting company in Chicago that had a station in big(ish)-market Milwaukee until they would take a meeting with me. I walked in thinking I absolutely looked the part with my shoulder-padded Ann Taylor blazer that was way too big for me and hair teased to epic proportions. I didn't want anyone there to know how young I was, so I tried to dress older. I even developed some weird thing with my voice that I thought made me sound mature and more legit.

I'm sure the station chief secretly laughed at my ridiculous getup and affected voice. "Where is your accent from?" he asked. "Um, Los Angeles," I said. Then he told me I didn't get the Milwaukee job. I was devastated. So devastated, in fact, that I didn't even pick up on the fact that he wanted to offer me *another* job instead.

Because I didn't have the aforementioned financial safety net, I would have taken *any* TV job I could get, including the one he was offering me in . . . business news. Yes, he offered me a job as a business reporter on the floor of the stock exchange for a nationally syndicated morning show in lieu of the Milwaukee one. It was a much bigger deal, but it felt like a death sentence at the time. As the daughter of immigrants, I knew nothing about money except feeling like I never had enough of it, so talking about it freaked me out. It was a topic I hated but one I was determined (and needed) to learn ASAP.

I felt like a fake when I started my on-air job as one of the youngest journalists to ever report from the floor of a stock exchange. But the truth is, we *all* do a little "fake it till we make it." *No one* is ever truly ready for any big career move that comes their way. We are all terrified that we are frauds and that it's only a matter of time until someone finds us out. It was only once I realized that I knew more than I gave myself credit for that I could quiet the haters inside my head and take on this challenge.

CONFESSIONS OF A
BOSS BITCH

Whacking Off

Before I started working at the Chicago Mercantile Exchange, I'd never seen a trading floor. The energy there is unlike any other: a combination of a raging nightclub, a horse auction, and a Middle Eastern bazaar.

My job was to write scripts about the latest business happenings based on the wire reports that came out every morning. I read them from atop a crate perched over the roar of a live trading pit so that the camera would actually see my face (there was a height restriction on heels women were allowed to wear on the floor . . . seriously).

I was so concerned with following the news writing style I learned in journalism school and coming up with clever puns that the gist of the actual story was sometimes totally lost on me. Except I didn't even realize it until my boss called me out on it.

He was the master of making me laugh even while he was criticizing me—which happened a lot. He frequently called me into his office to watch my on-air tapes together so he could critique my work. He made fun of what he called my "robot arms" and mimicked my awkward anchor cadence. But nothing was as bad as the day he played me back one of my stories and said, "Lapin, what is that story about?"

It was a story about Gillette coming out with a new razor. So naturally, I replied: "It's about a new razor."

He then pointed me back to the tape where I was on air saying, "It's a new razor that is sharp enough to whack off the hairs closer to the skin than the previous version."

I looked at him quizzically. "What's the problem?" I was proud of myself that I had used a visual word like *whack* instead of something obvious like *shave* or *remove,* and I told him as much.

He started hysterically laughing.

"What?! I thought it was more of a visual image and good writing."

"Lapin, you're in business news now. You are talking to *guys.* Never say 'whack off' anything," he said.

Oh. My. God. I was mortified. And even now, recalling this story, I am cringing.

"Whether you just made more male fans or not because you tried to be cute and clever with your words, the point is that you *weren't* thinking," he said. "The reason we are doing the story is that Gillette is a massive publicly traded company. It is rumored that it will be acquired by the even-more-massive $100 billion (yes, BILLION) consumer products company Procter & Gamble (P&G).† New products move stocks, and this is a big one. *That's* why we are covering the story."

I was speechless. I didn't know whether to laugh or cry.

"C'mon, Lapin, I know you know this is an important story, you don't need to try so hard."

"You're right; you're the boss," I said, defeated and deflated.

"Wrong," he answered. "I'm not there day to day with you. I'm not holding your hand. I'm not looking at every story and walking you through it. Believe it or not, I have more to do than mock your robot arms and unfortunate use of words. I don't want to be the boss of your every move. You're the boss of that. I'm just here to tell you when you're moving in a crazy direction."

I nodded, still trying to process what he was saying, and got up to leave.

"I'm keeping the Gillette story for our year-end blooper reel, Lapin."

I forced a smile and went back to work.

I kept repeating to myself, "I'm the boss, I'm the boss." But I wasn't excited by that idea—I was terrified.

It took me a few years to come to terms with what being a boss— without *technically* being the boss—actually meant. I came to see the boss mentality as a state of mind more than a title or anything else: one we can have no matter where we work or who we work for, whether it's a massive corporation or a three-person start-up.

You might think I'm about to tell you that the boss mentality means having unshakable confidence and a go-getter attitude at work every day. I won't do that because, let's be serious, no one loves going to work *every single day*. There are shitty days, shitty people, and shitty circumstances

---

† Gillette was indeed acquired by P&G.

that come everyone's way. Anyone who tells you they love work every. single. day. is either a damn liar or totally delusional. It's easy to get caught up in work drama, which can put you in a funk and make you hate your job and/or life. But if you adopt the mentality that you are the boss of *you*, it's just as easy to put your drama blinders on and fall in love with the work life you create for *yourself*.

As corny as acronyms can be, I am a big fan of them (and alliteration, as you'll see) because they help me to visualize what words and ideas mean. For me, *BOSS* stands for *Bold*, *Obsessed*, *Self-Aware*, and *Strong*:

BOLD. An important quality of a boss is the ability to make a decision. Right or wrong, be decisive. As they say, the road of life is paved with flattened squirrels who couldn't make a decision. Boss Bitches drive the car; we don't get driven over.

OBSESSED. Be obsessed with finding what makes you happy. Figuring out what you don't want to do is just as important as figuring out what you do want to do. Until then, love the shit out of everything you have an interest in.

SELF-AWARE. One of the telltale signs of the ultimate boss is someone who has total self-awareness of her flaws. We all have them. Boss Bitches don't hide them; we own them. We don't pretend we are something we are not; we flaunt the imperfect originals we are.

STRONG. Real strength is knowing that there are times when you haven't been your strongest, and that's okay. Forgive your former self for not knowing what you know now. Be kind to yourself for not being perfect and accept the fact that you never will be.

I didn't realize it at the time, but confronting my fear of business head-on and discovering my inner boss were the best things I could have done for my career. It was only then that I could use my perceived "stumbling block" at the Chicago exchange as a "stepping-stone" to my dream job at CNN.

I was all of 21 years old when I started working at CNN. And I was all of 25 when my entire division there was shut down. That meant that I was let go, along with twenty or so of my incredibly talented colleagues. I remember mourning the "good thing" I had going on there, but as is attributed to OG Boss Bitch Marilyn Monroe, "Sometimes good things fall apart so better things can fall together."

It might sound like a high-class problem, but getting and losing my dream job so young forced me to come up with newer, bigger, and bolder dreams. And, just as unexpectedly, the ones for the rest of my career would revolve around the very subject I once feared: business.

I was all sorts of *verklempt* (that's Yiddish for "jumbled up with emotions") when my agent told me about an offer to host my own two-hour global finance show on CNBC, one of the major financial news networks, making a starting salary of $150,000, which was double what I was making before. But better than the money (not that that wasn't nice) was having the confidence to speak the language of money fluently—and the readiness to speak it to the world.

Needless to say, I had come a long way from the 18-year-old money-speak scaredy cat I used to be. Covering the greatest financial crisis of our time during 2008–09 turned my proficiency in business news into real passion.

What I was *not* passionate about, however, was the call time. My show at CNBC started at four a.m. Yes, I had to be on the air, bright-eyed, with fake lashes, bouncy barrel curls and all, not just coherent but well-read and researched at four in the freakin' morning. That meant I "got up" at midnight to get to the station and get ready physically, mentally, and intellectually.

At first I was like, "Okay, that's not *ideal*, but it's such a great opportunity because four a.m. Eastern time means nine a.m. in London and five p.m. in Singapore." That meant pre–trading time in the States, the open of trading in Europe, and the end of trading in Asia. That lineup was like catnip to the business lover I had become.

In the two weeks I had before starting on air, I had become a mad-woman, preparing pitches for all of the series I wanted to do. I felt like a boss going into the job not only ready to rock my show, which was a combination of anchoring major headlines and interviews with CEOs and politicians, but also poised to create entrepreneurial reports after it wrapped.

I'd never lie to you: the "I'm the boss" mentality didn't come out all day, every day, but I tried to channel it most days. I was a totally different woman from the terrified and confused one I was when I walked out of my actual boss's office after being chastised for saying "whack off" on national television. Reminding myself that I was the boss of myself helped me keep a positive attitude during the less-than-ideal hours.

Over the next year, I launched special series like *Made in America*, which followed companies that kept manufacturing in the United States even if it was more expensive, and *States of Pain*, which took me from the governor's mansion in Seattle to the statehouse in Maine as I tried to figure out why states were in so much financial trouble. I also took my show on the road to LA and DC, which had never been done before.

Needless to say, I was burning the candle at both ends. I got to the studio at one a.m. and wrapped around nine or ten a.m., then would literally jump on the first flight to whichever source I needed for the series, do my interview, and jump back on a plane to make my call time back at the network later that night. There were times when I didn't sleep for days. The travel and my perpetual zombielike state took a massive toll on my body. But I didn't complain. I really wouldn't have had it any other way. The stories I came up with and the content I created made all the wear and tear worth it. It made the job my own.

I had done my best to embrace the idea of "being my own boss" even though I was not, in any official sense, the boss—and I was loving it. Until I wasn't. As happens frequently at most companies, the actual boss who hired me was replaced. I don't know if he left or was fired, but it didn't matter; he, my champion in the building, was no longer there. And, as also happens frequently at most companies, when a new boss comes in, they like to bring on "their people" and put their stamp on the place.

Still, I didn't think I was actually on the chopping block; after all, I had found ways to be innovative on a show for which that was generally considered impossible due to the fact that most guests didn't get excited about appearing on early, early, early morning television. I booked guests, broke news, and wrote stories that often became the most popular stories online that day. (One was, no joke, "The Business of Sex Toys." Yep, there's a business of *everything*, including *that*.) I knew my worth and I loved my job and the ownership I felt over it.

CONFESSIONS OF A
BOSS BITCH

Who's the Boss?

I was driving back to the airport in my jalopy rental car after covering a story in California when I got a meeting invitation from my boss saying he wanted to meet the next morning in his office after my show and that an HR representative would be there, too. If you've never had a meeting with human resources in attendance well . . . it usually means you're in trouble.

When my show wrapped the next day, I added a little extra concealer under my tired eyes and walked up to my boss's office. I was calm, almost numb, when I walked in to find him and the HR rep sitting in the couch area looking very serious.

"Hi, Nicole, thanks for coming in," said the HR rep, as if reading a prewritten and legally approved script (which she probably was).

"You're welcome. Just had a great show," I said, about to blabber all about it—but I stopped, because I knew they weren't having it.

"Nicole," my boss said slowly and sternly. "I had HR join us because I want to put you on notice. We have drafted this up in writing, so please take a look at it now and take it home with you."

On cue, the HR lady handed me a manila envelope with the little red tie thing on the closure. I opened it in silence and awkwardly attempted to read it while they watched.

I asked: "So, what does this mean?"

"It means I don't want you traveling anymore. I don't want you doing any series. As your boss, I want you to focus on the job you were brought in to do. I want you to sit there," he said, pointing to my set, "and read the news of the day. And that's it."

I gulped, trying to swallow the tingle in my throat that's usually the precursor to crying. "So, no stories at all? What about—"

"No." He shot me down on the spot. "You're not the boss here." It was clear that I had two choices: do the job he wanted or not do it at all.

I flashed back to meeting my amazing boss and mentor back in Chicago almost ten years before, and I saw his encouraging face saying, "Lapin, you're the boss of you." And perhaps too quickly, but with all of my heart, I turned to my new boss and said, "I can't do that."

There was silence. I'm sure it wasn't what they were expecting to hear. They were probably expecting a scared 27-year-old, grateful for her six-figure salary, to say, "Yes, of course, whatever you say." And maybe the 18-year-old me would have said that, but not the new me, not now.

"I quit." I got up and walked out. All I could think was, "*I'm* the boss, *I'm* the boss." And here's the thing, I wasn't at all terrified about the idea this time—I was excited as hell.

Once my dream jobs in television became realities, I went job hunting once again. This time, and even *more* unexpectedly, I decided that instead of trying to get hired, I would . . . hire *myself.* There was a time I never would have imagined that I would be involved in the business world in *any* way—not covering it, much less starting one of my own.

But, building a career is like folding a fitted sheet: no one knows how to do it and everyone wants a hack. There are weird wrinkles and unexpected challenges with *every* career. The best way to smooth them out is to create a life that makes you want to jump out of bed in the morning. So, let's carpe the fucking diem.

BOTTOM LINE†

Boss Bitch isn't meant to be a textbook. Still, a little review never hurts, and so at the end of each step, I'm going to debunk some of the business advice you may have gotten elsewhere and give you a chance to rethink conventional wisdom—and begin to think for yourself, as a Boss Bitch does.

> **Conventional Wisdom:** A boss is the CEO or the president or the head of your department.
>
> **The Real Deal:** Well, yes, technically. But being a boss is also a state of mind. It doesn't matter where you work, if you work for someone else, or you don't work at all. A boss mentality is all about how you feel and carry yourself.
>
> **Conventional Wisdom:** Work is work. Even if you like your job, more often than not it's going to suck. So suck it up.
>
> **The Real Deal:** Get this into your head now: no job is perfect. But I promise you'll have fewer sucky days if you embrace your inner boss, which means taking charge of your job, your career, and your life.
>
> **Conventional Wisdom:** A career is built in a straight line, where you work your way from an entry-level position up the ladder.
>
> **The Real Deal:** This is not your mama's career trajectory. Many of us will go from working for other people to working for ourselves and every combination in between. A career well had is one that feels more like a rope swing than a ladder, allowing you to move from point to point and enjoy the thrill of your own ride.

---

† Oh, and BTW, use the dictionary at the end of the book as a cheat sheet for business terms you might think you know but don't, or just don't know at all. (You'll see them noted with an * in the text.) FYI: the term *bottom line* comes from the business world; it means how much you or a company are making when all is said and done. There you go! You've already got one business term in your Boss Bitch bank.

BE THE CEO OF YOU
Run Your Life Like a Business

D o you find yourself thinking, "Ahhh! I have so much to do and so little time"? We can all feel like we are just running, running, running—from errands to work to family and friend obligations. But you have a choice: you can either let the day run you or you run the day. And Boss Bitches run *everything*.

CEOs* of companies know that great things take time. They also know that it's not about having or finding time, it's about *making* time. In Step 2 of "Being the Boss of You," I'll tell you how to make the most of your time by running your life like a business as the CEO of you.

YOUR TIME IS MONEY

Yes, it's cliché to say that "time is money," but sometimes clichés exist because they are true. It's also true that wasted time is worse than wasted money. You can get more money; you can't get more time. It's free, but it's priceless. And even though it's what we want the most, it's what many people waste the most of. Except us. Boss Bitches don't waste any of either (time or money) and have control of both.

BUYING TIME

Most business-minded people rank time as their number one most valuable asset: yes, ahead of their computer, their company's website, and even their physical office. Studies have shown that having just one extra hour in a workday was worth $500 to most people, with some placing that number even higher. So what's your time worth to you? If minutes are money, here are a few ways you can spend your most valuable asset wisely:

Get an assistant. Let's be honest: we all want one. Back in the day when I couldn't afford one, I made one up: seriously, I created an e-mail address—"assistant@nicolelapin.com"—and I used it to coordinate meetings and respond to press queries, thereby giving the perception that I was a bigger deal than I actually was. I have no shame in admitting that, because the truth is that a lot of us do wild things to "fake it till we make it."

Cut the e-mail addiction. Remember, connectivity and multitasking don't always equate to higher productivity. Resist the temptation to be hyper–plugged in; instead, schedule specific times throughout the day to check e-mail. I actually like to wait a good hour at the beginning of the workday before responding to any e-mails. Instead, I start my day with a handwritten list of what I want to achieve (along with a strong cup of coffee . . . or two). Only after the list is made and the coffee is consumed do I check my e-mail, and then I take a break from e-mail again until lunchtime. I find this helps me focus on the task at hand instead of getting sucked down an online K-hole (we've all been there . . . it's like the online equivalent of going into Target for one box of tissues and then emerging hours later with a full cart). Similarly, I keep my outgoing e-mails to a minimum by keeping a Google Doc open for each of my employees so I can jot down notes and reminders throughout the day. Then I send them the whole shebang at the end of the day as a nice, organized list. I know my employees love to hear from me (duh!), but let's be honest, it's not efficient for anyone for me to be poking them with one-off e-mails all day long. So unless it's urgent, I add it to their master list and then deliver it all at once so we can *all* remain head down and focused throughout the day.

Embrace your social addiction, responsibly. Many money experts will tell you to cut your Facebook, Twitter, and Instagram habit to get more done during the day. Well, I think that's crap. I regularly find story ideas, project inspiration, and even potential partnerships by exploring my social media feeds. Used correctly, social media can be a huge asset to the business of you. But just like your e-mail, schedule some time each day to update and scan your feeds. Pick a time when you are typically lower energy; for example, I like to go through my social media from two to three p.m. each day, when I tend to be a little sleepy and less focused. My social media time provides a nice mental break so I can power through the rest of the day.

Schedule EVERYTHING. My production company cofounder has a bum knee from running marathons and often needs to go to physical therapy. During those times, she has "personal" blocked out on her calendar so that no one can schedule meetings or calls with her during that time (BTW, I'll talk about gratuitous meetings in Section 3). So if you have personal stuff you need to take care of during the workday, schedule it. I trust her enough not to use that time to go shopping or fuck around, plus I need my people healthy, happy, and firing on all cylinders.

DON'T WASTE TIME BEING A DUMMY

It's not enough to protect your time from other people trying to claim it; you also have to save yourself from your *own* time suck. Yes—the curse of wasting your own damn time. Sometimes, it's an honest mistake: failing to schedule your day efficiently or setting a needless meeting with someone that really could have been a quick phone call. But other times, it's being just plain *dumb*—and that's on you, sister.

In some cases, *investing* a little time can actually help you *save* time.

Think of all of the hours of productivity you've flushed down the pooper over the years by trying to smile and nod your way through a project you knew nothing about, instead of just getting all of the information up front. This smiling-and-nodding syndrome—when you have no idea what's being said but pretend you do—is not just bad from a learning standpoint, but from an efficiency standpoint, as well. Don't get sucked too far into a project or even a conversation (I'll share a cringeworthy one with you later) without asking the pertinent questions about anything you don't already know.

CONFESSIONS OF A
BOSS BITCH

Stop Asking Me If I Have to Pee

"You ready, Lapin?" the guys from the crew yelled my way.

My face was pressed up to my computer monitor as I scrambled to do some last-minute research on the founders of a hot start-up I was about to interview. "Yeah, coming," I said as I grabbed my notes, the company's financial documents, and the diaper bag I always carried, which was full of my "you never know what's going to happen today" stuff (a poncho, snacks, makeup, etc.).

"Do you have to pee, NL?" my producer asked from across the room.

I thought he was just being funny, since I pack like I'm going on a long road trip every time I leave the newsroom.

"Har har, I'm cool," I said.

When we walked into the start-up offices, the PR woman introduced herself to me. We made small talk as I was getting mic'ed up before going into the interview.

Then she said, "You got to pee, NL, right?"

Now this was weird. Yes, the folks at work call me "Lapin" or "NL" all the time, but I'd never met this lady before. "She's getting pretty chummy," I thought. I mean, it *was* a little weird, but whatever.

"I'm all set, thanks," I said as I walked into the room set up for the interview with the founders.

I kicked the interview off by asking them about how they met and when they came up with the idea for the company. Then, I went into the hard stuff: "The company is experiencing heavy losses right now despite its popularity; is that going to turn around any time soon?"

"As a start-up, we have initial costs in the investment of the brand and company," one of the founders said.

"Yes, Nicole, those investments left us with losses at this stage of the game but, as you see from our pee, NL, we are already profitable, which is unusual for a company of our size," the other founder said.

"Wait a minute," I thought. These guys were definitely not asking if I had to pee. *Think, Lapin, think . . . PNL? What the F does that stand for?*

I didn't straight-up ask what it meant, but rather: "How do you interpret the 'PNL'?"

"Well, the profits are on the rise and the losses we hope will be reduced significantly in the next year," one of the guys responded.

And suddenly it dawned on me. "Ohhhh . . . ," I thought, "*PNL* stands for *Profits 'n Losses* (like Kibbles 'n Bits)." No one was asking me if I had to pee. No one was actually calling me "NL." Everyone was just talking about the profit and loss* statement: the "P&L" of the company. While I *thought* I'd done all my homework in preparing for the interview, clearly I'd missed something.

Face-palm. Lesson learned. When out in the field—whether as a reporter or wherever your business takes you—you can never be *too* prepared. And if you're not, avoid the storm as soon as you feel the first drop (sorry, I had to).

As I learned (the hard way), sometimes being prepared is as easy as knowing the lingo. So turn to the dictionary at the back of the book (which you don't need a dictionary to understand) for some commonly misinterpreted business words and phrases to help you avoid wasting time and looking like a dummy, like I did.

BACK TO SCHOOL AGAIN?!

Urghhh . . . you're in a work lull. A rut. And you think the best way to get out of said rut is to go back to school? Wrong. Deciding to go back to school is not the right decision if it stems from a place of avoidance, as in avoiding any life and career problems you're having. Of all of the business decisions you'll have to make in your life as the CEO of you, the one about whether or not to invest in going back to school is one of the biggies. That's because it can be one of the biggest time sucks and money drains.

"But, Lapin, I *need* an advanced degree to get ahead," you're thinking. Yes, it might be tempting if you are going through a pause in your career to go back to school, but do you *need* it? Maybe . . . but likely not. Really ask yourself what career benefits you'll get out of it and if those are worth the time and money.

I'm a numbers girl, so let's crunch a few. It's been said that by getting an advanced degree, you can make $800K more over your lifetime versus a counterpart who doesn't have your wicked graduate-degree brain. With the average cost of your extra schooling at around $100K, the $800K return sounds tempting and maybe even too good to be true. That's because it is.

If you are interested in this additional schooling purely from a moneymaking perspective (yes, yes, I know you are meeting fabulous people and reading fabulous books on a grassy knoll), then I have an even better option for you. Let's say, instead of going back to school, you take that $100K and invest it over the next fifty years at 5% (which isn't even an aggressive assumption; in the investment world, that'll make you 10% over time). You will end up with around $1,150,000. That's a full $350K *more* than you would be making with that fancy-ass degree. And let's be honest, that $800K figure is pretty optimistic in our post-recession economy, where there is much less of a job premium for people who have their MS versus their BS. And those little letters basically sum up how I feel about the "it's an investment" argument for grad school . . . it's BS.

More important than the money you will spend is the time it takes to earn a degree. A year or more of your life. Is *that* worth it? Depending on what you want to study and where you want to go with that degree, the answer could be yes (for example, getting your masters in engineering in today's tech world is a pretty solid investment, especially as a woman). And, sure, specific industries require advanced degrees: it's pretty difficult to sit for the bar exam and become a lawyer without going to law school, and you're probably not going to get a job as a surgeon without a medical degree (at least I hope not). All I'm asking is that before you pony up the time and tons of paper for, well, another piece of paper, make sure you can really justify the debt monkey you are putting on your back. If you can, then great. But really, really try to prove it to yourself—not just with anecdotes, but with numbers.

Boss Bitches don't need a classroom to get an education. In fact, investing in yourself in alternative ways might just provide better real-world learning than you would ever get at grad school, anyway. I'll dig into specific tips for this when I talk about networking in the next section, but if you want to meet smart people who could help you in your career, you have tons of other options before spending major time and money on a fancy degree.

Get the degree of life, instead. That's what employers really care about. As an employer myself, I can say that what I look for in the job candidates I meet is experience, not the letters after their name. I don't care if you got your education at an Ivy League school or instead by busting your ass as a gopher for someone cool. In fact, I prefer the scrappy nature of the latter myself.

My father's favorite quote on this subject was one from Mark Twain: "Don't let your schooling interfere with your education." One of mine is from the movie *Good Will Hunting*: "You dropped one hundred and fifty grand on a fuckin' education you coulda got for a dollar fifty in late charges at the public library." I say: moxie and street smarts are the most killer MS combination out there.

THE MOST IMPORTANT CLOCK TO MANAGE: YOUR BIOLOGICAL ONE

Breaking news: you picked up the only book that talks about planning your business and your family situation. It's crazy to me that these two things are not discussed together more often, because nothing affects how you spend your time and thus your career more than your decision to have (or not have) a family.

Think of it this way: your twenties and thirties are your peak earning years, the time when you hit your stride professionally and start dominating the business of you. But this is also the time for making major moves in your personal life, and with that comes a ton of decisions that, for women in particular, *will* have a major impact on our careers. Decisions like: Whether or not to get married. Who to marry. Whether or not to have kids. When? How many kids? And where does work fit in?

No matter how much we think we can "do it all" or how much support we have from a partner or maybe a nanny, having kids drains us of the time, energy, and focus that we could otherwise be putting toward our careers. This isn't to say there is anything wrong with slowing down or taking time off to grow your family. If that is what you want, absolutely, get it, girl! But it *is* to say that we should look at that decision through the same lens with which we'd look at any other professional decision: the one where *we* are the boss of ourselves, and no one, I mean no one, else gets to decide our destiny or our future.

I know that's not a very romantic way of looking at it, but it's true and not something to be precious or anything but super realistic about. Rather, it's something that's never too early to be thinking about and planning for.

CONFESSIONS OF A
BOSS BITCH

Freezing My Clock

From my late teens to my late twenties, I had no life besides work. I was a work addict for a solid decade. I had nothing on my mind besides working and then working some more. And then, when I was 27, I met a boy—and it got serious. Fast. We moved in together after just a few months.

We were inseparable right away. We integrated our lives quickly, and it felt like "this is it, this is my husband." We never really talked about marriage and kids, I just felt those goals were mutual and understood. Then, about a year in, I realized they might not be. We were at a party and his friend commented that my guy wasn't ready to get remarried and have more kids (he already had a daughter from his first marriage). Instead of dutifully correcting his friend, as I expected him to, my boyfriend nodded in total male sympatico. Wait, what?! I felt like I had the wind knocked out of me. I was shocked and sad. When I brought up the subject later that night, he avoided a real conversation—and kept that up for the next three years.

I went through a phase of saying, "Well, I don't even want to get married or have kids anyway, so there." Of course, it wasn't true, but I still tried to convince myself. It was a defense mechanism that worked well enough for about two years. And then . . . I turned 30, and I had a panic attack. I couldn't suppress my intense urge to have a family of my own anymore.

I became baby crazy. All I could think about was babies, babies, babies, and every time I saw a woman with a stroller on the street my heart sank with longing. I went from trying to believe I didn't want any kids because my partner was noncommittal to wanting four or five. The more he didn't want to talk about my desires for a family or commit to it, the worse I felt. I was so mad at him.

I wasn't wrong for wanting what I did. But I *was* wrong about who I was mad at. I shouldn't have been mad at him. I should have been mad at myself. I had waited for my guy to decide my future. I was so consumed with being a Boss Bitch at work and taking control of my career that I had totally neglected to apply that Boss Bitch mentality to my relationship and to the major life choices that could define my happiness.

After four years of no ring and no baby from my relationship, I got to a point that taking my chances at being a mom someday was no longer an option. So I decided to quit being frustrated by waiting to see what *he* wanted to do, and I finally took control of *my* life and my reproductive future with the same determination with which I've taken control of my career.

I did my homework. I weighed my options. And I decided to freeze my eggs. I felt time slipping away, and my biological clock ticking, so I took matters into my own hands and stopped the clock. Being a Boss Bitch at work and being a mom— someday—didn't have to be an either/or proposition; I could have both, and *I* was in control of making that happen.

It's taken me a while to realize that taking control of my body *is* taking control of my life and my career. As women, our bodies do a lot of awesome things. One of the most awesome, of course, is having kids. And while starting a family might involve another decision maker, the main decision maker is always *you*. Your life is a dictatorship, not a democracy.

Of course, the decision I made won't be for everyone. It's a difficult one not only emotionally and physically but financially. But it was an investment in me.

Whatever you personally choose to do, don't be in denial about your desires. Embrace them, express them, and plan for them. Thanks to today's amazing advances in modern medicine, we don't have to let anyone—not even nature—determine our destiny. And while you personally may not want to or need to take the steps I did to ensure that, just knowing we have those options is as empowering as fuck.

I'm not sure if I will have the family I always imagined for myself. Whatever it ends up looking like, I know now that it won't be a fairy tale in the traditional sense. Take a classic fairy tale like "Cinderella." As a kid, I always saw Cinderella as some helpless girl who was saved by a man. But now, as an adult, I see her not as a girl who asked for a prince, but as a girl who asked for a party dress and a night out. My "fairy tale" looks more like that now; I rethought those classic stories and while my dreams of having a family haven't yet come true, they are realistic. Sure, there is still a prince, but I'm not the princess who needs saving. I'm the queen who's got this shit handled.

My story is still very much being written and edited in real time, as all of our stories are. The location and scenery will undoubtedly change over time. We might move from the workplace to the home to the home office to the corner office—and maybe back again—throughout our lives. And while you, yourself, will no doubt change, too, through it all you are the constant. You are the she-ro, the CEO of your life, and can never be demoted, terminated, or stripped of that role.†

---

† Download my free ebook *The Boss Bitch Guide to F-Words: Family, Fertility, and Finance* at bossbitchbook.com.

FYI

CELEB MOMMIES—THEY'RE JUST LIKE US!

In today's new normal, there are multiple ways to balance being a mommy with being a Boss Bitch. From "mom-preneurship" to career breaks, more and more women are doing the kid thing on their own schedule—while still bringing their A-game to their careers. And few women are as skilled at balancing the mommy role with the A-list role as these ladies:

Kristi Yamaguchi. The Olympic figure-skating champion hung up her skates for full-time motherhood, then launched her own lifestyle brand, Tsu.ya, for other stylish mothers on the go.

Jessica Alba. The actress started her company, Honest, when she faced a lack of eco-friendly products for her newborn daughter. That initiative turned her mommy project into a billion dollar company.

Reese Witherspoon. This powerhouse started acting when she was 15; got married (twice) and had three kids; then launched her own Southern-charm-inspired clothing brand, Draper James.

I don't have a tattoo (yet), but if I got one it would say, "There will be time." It's a line from a T. S. Eliot poem (yes, I'm a nerd, but you already knew that). I tell you about the tattoo because it's the saying that has the most meaning to me (so much so that I would write it on my body for the rest of, well, time). To me, it means that there will be time for everything I want to do in life, whether it's starting a business or starting a family or both.

Yes, we are always reminded that time flies. But guess what? You're the pilot, so let's fly, bitch.

BOTTOM LINE

Conventional Wisdom: You need to work your ass off to be successful.

The Real Deal: Well, yes, but remember the four-hour-workweek idea that was all the rage? It was all the rage because there is a lot of truth to it. Think about how much time you putz around on your computer without actually getting anything done. So work your ass off, just do it with blinders on to all the other online traps that take you down digital roads from which you don't return for mindless hours, and you'll be amazed how little time it actually takes to be successful.

Conventional Wisdom: You can't really plan for a family, because you have to let nature and love take their course.

The Real Deal: No, you don't want to be that girl who sticks to a rigid timeline for getting married and having kids. But you should be able to articulate what you want; otherwise you'll have a tougher time making those dreams a reality. Do you want to get married? Do you want to have kids? If so, how many? And when-ish? The answers to those questions will have a big, if not the biggest, effect on your career. Reserve the right to change your mind but answer the questions for yourself. Part of running your life like a business is being the CEO of your family. But before you do, you have to figure out what that looks like.

Conventional Wisdom: The secret to "having it all" is balancing a family and a career.

The Real Deal: Bullshit. The secret to having it all is realizing that you already do.

BEING THE BOSS AT WORK

STEP

THINK LIKE A BOSS

How to Be Entrepreneurial Within an Existing Company

I worked for major companies for most of my young adult life. They were big and mighty, like CNN and Bloomberg, and I was happily surprised every day when I walked into the building to find that my badge *actually* worked.

The CNN Center felt like Disneyland to me, and not just because the public could actually take tours—that they paid for!—to come watch us work (no joke), but because I was in *my* happiest place on earth. I could walk from one of the many CNN newsrooms, like Headline News or CNN International, to another in a matter of minutes. Bloomberg had the same kind of awe-inspiring feel. The headquarters in midtown Manhattan look like the swaggered love child of Google and Goldman Sachs. I was beyond lucky, and I knew it. But I also knew I wasn't going to work at those companies forever, even as I was having the time of my life. I set my Boss Bitch sights on playing career chess, strategizing not just the next move but a few moves ahead.

In Step 1 of "Being the Boss at Work," I'll teach you how to get the most out of working for a company by being entrepreneurial and creating your own brand within theirs. Doing this will require chess-like strategy. In the same way you wouldn't expose your queen to take a pawn, creating your personal brand shouldn't come at the expense of your job. There is a way to satiate your boss appetite without biting the hand that feeds you. Check. Mate. Let's play.

YOU GOT YOUR BACK

Maybe you have a great job but already know that someday you want to go off on your own. Or maybe you're planning to take time off to be a mom soon. Or maybe you want to work at the same company forever. All of those feelings are cool and perfectly valid—because they are *yours*.

As you've gotten to know me, you've probably learned that I like to crack the planning whip, but with the caveat that plans change all the time. The same general idea applies here. You might think you want to work forever for the company you're at now. But let me ask you: What idea have you *ever* had that has lasted forever? A guy you just *knew* was for keeps only to get over him a few months later? That perfect apartment that you were *never* going to leave but grew out of in a few years? Need I continue with more examples of this? Didn't think so. We've all had the experience of being *so* sure of something that is a distant memory and maybe even laughable now.

We change our minds. Circumstances change. The economy tanks; an industry hits the skids. Change just happens, and I want you to be ready when it does. Your work life *might* play out exactly as you hope, but more likely than not, it won't. That's why you need to have your own back no matter what.

THINKING OUTSIDE THE CUBICLE

I get it: it's easy to get into a routine, to go on autopilot at your job. Some days you're just not interested in doing much more than what is required of you. So you feed the beast, grease the machine. You get it done—and at the end of the workday, you can't get outta there fast enough.

There are going to be those days regardless of whether you work at a goliath of a company, own a small business, or work from home. It can be something frustrating at work itself, or it's some drama elsewhere that's bringing you down and not allowing you to take your A-game to work. Whatever it is, it happens to all of us. As I told you in the first section, my goal for myself and the one I want for you is to keep those days to a minimum, and that's where being the boss of you comes in.

ARE YOU A DUCK OR AN EAGLE?

One of my favorite quotes is from a teenage poet: "There is a freedom waiting for you, on the breezes of the sky,/And you ask, 'What if I fail?' Oh, but, my darling, what if you fly?"

Maybe I'm drawn to bird analogies because I always aim to fly even if I fail. I visualize myself as a bird, but not just any old bird. I like to think I'm a flamingo rather than a pigeon. An eagle* instead of a duck.*

The duck-vs.-eagle idea is not mine. It's actually a pretty popular leadership concept. The gist of the philosophy is that ducks are people who complain about how things are but do nothing to change their situation "because that's how we've always done it." They tend to hang around with other ducks—quack quack quack, complain complain complain. Eagles, on the other hand, soar above the rest of the flock; they are the folks who see a problem and then take it upon themselves to fix it.

SOAR, BITCH, SOAR

This idea of being an eagle in your workplace is embodied in my girl Doris. Doris is a bathroom attendant at one of my favorite restaurants. The first time I met Doris, she made a point of introducing herself and asking my name. "I've seen you here before," she said. She was warm, motherly, and seemed genuinely pleased when "one of her girls," as she said in her buttery Southern accent, stopped in to see her.

I'll never forgot the time she looked me straight in the eye and said, "Aw, baby girl, I brought in these special pointed Q-tips that get the smudged eyeshadow in your crease and under your eye, and I tell you this out of love, but I think I'm going to give you one for a whirl." I looked in the mirror, and she was right: I was definitely in need of cleaning up my eye area. I love girls' girls who actually tell you when something is awry with your "situation": an open zipper, schmutz on your pants, or something crazy with your hair or makeup. Doris was that girl—and then some. She stood next to me in front of the mirror, directing me with the fancy Q-tip, making sure I didn't miss a spot. "Well, there you go: now you are even more perfect than the perfect you were when you walked in, if that's even possible."

Doris made me instantly happier. When I got out of the stall, she had one of those fancy monogrammed napkins that you usually see in nice powder rooms waiting for me. It had an N on it. "An N," I thought. "That couldn't possibly be for *Nicole*," I said. "Oh, yes, my dear Nicole, that is for you to make you feel at home when you are a guest here," she said. I was so confused and so impressed at the same time. Then I looked under the sink and Doris had an accordion folder with tabs for each letter of the alphabet. Doris had actually made a special folder for napkins with all letters of the alphabet to make every one of "her girls" feel special.

I had never seen a setup like hers. Doris thought of *everything*, from the special Q-tips and napkins to having every flavor of mouthwash in case, as she said, "someone doesn't like the blue one or the yellow one, there will always be an option because, honey, we all get a funky mouth." One time when I saw her, I had a little period emergency. I quietly asked her for help with my "lady time that just snuck up on me." And she said, "Don't you worry, darling: a tampon? Super or regular? Or a maxi? With wings or without? Whatever makes you feel most comfortable, I got you."

Doris was officially my she-ro, and I wanted to learn more. "Have you always done all this?" I asked her, gesturing around her sink area. Doris told me that when she first started at the job, she hated it. She didn't want to be in a smelly bathroom; she didn't want to hand mean girls towels just to barely get an acknowledgment or a tip. "But then," she said, "I changed my attitude. I turned my frown upside down. I started putting in extra time and energy into making this my dream palace. The more I did, the more 'my girls' responded favorably. The more I got to know each of them, Nicole [obviously she remembered my name], the more I loved my job. Not only did the pride I took in my work turn into happiness, but I now wake up in the morning excited to think about the new, fun, personal things I can do. And the more 'gifts' I receive, as well. I've even had a few of 'my girls' hire me for their private events. It's been a win-win-win."

Doris is clearly an amazing Boss Bitch. And she was right: her attitude changed everything for the better. It sounds odd, but I even found myself going back to that restaurant more because of Doris than the food or the ambience, which were nice, but less memorable. I made sure to bring cash into the bathroom for her. She called a tip a "gift." It was the first and only time I heard that, but I thought it was awesome. She had a small, sweet sign in an ornate gold frame that said: "Your presence is my present, my friend. And any gift from a friend is a wish for their happiness. Love, Doris." It was so thoughtful and classy. On the bottom, in tiny letters, she handwrote, "Square, Check, Cash, or Cookies. All gladly accepted." Yes, my girl Doris had a Square to take credit cards. I don't think anyone left that bathroom without a hug, and I never saw anyone leave without happily giving her a "gift."

I've thought a lot about my eagle Doris in the years I've been going to that restaurant. Here are the business lessons she taught me:

1. *Choose to differentiate yourself.* Doris has brought to life another one of my favorite sayings: "Nothing changes if nothing changes." She changed her attitude. She stopped complaining. She created a memorable experience. She gained fans, not just customers. No one did this for Doris. Doris *decided* to do this for Doris.

2. *Color brightly inside the lines.* Pre-"eagle" and post-"eagle," Doris still technically had the same job. She worked for the same restaurant. But she made her job hers; she created a brand built on positivity, and she reaped the rewards.

3. *It's all about the little things.* Doris was thoughtful in every aspect of her job. It didn't cost a lot to go above and beyond the call of duty, to make her personal touches. But that small investment paid her back and then some.

Doris didn't have an MBA, but she created one killer business model and brand for herself. She didn't just do her job. She owned it and made it soar.

EVERY BOSS NEEDS HER BRAND

What are the three important words for every Boss Bitch? They might not be the ones you think. They are: "Who are you?" (But, yes, "I love you," too.)

The first thing to consider as you start building and then bolstering your personal brand at work boils down to a seemingly easy—but sneak-attack existential—question: Who am I? Yep, that's it, but those three words are the secret and first step to *everything* in personal branding. So: Who are you?

I know this can start to get a little touchy-feely, but it's important to do a little soul-searching when figuring out what your professional brand is so it feels authentic to you. Before you can describe who you are and what you stand for to anyone else, you have to figure it out for yourself.

Every Boss Bitch brand is different; it's time to make yours your own. For you skeptics out there who think, "I'm doing fine at my job just the way it is, thankyouverymuch. What do I need a brand for?" Welp, I hate to be the Doomsday Bitch, but what if you get fired or laid off from your current gig? Think about it this way: you could be jobless and brandless. Or you could be jobless with a killer brand. I think the latter puts you in a much better position of power . . . just sayin'.

SO, WHAT'S YOUR BRAND, BITCH?

You'll see throughout this section that it's very important that your brand is compatible with the brand of the place you work at right now. Like in a relationship, it's all about having shared values. Do you and your company value the same things? Think of it like a Venn diagram made up of their values and yours.

While you obviously have tons of admirable things to bring to the table at any company, those in the "sweet spot" will get you noticed and promoted (in fact, they're likely what made them hire you in the first place).

And to continue the relationship metaphor, the more you and your employer reflect those values in each other, the more you will continue to grow together—making you even more essential to your company (and valuable to others). That means, in two words: job security.

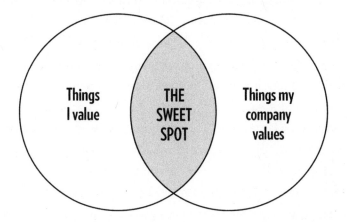

No, you shouldn't change yourself or your personality drastically for any job (or any relationship!). But you *should* accentuate those parts of yourself that align with the company's brand and culture. And don't just shade the overlap of the Venn diagram, highlight it!

BRAND YOURSELF 101

First, think of three things that are important to you from a work perspective. Maybe you've never thought too hard about what you hope to get out of a job, and that's okay. But now's the time to do it. It could be anything from, say, using your analytical skills to traveling to bonding with like-minded colleagues. Whatever it is, list it out. If you don't, there's no way to measure your progress.

Now think of three things that are important to your company. You probably know this pretty well. It could be reaching the greatest market share, innovating new products, or having a reputation for outstanding customer service. List these out, too, don't just "know them by heart." The best way to figure out what's in the overlap is to visualize it.

Don't freak out thinking about diagrams. Just do something like this:

Example: *I work as a production assistant.*

Three things that are important to me from a work perspective: *creating TV content, discovering emerging music, traveling to new places.*

Three things that are important to my company: *producing a lot of content across multiple platforms cheaply, securing international distribution, and having a start-up culture.*

Look for where these things overlap and how you can leverage those that are important to your company to do more of what's important to *you.*

Analysis: If you love TV and music, what about focusing on creating and then pitching a music video or music-related content specifically? Since your company has a start-up feel, internal pitches will probably be warmly received. In fact, like a lot of nimble start-ups, the founders will probably love it if you propose that you "own" (and "rock") the music vertical* from start to finish. Or if you love to travel and they are looking for international distribution, you could offer to take some strategic meetings abroad while you shoot a music video there (I think that's knocking out three birds with one proverbial stone). Chances are they might be into the idea but might not be able to foot the bill. Don't write it off. A smart Boss Bitch will think one step ahead and save up her frequent flier miles to take care of the trip herself, then conquer the meetings and the shoot and come back with a ton of value for the company—not to mention, way more experience and personal value for herself than any amount of miles used otherwise would get her.

BRAND YOUR NICHE

Let's say you're not currently working in the industry of your dreams. Luckily, there's a Boss Bitch way to make your current gig a little more dreamy.

Think of your three favorite industries. Most people will identify maybe one or two industries they can see themselves working in, but I say choose three that might suit your personal goals and skills. For me that would be: media, business, and investing. Just do me a favor, for the sake of this exercise, and try not to pick three *completely* different things like neuroscience, professional golf, and nonprofit work. That's going to make for one tough (but not impossible) career path.

Then, think of any overlap with the industry you're in right now and where you ideally want to be. That shaded part is what's going to be the best niche to structure your budding brand around:

> Example: *I am a junior publicist.*
>
> My three favorite industries: *fashion, celebrity gossip (I think that's an industry at this point!), and women's magazines.*
>
> The industry I'm in right now: *brand PR and marketing.*
>
> *Analysis:* If you live and die by the latest fashion and celeb news and maybe you secretly want to start your own gossip blog or column later on, then try to focus on creating sources within those types of publications, aka the "weeklies" of the world (*People, OK!, InTouch, Us Weekly,* etc.) and women's magazines or websites you love (*People StyleWatch,* Refinery29, Popsugar, etc.). Try to reach out to writers or even assistants there (if you take nothing else away from this book, remember: assistants move around and up). It's relatively easy to track down anyone with a smidge of effort. Can't find their e-mail? Ping them on Facebook or Twitter or LinkedIn. Try to start a dialogue in any way you can. If you don't live in a major city where many of them are located (which in this case would be Los Angeles, NYC, or San Francisco), plan a one- or two-day trip and try to set up in-person meetings "boot camp"-style. There are also freelancers across the country that you can reach out to who might be in your area or willing to jump on a call, since you can provide them with content for the publications for which they contribute. This 1) broadens your network in the niche

that you love, 2) provides a ton of value to your company, and 3) makes the people or brands they represent happy because now you have a contact at the outlets from which they are seeking press. Everyone wins.

BRAND YOUR OFFICE PERSONA

Delivering value in a workplace isn't all about formal skills and leadership abilities; sometimes, there's a lot of professional value in bringing your shining personality—in all its quirkiness—to work. Come up with one fun fact about yourself. Keep it clean, but don't be afraid to think outside the corporate box. Do you like to play the drums? Were you the all-conference track-and-field champion in high school? Have you seen every episode of *The Simpsons* ever made—twice? Write down what makes you, you.

Now think of an odd perk of your job that no one told you about during orientation. Maybe there's a Ping-Pong table in the basement, or a secret storage closet where cool stuff gets stowed away, or a lending library on a bookshelf on the fourth floor. Whatever it is, let's look at how you can brand this oddball stuff:

> Example: *I am a receptionist at a dental office.*
>
> Fun fact about me: *I make a mean flower arrangement, like full-on professional-style, with banana leaves lining the vase and everything.*
>
> Odd quirk of my job that's outside of the description: *My dental office gets tons of shipments in interesting-looking containers that are thrown away—and my hippie recycling heart breaks every time.*
>
> *Analysis:* Own your front-desk domain. Start taking those cool containers the office gets and create makeshift vases. Let's say the office gets a floral arrangement from someone happy with her whitening or whatever every once in a while. Once that bouquet starts to wilt, pounce on it with those mean arranging skills and make it into something cool and decorative.

Flowers are expensive to buy at the store (it's an addiction of mine, so I know this all too well), so if you do need fresh flowers, pick some from a friend's garden or peruse the discount buckets at Trader Joe's. The added loveliness will definitely be noticed by your office mates, not to mention patients at check-in, and you'll become known as the receptionist with the mostess.

You never know if or when a random skill will turn into something that will set your brand apart. You might be "discovered" by some of the office's high-end clientele, who might ask you to create floral arrangements for one of their parties, leading to some extra cash (a great "side hustle,"* which I'll talk much more about in Section 3). If nothing else, you'll beautify the office, put a smile on any potentially grumpy person's face—which can be frequent since most people don't enjoy going to the dentist—and score a big W for recycling!

These thought exercises are intended to help you start putting your toe into the branding water and figuring out who, exactly, you are while still swimming upstream at work. Remember, as with anything in life, you can—and should!—revisit these questions again and again, constantly refining your answers and coming up with more creative ideas to make you love your job (and make the people there love you back).

PLAY TO YOUR WEAKNESSES

BITCH TIP

When crafting your personal brand, the natural instinct is to lead with your strengths. But don't forget about your weaknesses! In fact, instead of attempting to *diminish* your weaknesses as conventional wisdom suggests, I advocate the opposite. (Shocking, right?) Sometimes you should play up your weaknesses; after all, it's hard to change those fundamental things about yourself, so why not be aware of them and try to make them work *for* you instead?

Maybe your "weakness" (I put it in quotes because weakness is in the eye of the beholder) is that you're "that girl" who's always compulsively tweeting throughout the workday. Fine! Be "that girl" and turn the negative connotation into a positive one by offering to come up with a new social media strategy for your team. Maybe you have a swearing problem. Fine! Write a book full of curse words (wink, wink).

HELLO, BRAND. IT'S ME, YOUR BOSS BITCH.

Look, I get it: all this personal-branding and "Who am I?" stuff can feel daunting. I know it's a lot to think about. But being proactive will help to calm any potential anxiety attacks around building your brand. Keep in mind that 1) it doesn't happen overnight: brands, especially the best ones, develop over time and through *a lot* of iterating; and 2) I had the same freak-outs and made it through them—so you can, too.

My brand has changed and evolved over the years, as any good one will. When I first started thinking about what it might look like, I was in my early twenties and had no idea what I was doing. I didn't articulate my brand properly or make the most of developing it at the job I was in at the time.

After I floundered through various half-baked ideas, it was time to get real. So I hired a "personal brand consultant." Yes, that's a real thing, and they're not cheap. But, lucky you, instead of paying for that pricey service yourself, I'll just tell you all the best stuff I learned.

The first thing you have to realize about getting into the nitty-gritty of your brand is that it has to be completely honest and authentic to you, or it's not going to work. Going through the exercises in this section will feel a lot like going to a shrink, but when you think about it, developing a brand gets to more or less the same goal of figuring out who you are (on the business side, at least).

Here were my answers to the first exercise from my personal brand consultant:

Adjectives I use to describe myself	sassy, smart, honest, fun, aspirational
Adjectives others use to describe me	intense, driven, young, funny
Untapped skills	swearing

(This was the exercise that led to *Rich Bitch* and *Boss Bitch* in all their swearing glory, BTW.) Okay, your turn:

Adjectives I use to describe myself	
Adjectives others use to describe me	
Untapped skills	

Next, you have to start talking about your brand *as a business or product,* which is different from how you talk about your brand as a person. If you think about it, every great product—whether it's your favorite brand of jeans or skin-care product or protein bar—has a distinctive slogan or logo and a unique look or color scheme, and evokes certain feelings or emotions in its customer. It was weird at first, but my brand guru told me that I needed to start viewing myself like I do my favorite brands. What did I love about them? What made them special? It wasn't enough to figure out the "Who am I?" question, but I needed to start answering the "Who am I to the world?" one as well.

So on my next visit to Lululemon, instead of just running to grab my go-to high-rise leggings then peacing out, I started paying attention to the store itself. What did I like about how it made me feel? I noticed the logos placed in subtle places on each item of clothing, the motivational sayings, the posters highlighting awesome local fitness gurus, the red shopping bags that no one throws away because they are so cool. Those things aren't accidents. They are thoughtfully planned as part of a branding strategy—and it works. That strategy and attention to detail are part of any good brand, including yours, which brings us to my answers to the second exercise:

My personal motto	"Get it together and get it all."
How I want to make others feel	Comfortable talking about scary, taboo topics. Comfortable in their own skin. Empowered to grab life by the balls.
Colors I associate with	black, white, gold, gray

This last activity led to the signature I use at all of my book signings: "Get it together and get it ALL!!! XO, Nicole." Hopefully, I get the chance to sign a book for you that way. I add little custom tidbits when I sign in person, but it's no mistake that they all feature my same personal motto.

This exercise also led me to finally get super raw in the way I tell stories. I used to be so guarded about admitting my faults until I realized that the only way to make others feel comfortable with scary topics like money was to be unapologetically crazy-real myself. I have blinders on to anyone who is offended by my swearing and brutal, sometimes crass honesty; that's just me, and if you're not interested in working with me, warts and all, then, well, I'm not interested in working with you. I don't mean that in a bratty, "so there" kind of way. But the strongest brands can't be all things to all people. A narrow but well-defined brand has a better chance of resonating with more people than one that aims wide but is too wishy-washy and diluted. So that's why, instead, I focus on connecting with my customer (you!) as *myself*, in all my swearing glory, because you get me, and I don't waste time trying to reach those who won't.

And, last, the color question is not a throwaway one. Big companies, like Lululemon, have exhaustive brand books so that everything from their website to press releases to bags looks the same every time it appears. There are a zillion shades of red, so Lululemon doesn't pick one at random; they even have an exact HTML color code. From this exercise, I used black, white, and gold for my logo (my specific golden yellow is #FFDF00). You may never want to have your own company, but since *you* are your company, when it comes time to choose a color to represent you, be thoughtful and consistent about it.

Okay, your turn:

My personal motto	
How I want to make others feel	
Colors I associate with	

Finally, my branding guru had me write down my one-, three-, five-, seven-, and ten-year business goals and then think through how to develop a brand that got me there while looking to others I admired for inspiration.

Here were my answers to the third exercise. (BTW, there were many more exercises for my four-figure branding bill, but these are the most essential for getting started.) Keep in mind, I completed this first round of branding before *Rich Bitch* even came out; these goals are now in my rearview mirror, and I'm on to the next batch, but I share them as a reminder that your business goals and brand should be compatible.

My 1-year business goals	Sign a book deal for *Rich Bitch*. Join a major talk show as the in-house financial correspondent. Become known to the rest of the media community as the go-to money expert.
My 3-year business goals	Have *Rich Bitch* become a bestseller. Create a dialogue about the title, concept, and content that extends beyond the book to the press, events, and social media. Use the platform to leverage new professional opportunities for another book and TV show.
My 5-year business goals	Sign my second book deal. Have a money column in a major magazine. Have my own network show that is based in business content but with a mainstream bent.
My professional crushes	Katie Couric, Tyra Banks, and Sara Blakely

This became my road map to staying super focused on my business goals. And, yes, I happened to accomplish them on time, but I would be the first person to admit it if I hadn't. Year one, I *did* sign my book deal and join *Wendy Williams* and *The Insider* as the regular financial correspondent while appearing on a ton of other shows like *Dr. Oz* and *Good Morning America*. By year three, I *did* have a *New York Times* bestselling book that was covered on almost every TV, print, radio, and podcast outlet I targeted. That definitely didn't happen on its own: I was an (overly) obsessed spreadsheet nutcase about it. There was a little bit (okay, a lot of bit) of luck, like when I got a hookup with billboards, for example. But everything else was planned, and I held myself and my team accountable. Those things allowed me to lay the foundation for my second book deal (duh, this one), a monthly money column in *Redbook*, and my own money show on the CW, *Hatched*.

So what do Katie, Tyra, and Sara have to do with anything? Writing down my professional girl crushes forced me to figure out exactly *what* I admired about them. With Katie, I not only thought she created a versatile on-air persona—from morning news at NBC, to the evening news at CBS, to her own syndicated talk show, to anchoring at Yahoo! News—but I also loved how honest she was by talking about the death of her husband and getting a colonoscopy on air to raise awareness about the cancer he died from. With Tyra, I loved that she kept it classy on air no matter what topic she discussed. With Sara, I admired her authenticity and accessibility when articulating her brand . . . and what a brand it is! It's the "Q-tip" in its product category, meaning that no matter if it's another cotton swab or not, you say it's a Q-tip, right? Same with Spanx in the shapewear market. Over the last five years, I've been lucky enough to meet these three Boss Bitches. And yes, they are awesome in real life, too.

Okay, your turn:

My 1-year business goals	
My 3-year business goals	
My 5-year business goals	
My professional crushes	

These exercises are just jumping-off points. After all, it's *your* brand to define, so do it however you want. You're in charge! Go to town adding any other important elements that apply to your area of expertise. Are you an aspiring chef? Make note of the flavors and spices that define your secret sauce. Interior design maven? Jot down the periods and patterns that make up your favorite palette.

And just like anything else in life, you're allowed to change these elements as your personal brand changes; in fact, you *should* change them up every so often to reflect your ever-evolving self, as long as you keep writing them down so you stay on track. They may not seem like much on their own, but combined they paint a pretty comprehensive picture of who you are professionally and how you define that brand for the world. And they provide a nice cheat sheet to use again and again: from designing your website to crafting your social media content and design. You might not be at a place now (or ever want) to start producing marketing or business materials, but start thinking about these brand elements *now* so that you're that much further along if and when you are.

STAYING ON POINT AND ON BRAND

The best brands are the ones that resonate with everything that has their name on it. So now that you have your blossoming brand in hand, make sure it is felt by everything you touch.

ELEVATE YOUR ELEVATOR PITCH

Every successful company has a rock-solid fifteen-second spiel; what's yours?

If you don't have one, you should. I've seen a lot of women squirm and feel uncomfortable when faced with distilling who they are into a fifteen-second pitch. Enough already! It's time to stop squirming and start selling the sizzle. I'm sure you're building a banging brand, but whether other people think so is a direct result of how you express it in an elevator pitch.

My style is always: I'll show you mine if you show me yours. So here's my elevator pitch: "I'm Nicole Lapin, cohost of *Hatched* and author of *Rich Bitch* and *Boss Bitch*. I am the financial expert you don't need a dictionary to understand."

Here's what another Boss Bitch, designer Rebecca Minkoff, says her brand is: "I'm Rebecca Minkoff. My greatest creations are my two children. Second, I have a business and it is fashion-based, but what we are really striving to do is make a product that is accessible, that makes us feel confident, and that won't break the bank. It's also about empowering more women to be self-made."

Keep it short, sweet, and to the point. Of course, I'm many other things besides a money guru for the everywoman: I'm also a passport stamp collector, an LA lady, a margarita aficionado, to name a few. These are all labels, though, that don't cut it for the core "Who am I?" brand answer.

Similarly, I'll bet your "list" is pretty long: wife, mother, marathoner, teacher, cupcake connoisseur . . . you get the idea. The question is, which of those things are part of the story you want to tell the *professional* world? If you're looking to start your own mom blog, the second of those might be the one you lead with, for obvious reasons. If you're trying to get your side hustle on to make extra cash by pitching your favorite sneaker company to be a brand ambassador, then the third one might be the most appropriate. The point is that, while you are undoubtedly many awesome things, you want to highlight only those that are most relevant to your brand when pitching it.

ROCK YOUR RÉSUMÉ

Another important Boss Bitch tool is a polished résumé. You already know that you need to make sure it has no errors and is formatted in an easy-to-read way, but also make sure that you are not all over the place with your skills and the examples you include. In other words, I know you have a ton of mad skills, but the ones you list need to be apropos to wherever you currently are and where you want to go in your career. Are you applying for a job at a boutique? No need to list your time spent as a lifeguard. Also, while you might have sick origami skills, leave that gem off in favor of, say, your fluency in Spanish. Think about how to translate your burgeoning personal brand into as much of your résumé as possible.

YOU ARE YOUR URL

Regardless of whether you are between jobs or not, always have your *own* professional-looking e-mail domain. Without question, it is time to ditch that Hotmail address that alludes to some inside joke (or, God forbid, has the word *babe* or *chick* or *diva* in it) and upgrade to something polished, professional, and easy to remember. firstnamelastname@gmail.com is always a safe bet, or upgrade and purchase yourname.com on GoDaddy (many domains are $20 per year or less) and then use that as your e-mail— e.g., nicole@nicolelapin.com (which is my real e-mail, BTW, so shout at a sister!). This will be the first mode of contact you provide many people with; make sure it's smart, not obnoxious.

WATCH YOUR OWN BIOPIC

Every Boss Bitch needs a bio at the ready, something about a paragraph long (featuring just the highlights). You'll also need a go-to headshot. Yes, a headshot. This is not just for people like me who work in the media or some other visible field; everyone should have one. Trust me, no matter what you do, if you get invited to a conference and need to be in the program, or join a club or an association and want to be listed in their directory, you'll want a headshot. It doesn't have to be all glam (in fact, it probably shouldn't be unless you work in fashion), just something simple and professional (*not* cut out from a group photo where you can see the arm of the person next to you). It's also a good idea to include one on any professional online profile. Try to keep the photo you use across social media the same, especially if they are public and you use them for work in one way or another.

I'm not going to tsk-tsk you on shit you already know shouldn't be on your public social media; you've heard enough horror stories already. Just don't be "that girl." Instead, be the Boss Bitch that has a consistent and professional presence throughout (including industry-specific platforms like IMDB, CrunchBase, and Doximity if they make sense for you). Your bio blurb on Facebook, Twitter, Instagram, and whatever other sites you're on should be the same, too. Remember our conversation about colors and fonts or even a logo (you don't need a family to have your own crest!) that represent you? Try to incorporate some of that across all of your social networks. Be obsessed with your image online—but, as I know from personal experience, don't become obsessive.

CONFESSIONS OF A
BOSS BITCH

That Time I Got Busted Googling Myself at Work

It was Christmas Eve, and I was at the anchor desk for the evening newscast. Believe it or not, I loved working holidays. I don't have a family of my own, so I would always volunteer to go in on Thanksgiving or Christmas or New Year's, when most of the bigger-deal people would want to take time off. By working those days, I got to fill in for the higher-profile jobs.

"Are you ready to swap out?" asked the anchor on after me, who didn't even want to be there but got the short end of the time-off stick, as she was relieving me to do her show.

"Oh, yes, of course," I said, looking uncomfortably at the mess I'd made of the laptop on the anchor desk. "Sorry. I got some cranberry sauce on the keys. I'll get one of those wipe things to get it out."

"It's fine," she said, clearly not happy to be there. "I have to log in and research a couple of things."

"Of course. Let me sign out of my e-mail," I said, X-ing out of my browser.

I was thinking, "Sor-ry, sister—just because we are working on a holiday doesn't mean we shouldn't eat like it's one!" I took out my earpiece and went to the break room to finish up my plate o' festive goodness.

After her show, she came over to my table. "I didn't wipe off the keyboard," she said snarkily, "but I did wipe out your search history. Enjoy your dinner," she said as she turned to leave.

Those laptops you see behind the news desk on TV aren't there for show; anchors use them to research stuff, look at scripts, or check important e-mails. I, however, was using it for something else, too. While I was on set, I researched, yes. I looked up scripts, yes. I looked at important e-mails, yes. I Googled myself, yes. I actually Googled myself . . . a bunch of times.

I had never thought to clear my history so that no one else could look at what I was searching for online. And while a lot of things we search for online are embarrassing and likely not things you want to share with others, Googling yourself (multiple times at that) is probably one of the worst.

I was busted. And mortified. Surely she thought I was a total self-absorbed narcissist. But in fact it was the opposite. The truth is, I wasn't the most self-confident person when I started on air. And the more exposure I got, the more self-conscious I became. Googling myself became an obsession that I indulged any time I had Internet access. As my career on air grew, I got to a point where I Googled myself no fewer than five times per day.

This incident was a wake-up call. My searching had become obsessive, un-healthy, and now had resulted in embarrassing myself in front of a colleague I admired. It had to stop.

Monitoring your personal brand is one thing, but as I learned the hard way, it's easy to take it way too far. The only thing I do now is have Google Alerts on my name. That way, I can see immediately when an article I wrote has come online so I can share it with my network. I never randomly Google myself anymore, so I don't have to worry about having another embarrassing search-history encounter. One of those was enough for me to avoid another potentially sticky situation at all costs.

LOOK THE PART

If you want people to start treating you like the boss that you are, you should look the part, and don't be shy about caring about your appearance at work, says a mentor of mine, Mika Brzezinski (you know her from MSNBC's *Morning Joe*, as well as her wildly successful *Know Your Worth* book series and campaign). "Clothing is the package in which your professional value is delivered," Mika says. That doesn't mean it should distract from your credentials; on the contrary, she suggests wearing simple outfits to meetings and interviews. "You don't want to be overdressed and appear as if you don't need the job. You don't want to be underdressed, either. It's a fine balance."

TO BUY OR NOT TO BUY?

Dressing to impress at work doesn't have to come with a hefty price tag. It's all about clean and simple—which is a look every budget can afford. After all, you should focus most of your time, money, and energy on becoming a brand, not wearing one. But if you do want to invest in something expensive to step up your corporate closet, crunch the numbers to see if it makes financial sense. Don't freak out by this equation I came up with; it's easy to plug and chug whatever you're eyeing to see if you should buy it or skip it!

ORIGINAL COST / USES PER YEAR = COST PER WEAR

COST PER WEAR + MAINTENANCE PER YEAR = X

ORIGINAL COST – X = VALUE PER YEAR

IF THE VALUE PER YEAR IS
> 65% OF THE ORIGINAL COST—THEN BUY IT!

IF THE VALUE PER YEAR IS
< 65% OF THE ORIGINAL COST—THEN SKIP IT!

Here's an example: you want to buy a $200 blazer. Let's say you want to wear it in different ways twice a week in and out of the office, or 104 times per year. Divide $200 by 104 wears and you get a price of about 2 bucks per wear. Then factor in maintenance, aka dry cleaning, at around 50 bucks a year and subtract that from the original $200 price tag. Since that number ($148.08) is greater than 65% of the original cost, factoring in maintenance costs and the amount you will use it, it's worth it. So buy it!

However, if you are looking at a $500 dress that you might only wear two times per year for nicer work events with maintenance costs of hemming and dry cleaning of around $50 per year, then the value you are getting is 60% of the original cost. Not worth that hefty price tag. So skip it!

You know the old saying, "Dress for the job you want"? I don't totally agree with that (otherwise I would show up in Victoria's Secret angel wings—just kidding). I suggest, rather, that you dress for the job you have and strut in those work-appropriate shoes to where you want to go.

PUT YOUR BRAND TO WORK

As you are thinking about your brand, connect the dots carefully between the job you have and the one you want. You can go about that in two ways: 1) be innovative and piss people off, or 2) be innovative and respected for something that makes you stand out without burning any bridges you might need to cross in the future. Boss Bitches choose door number two.

Let's say you are a gynecologist but want to be a tech entrepreneur. Sounds weird, right? Well, I didn't make that up; it's actually what my gyno wants to do (yes, we talk when she's not in my hoo-ha). She loves what she's doing now but sees a lot of white space for apps that provide microloans to women looking to fund reproductive health issues that they can't afford or their insurance doesn't cover. Moving in that direction full-time would be a total 180 from what she's doing now. But there *is* a bridge that will get her from the scrubs to the hoodie—if she's strategic.

Right now, her focus is on kegels, the super-fun exercises you do to strengthen your pelvic muscles. She is starting research on an app that focuses on kegels. Because that is already her niche, she'll win the respect of her industry. That allows my gyno to gain great experience in the app-building and -designing world without getting the panties of her colleagues and supervisors in a bunch. And if, for some reason, while exploring her kegel app she decides she hates tech entrepreneurship after all, she hasn't pissed off her professional community and jeopardized her position in her field.

BEING INNOVATIVE IN A COMPANY
(THAT DOESN'T ENCOURAGE INNOVATION)

Defining your brand forces you to find your own value, and, if done correctly, can also *force your company to value you more as well*. Your brand is valuable to you because it's yours. It's portable, so you can take it with you to any workplace during the course of your career, even if you end up searching for a job and hiring yourself. But while you are at your current job, the more value you add for your employer, the more you go from being a commodity to being irreplaceable (or at least not easily replaceable).

To add value, you need to start thinking like an eagle, asking questions like: What problems exist here and what creative solutions can I come up with to solve them? What's the one idea that no one is thinking about but if they did, it would transform the business? By venturing to answer these questions, you are already wearing your innovator cap.

What if you work for a company or in an industry that doesn't particularly value innovation? One where you get stuck in the same (boring) routine because there's no desire to change the "that's how we've always done it" approach? As Doris's story showed us, no industry or job is an excuse for acting like a robot. As Steve Jobs said, innovation differentiates leaders from followers. And we Boss Bitches are leaders who can innovate wherever we are. Here are a few ideas for thinking differently in whatever role you are in now:

> *If you're a real estate agent,* don't just sell properties. Get to know who the best contractors and service people are in the area so you can recommend them to clients. Sellers and buyers both always need to spruce up a property with a paint job or repairs or landscaping, so why not get the reputation for being the one who can hook them up with the very best? The repeat business will get the customers discounts on the work, and you'll get repeat clients when word gets out about how you made a difficult process easy peasy. You'll sell those snazzed-up houses faster, too.
>
> *If you're an accountant,* don't just emerge during tax time. Instead, why not create a monthly "Did You Know?" e-newsletter that shares helpful tips throughout the year? Better yet, customize your bulletins and call a client when a change in tax law could benefit them. Your clients will feel taken care of, your job will be easier come April, and it will pay off in referrals and more business for you.
>
> *If you're a dog walker,* don't just walk dogs. Give each new client a small notebook to keep by their door, with your business card taped inside, then jot down how the walk went every time you visit. They'll appreciate the update on whether pooch went number one or number two (if you're a dog owner, you'll totally get this), and the log

can serve as a daily reminder of the impact you have on their lives (which will come in handy when a neighbor asks for a referral or when holiday tipping time comes around).

WHAT'S YOUR SCHTICK?

Can't think of a "schtick," aka the thing that makes you stand out within a crowd or an industry? Here are what I affectionately call "schtick starters":

Schtick: A signature something.

Example: Simon Cowell's signature black T-shirt. Gwen Stefani's signature red lips. Angelyne's signature pink corvette (if you're an LA girl like yours truly, you'll get this immediately; if not, look it up. I promise it's worth the search). Whatever your signature is, make sure it's brand-appropriate but still noticeable enough to make you memorable.

Schtick: The "best" at something.

Example: If you are a nail technician, become known as the "best" foot massager in the place. Or, if you work in marketing, become known as the best PowerPoint deck presenter. Obviously, who wouldn't request the "best" foot massager? And, likewise, who wouldn't want to put the "best presenter" on their big account? You don't need to be the best at everything, just have your one "thing" and make it known.

BEING INNOVATIVE IN A COMPANY
(WHERE INNOVATION *IS* ENCOURAGED)

These days, lots of companies, especially in the tech world, have built their own brands around being "innovative." Even outside of the tech world, more industries are modeling themselves after the likes of Google by allowing employees the freedom to create their own work structure. However, this can be both a blessing and a curse, because having *too* much autonomy and not enough structure can lead to a lack of productivity.

While nap pods and game rooms sound super cool, thriving at innovative start-up-like companies takes a lot more discipline from you than you might think. I've worked at innovative companies where, if you weren't on top of your own shit, you could get sidetracked by having *too much* freedom. Instead, use the flexibility to your advantage by thinking of yourself as a "corporate entrepreneur" and finding ways to come up with solutions to problems that will benefit your team or company—and help you make a name for yourself in the process.

CONFESSIONS OF A
BOSS BITCH

Don't Try to Be Something You're Not

As I told you in the first section, I was hired at CNN when I was 21. And even though I should have been proud to land that dream job at such a young age, the truth was, I didn't want my coworkers to know how young I was. I thought no one would take me seriously or believe I had the amount of experience I did. I was in the mix with legendary correspondents and anchors who had covered several presidents, Supreme Court justices, and wars. I felt like I was punching *way* above my weight.

I would sidestep whenever my age came up in conversation. My palms would sweat, and I would look away and try to skirt the subject by saying something unclever like, "You never ask a woman her age!" Then I would deflect the conversation to something else. (Of course, now, more than a decade later, I love when people think I'm younger than I am . . . but I digress.)

After a couple of years of being cagey, I realized that there was *no way* to compete with or differentiate myself from my illustrious colleagues in terms of experience. While I'd put some time in doing local and national news, I'd never had a "beat" at the State Department or a niche as a "war reporter." I was fighting a losing battle. Instead, I set out to create a brand that I *could* "own" with credibility. Ironically, it turned out to be the thing I tried to hide most: my age. I created a beat that only I could have by virtue of it.

Mind you, CNN is a company that is rooted in innovation. It was the first twenty-four-hour cable news network. In the early days, people thought it was a joke, dubbing it "Chicken Noodle News" because they were the first to go above and beyond what TV news was always thought to be: the evening newscast. The company culture was one that fostered creativity so much so that we didn't even say "think outside the box"; we said "think outside the octagon." So I felt safe to do just that.

I started a series called *Young People Who Rock.* After all, who better to report on young people who rock than a young person who, if I do say so myself, rocked?! I conducted weekly interviews with a different young person or people under 30 doing amazing things in the worlds of business, politics, entertainment, or social activism. I interviewed the youngest US congressman, CEOs in their twenties, and even then-tween Justin Bieber. (Forget all this business stuff—doing the first interview with the Biebs is still and will always be one of my most favorite accomplishments.)

Of course, no one gave me the idea for the series. No one I worked with or for said, "Hey, Lapin, you should do a series on young people" or "You should really find something that makes you stand out here." Nope, none of that. Lapin made it happen (not that it was easy).

It took me a full six months to "sell" the idea. I wrote proposals. I came up with a list of people I could interview and an online blog to complement the on-air pieces. After many months of not taking no for an answer, I finally got a green light for a scaled-down version of my proposal. As the saying goes, I shot for the moon; when I didn't get there, I still landed among the stars. The opportunity wasn't the one I originally aimed for, but I was determined to "rock" the one I got.

My *Young People Who Rock* series lasted for two years. And my perceived Achilles' heel—my age—became one of my biggest strengths and brand assets in that job and for years to come.

SCREAM AND SHOUT AND GET YOUR BRAND OUT

Once you've created a brand that fits you within your current role *and* hopefully gets you closer to your ultimate career goal, it's time to think about telling the world about it. There's no shame in self-promotion—if done the right way.

The thing to keep in mind about personal PR is that you also have to be careful about upsetting the people you work with. There's a delicate balancing act between looking out for yourself and being perceived as just being in it for yourself. Before you do anything, think about how your (actual) boss is going to take it, and how it might affect your company's brand, not just your own. Hello, Captain Obvious, you can't build a brand within a company if you don't have a job there anymore.

If it passes the promotional sniff test, then go to town with putting yourself out there. Have you heard of Dr. Pimple Popper, aka Dr. Sandra Lee? Well, if you love seeing gnarly stuff come out of pores (like moi), then check out her videos on YouTube. They're nothing fancy, no gimmick, just videos of her being awesome at what she does: popping pimples. I, and millions of others, can't look away, even if it's cringeworthy. The innovative thing about her brand isn't that she's doing anything new within dermatology; she's actually doing the same thing that countless other dermatologists do on a daily basis. What *is* amazing about her brand is the way she invites the world in to see her doing it. She keeps it classy so as not to be mocked by her professional peers while also gaining tons of press on major women's websites and publications. Getting her pimple-popping skills out there in a creative way has made her one of the most sought-after dermatologists in the country . . . for all the right reasons.

BE YOUR OWN PUBLICIST

BITCH TIP

You don't need a schmancy publicist to get the word out about how rad you are. In fact, there are lots of super-helpful (free!) websites that let you publicize yourself. Here are a few of my favorites:

HARO (Help a Reporter Out, helpareporterout.com). You're clearly an expert in your field, whatever that field might be, so use HARO to connect with people in the press looking for someone like you. The site is basically a matchmaker for reporters and experts. When a reporter needs a source for an article she's working on, she puts a query out on HARO asking for people with certain knowledge or experience to respond. Browse the queries by your industry, then write a thoughtful response outlining your expertise in the desired area. If the reporter likes your response, you could land an interview for a story, which typically also includes a quote from you as Madame Expert and a link back to whatever work of yours you want to promote.

Muck Rack (muckrack.com). Set up a free Muck Rack profile featuring any of your written work, as well as your areas of expertise, so that interested companies and publicists can find you easily when they need a comment from your industry. You'll also get a daily roundup of the hottest topics so you can align your brand with what's in demand.

Google+ (plus.google.com). Hopefully, you learned from my super-embarrassing "Googling myself" story and aren't using the search engine to compulsively monitor images of your face (le sigh)—at least not from your work computer. But the reality is that clients, employers, recruiters, and, yes, dating prospects are turning to Google more and more to do their homework on little old you. So set up a Google+ profile to help control what they see, i.e., your brand. Google's algorithm ranks your Google+ profile higher than other mentions of you on the Internet, for obvious reasons, so this is one of the best ways to make sure you're leading with the good stuff. Keep it up-to-date with contact information, current projects, and, yes, one or two (tasteful) photos to control what people see when they search.

One caveat to this: No amount of PR alone will make a product great. And you, my dear, are your own product, no matter what you do. If you are not just good, but great at your job, you will get word-of-mouth buzz that no publicist can get you. When *Rich Bitch* came out, I went balls to the wall with press for it. I had a couple of expensive publicists who helped me get on a bunch of talk shows and in a bunch of magazines advertising the book during the first month after it was published. But then when all of that went away and the press moved on (as it does) to the next shiny new thing, what made my book successful is quite simply that it's a good book (I'm biased, obviously) and something that my readers told their friends about. Word of mouth was the best press of all. If I were able to print an emoji in a book, I would insert the "preach" one here.

Contrary to that popular saying "Act like a lady, think like a boss," you have to *act* like a boss, too. Anyone can think their ass off. But Boss Bitches don't just think about goals: we act on them and make noise while we're at it. We're a lot of things, but "quiet" isn't one of them.

BOTTOM LINE

Conventional Wisdom: Working for someone else means you're going to have a lot of shitty days at work—that's just how it is.

The Real Deal: Nope. The daily grind is a grind only if you let it be. Do your job, of course, but there's always a way to do it better. Take a step back from your daily routine and think about how you can own and make it yours. You'll make your actual boss happy, and, more important, you'll make your real boss—*yourself*—happy, too.

Conventional Wisdom: I can brand myself in an aspirational way and create the persona I always wanted.

The Real Deal: Obviously, I love being aspirational and am bullish* on you being whoever you want to be. But when it comes to branding yourself, you have to be nothing but real with yourself and your targeted field or it's not going to work.

Conventional Wisdom: Self-promotion is obnoxious. Keep your head down and do your job, and you'll be justly rewarded.

The Real Deal: Oh, puhleeze. Don't assume the world is going to see your light if you keep it under a rock. Toot your own horn when and where it makes sense, and you may find yourself in a bigger, sweeter ride as a result.

TALK LIKE A BOSS

Being Queen (Worker) Bee

One of my favorite lady empowerment campaigns out there (which is also spearheaded by one of my all-time favorite OG lady bosses, Beyoncé) is Ban Bossy, which you might recognize by the tagline delivered by Miss Sasha Fierce herself: "I'm not bossy, I'm the boss."

While I don't necessarily love the idea of "banning" any words, I do like the idea of reclaiming the negative perception of women who speak up, especially with conviction. Studies have shown that a majority of women, a far higher percentage than men, are scared of speaking up at work. Why? Because *both* men and women tend to view talkative women negatively, read: as bossy. (Urgh . . . c'mon, ladies!!)

Being a statistic isn't cute. There are few things more important to succeeding in business than mastering the way you communicate. So that's why, in Step 2 of "Being the Boss at Work," I'm going to teach you how to present yourself and your ideas smartly and strategically so that you get what you want at work. In other words, now that I've got you thinking like a boss, it's time to start acting like one, too.

DON'T SCREAM OR SHOUT, BUT LET IT ALL OUT

Boss Bitches know how to speak up for themselves and stand up for other Boss Bitches. We think of our voice not as something to be ashamed of, but rather as our biggest asset (as men do). The way you communicate is an extension of who you are (aka your brand), what you stand for, and where you want to be. Of course, there are many forms of communication in the workplace—from interpersonal to digital—so let's make sure all of them are on point, starting with good old-fashioned face-to-face ones.

STOP SAYING SORRY!

How many times do you find yourself apologizing throughout the day? Do you say I'm sorry when it takes you a few hours to respond to an e-mail? When you start to speak at the same time as someone else? When someone else bumps into *you*?

You might not even realize when you are doing it. I only realized how frequently I was apologizing after I literally kept a tally for each time I said it in the course of one day. I found, much to my horror, that there were *sorrys* everywhere. My world-record number: fifty-three. Yes, I said I'm sorry fifty-three fucking times. In a day. I was shocked and embarrassed by the number, but the silver lining was that I became aware of my excessive apologizing right then and there—and you better believe I did something about it. I encourage you to count *sorrys* for yourself, because only once you are mindful of how much you are saying it can you finally stop apologizing for things that aren't deserving of an apology.

I'm sure you're not surprised to learn that studies have shown we ladies are more likely to say I'm sorry than men. The interesting thing about those studies are that men don't have a problem apologizing, they just have a higher threshold for the stuff they deem worthy of an apology. Bumping into someone coming out of the elevator or not returning a call right away doesn't make their *sorry* benchmark. But for many of us ladies, it does.

So why do we as women say we are sorry so much? Part of it might be out of habit. Part of it might be a desire to seem more likable or express empathy. Some women I speak to tell me that it's about not looking overly aggressive or not wanting to assert too much authority. I get it: it's nerve-racking to interrupt your boss or badger someone for something that hasn't been done. But are you *sorry* for it? Whatever the core reason, it makes us look like we lack self-confidence. Let's vow to apologize *only* when we actually do something wrong.

Now for some role-playing. Let's say you just started a new job and you have a kick-ass idea for improving efficiency that would save the company money. How do you make your pitch to your boss?

SCENARIO 1

YOU: [*timid knock on boss's office door*] I'm sorry to bother you, but I wanted to run an idea by you, if you don't mind.

BOSS: [*continues looking at computer screen*] Shoot.

YOU: Sorry, this is probably stupid, but I was thinking we could, maybe, if you think, um, we could maybe update our software for the . . .

BOSS: [*still looking at computer screen*] Software is IT's problem. I need that memo I asked you about.

YOU: But, oh, um, okay. Sorry.

SCENARIO 2

YOU: [*knock*] Do you have a minute?

BOSS: I might even have two.

YOU: [*still standing in the doorway*] What do you think about getting the AlphaDigital 3.0 upgrade? It would double our invoicing speed and improve overall cash flow.

BOSS: 2.0 is running fine. I picked it myself.

YOU: You were absolutely right to choose it. I researched the new version, and it would be that much better.

BOSS: We're watching expenses.

YOU: It will pay for itself and then some in the first month. I checked it out before coming to you.

BOSS: Great. Make it happen.

In the second scenario, not only do you get what you want, but you get to walk away empowered with the confidence that you conducted yourself like the Boss Bitch you are.

Now, I know bad habits are tough to break. We say *sorry* so much we might not think much of it. But it's a crutch, and a crutch we don't need.

A good way to do that is to remember the acronym KISS: Keep It Simple, Sister (okay, the last *S* conventionally stands for *stupid*, but I like my version better). Get to the point as clearly, quickly, confidently, and respectfully as possible, that way you don't feel the need for filler *sorrys*.

Aside from interrupting a superior, here are other times we tend to say *sorry* in the workplace—with a possible alternative to say instead:

Being late for a meeting

What you might be inclined to say: "I'm so sorry, I had XYZ to do [sometimes we make this up because what we're really doing, like maybe tracking down a tampon, isn't appropriate to say]."

What you should say instead: "Thank you so much for your patience. I know your time is valuable, so let's dive in."

Asking a question

What you might be inclined to say: "I'm sorry, can I ask a question?"

What you should say instead: "Here's my question."

Not liking something

What you might be inclined to say: "I'm sorry, I just didn't think it was that good."

What you should say instead: "I personally didn't care for it, but here's an idea to improve upon it."

Grabbing something or getting by someone

What you might be inclined to say: "I'm sorry, I'm just going to reach by you to get that. I'm sorry, I'm just going to scooch around you."

What you should say instead: "Do you mind handing that to me?" or a simple "Pardon me!"

Someone asking you a question to clarify something you said

What you might be inclined to say: "I'm sorry for the confusion. What I meant to say was XYZ."

What you should say instead: "Let me clarify what I was saying about XYZ."

Nailing workplace communication isn't an overnight thing, especially if you're conditioned to be timid. There's no shame in writing out phrases like this in advance before you walk into an important meeting or a difficult conversation. Or practice with a friend. Chances are, she'll need the help, too.

Boss Bitch Amy Schumer has a *hilarious* skit showing a panel of top women in their fields apologizing for the silliest things: for coughing, for their microphone not working, for asking for water, for being allergic to caffeine, for talking over each other, for having coffee spilled on *them*, for getting bumped *into*, for getting hurt, for the moderator mispronouncing or misstating their name or title. What makes this skit (and any great comedy for that matter) funny is it's based on reality. I totally could imagine seeing each of these individual things play out in real life, but when strung together, it highlights how farcical those moments really are.

The only way to get rid of the stereotype is, hello, by not making it a stereotype anymore and just not apologizing so damn much. To be fair, I probably apologize about five times a day now, maybe ten on a particularly rough day. I still apologize to express empathy and, of course, if I do something wrong. But I do it far less. #sorrynotsorry

BAN *THESE* WORDS

Again, as a fighter for free speech and no filters, I don't love the idea of banning words. However, I believe we *do* need to avoid certain words and phrases that make us self-censor and apologize for what we are saying in the workplace. They include:

Qualifiers

"Kind of"

"Probably"

"Maybe"

Example:

Say this: I think the presentation should include this chart.

Not this: I **kind of** think that the presentation should include this chart.

Fillers

"Um"/"Ah"

"Like"

"I mean"/"You know what I mean?"

Example:

Say this: I don't believe the numbers reflect the results.

Not this: **I mean**, I don't believe the numbers reflect the results, **you know what I mean?**

Seeking Affirmation

"Isn't it?"/"Doesn't it?"

"Don't you think?"

"Right?"

Example:

Say this: The projection is a little off.

Not this: The projection is a little off, **isn't it?**

JUST SAY THANK YOU

Now that I have you thinking very carefully about the words that no Boss Bitch should use, let's talk about a couple of little words you *should* start embracing more than you do now: *thank you*.

I have often said that any math you need to get your finances together you learned in grade school. Well, sometimes when it comes to talking like a boss, the same sentiment applies: remember to say thank you.

Another Amy Schumer skit (yes, girl, I love you) also highlights this crazy thing that women do (er, don't do) when we get compliments: say thank you. The female friends featured in the skit compliment one another with things like "Look at that cute little dress!" Instead of responding with the appropriate *thanks*, each woman puts herself down in extreme and ridiculous ways. (My favorite: "I paid like two dollars for it; it's probably made from old Burger King crowns.") Sound familiar?

Self-hating responses to praise is an epidemic not only in our personal lives but also in the workplace. Are you guilty of not being able to take a compliment from a boss or colleague about your work?

Do you have these types of reactions to compliments?

- Make the compliment seem like it was nothing at all, downplay it, or, worse, deny it.
- Wonder about the motivation of the compliment.
- Assume the compliment giver is just being nice or feeling sorry for you.
- Don't acknowledge the compliment and immediately dish one back.

If so, here are some suggestions for how to change that reaction to one rooted in self-confidence rather than self-loathing. You know how much I love tangible examples and role-playing. So let's do some more:

Compliment Example #1:

Someone at work says: "You did great putting that portfolio together!"

You used to say: "Oh, really? It was no biggie, way easier than I thought."

Now you say: "Thanks!"

Compliment Example #2:

Someone at work says: "You rocked that presentation!"

You used to say: "Really? I don't think so. I stumbled and stuttered so much."

Now you say: "Thanks!"

Compliment Example #3:

Someone at work says: "You aced the coordination of that event with such short notice!"

You used to say: "Yeah, it was probably dumb luck."

Now you say: "Thanks!"

Are you seeing a trend here? Whether it's praising your stellar deck*-making skills or your new 'do, you get compliments. Because you're awesome sauce. Accept them. Say thank you! and move on with your awesome self.

JUST SAY NO

This section is not about the D.A.R.E. program slogan from middle school. It's another little word to try and say more of at work, along with *thanks*. And that word is: *no.*

Saying no might sound contrary to what I stand for as a fearless Boss Bitch, but remember, I'm all about laser focus and doing less, better. So, by all means, say yes! to projects and committees and other extracurriculars at work, but only when it's a hell yes or fuck yes. If it's anything less, it's a no.

Being hungry for success no matter where you are in your career is a necessary quality of any Boss Bitch. I still feel as hungry as the day I started in TV making less than $20,000 a year. I love the saying, "If you are persistent, you will get it, but if you're consistent, you will keep it." To me, this means that you can't be an eager beaver then retreat into your beaver hole, tapped out and exhausted, after you get whatever you were eager for. You have to be consistently eager. And to do that, you have to maintain a workload you can keep up with.

In the workplace, we're playing a constant game of "What have you done for me lately?" As they say, you're only as good as your last success. Did you do something stellar last year? Kudos. What about last month? If you don't keep on churning out those successes, then, in the eyes of a lot of bosses, you haven't accomplished anything tangible lately. Being known as a one-hit wonder at work doesn't equal a home-run career.

Hey, we all want to be seen as these superhuman creatures who can handle any assignment we get. But the truth is, no matter how superhuman you are, you simply can't do everything that comes your way—at least not well. Perhaps you also think that by biting off more than you can chew you'll amass a ton of experience and contacts, even if the quality of your work suffers because you spread yourself too thin. But wouldn't it be better to do both: produce a clear shining accomplishment while also getting some great experience? How? By going deep instead of wide.

Diving deep into one or two extra projects will almost certainly be more beneficial to your personal and professional growth than treading shallow water in a bunch. By doing the latter, you're not likely to produce real results or strong subject matter expertise, but rather, you'll pass out from exhaustion trying to keep pace.

This doesn't apply to the small, annoying mundane stuff that you have to say yes to (because your boss or a client said so) even if you're lukewarm about doing it, especially when you are starting out in a job or field. That stuff is a must, but beyond that, what is worth your most valuable asset—your time? Anything that makes you jump out of your chair and say hell yes.

Seriously, it's that simple. Here's your test: When asked to take anything on, just ask yourself, "Do I want to take this on?"

- If the answer to that question is "OMG YES! HELL YES! This is the best opportunity ev-er," then your answer to the opportunity is yes.
- If the answer to that question is "Yeah, I guess this *could* be interesting," then your answer to the opportunity is no.
- If the answer to that question is "Well, maybe. I need to make nice with this person, and I think I could squeeze this in," then your answer to the opportunity is no.

(This also works for romantic quandaries, but I'll save that for another book.)

The "hell yes" test is basic but effective. In fact, this is the very test used by successful entrepreneurs and powerhouse CEOs. They realize the truth to the cliché that "time is money." As we talked about in Section 1, whether we have a lot of money or not, time is the only currency we all have. It's the great equalizer because we all have the same amount of it. We control how we spend it. So spend wisely, bitch, on things that have you jumping up and down with excitement, not stuff you are "meh" about.

Are you a yes-woman, typically? Are you the motherly, "I'll take care of everyone" type of lady? Well, that's lovely, but sometimes you have to put your oxygen mask on first before helping others. Does that prospect make you nervous? Are you scared that if you say no too much, people will hate you or talk shit about you behind your back? Don't be. Here's a cheat sheet of how to say no without sounding like an asshole to various people who might ask you to do extra work stuff.

YOUR COWORKER

Asks you: "Hey, can you help me with this recruiting project?"

You say: "I would love to be helpful, but so-and-so has me on deadline, so I don't have the bandwidth to make this the success it should be. When that project is done, I would love to find other ways we can collaborate!"

Why you say this: Having coworkers in your corner and collaborating together is a very important part of thriving at work. So tread carefully with this one because you'll likely need their help at some point, too. If you really can't give them the help they need without compromising your own commitments, then say no. But beware that you should only use this method if you are indeed really slammed. If the person asking you for help finds out you were lying, you could burn some important bridges—and they sure won't want to help *you* down the road.

YOUR CLIENT

Asks you: "Are you able to attend this event?"

You say: "I am so flattered you thought of me for this event. I can't make this one, but please keep the invitations coming!"

Why you say this: Clients are queen in any business. They are your source of, well, money, so you want them to be happy. You may be worried that if you decline this ask, they will never ask you again. But what you should remember is that you are thinking about this ask a thousand times more than they are. In fact, it's likely a throwaway invitation (sorry, ego, but it's true), and they probably already have someone else lined up to go as a backup.

YOUR BOSS

Asks you: "Can you take on this project for Client 3?"

You say: "I'm not confident that I can take on another client while devoting the time and energy required for my other clients. I would love to revisit after the current projects with Clients 1 and 2 are wrapped up. In the meantime, I would be thrilled to learn more about the client and try to be as helpful as I can by brainstorming with you for the best strategy of success for Client 3's project. Let's set up a meeting to discuss, and I can also get you up to speed with where we are with Clients 1 and 2."

Why you say this: Saying no to a superior is tough, there's no doubt about it. But if you are really unable to take on something else without letting your current projects down, then you have to say no. Here it helps to remind yourself that you are doing both you and your boss a favor, because if you accept the project, you risk doing a mediocre job at all of them, which not only hurts the project but also affects your overall performance and reputation, and will likely come back and bite you in the ass during review or bonus time.

Remember, saying no the right way doesn't mean that you are unwilling to go above and beyond. Rather, it shows that you value your time, the asker's time, and the importance of the ask. It underscores that you are thoughtful and cautious about taking on something you could only deliver on half-assed. Don't half-ass anything. Whatever you do, always use your full ass(ets).

MASTER YOUR DIGITAL DOMAIN

Of course, it's not just the verbal communication that you have to stay on top of at work, it's the electronic kind that can be just as important, if not more so, to nail. Before you send anything work-related, think about how it represents you and the brand you thought about in the last step. What does it project to those around you about who you are and where you want to be? Is the answer less than flattering? Well, then move those adorable fingers away from the Send button.

E-MAIL ETIQUETTE 101

E-mail has been around long enough now that it's hard to believe that people still need tips on how to write an effective one. But you'd be shocked how many people send me e-mails that are vague, unhelpful, or flat-out unprofessional (or all of the above). Don't be that girl.

Write a super-clear and direct subject line. Duh, it's the first thing people see, so make it count. We all open e-mail mostly based on subject title, or at least use it to decide which we open first.

If it's *actually* urgent, write "URGENT" in the subject line. If it's not, use something specific, accurate, and direct like "Recommendations for the Press Kit" or "Wednesday Morning Meeting *Canceled*." If you are following up with a person you just met, use their name in the subject line. Do you notice that marketers will do that to entice you to open their solicitation because it pops out like they know you? They do that because it works. Try something like "Great to Meet You, Ellen." If the contact is a little more on the personal side rather than a potential hirer, I like to think of something catchy, like "AWESOME . . ." in the subject and the first line of the e-mail saying ". . . to meet you!"

Add the e-mail addresses LAST. Oh yeah, I've been there, and I'm sure you have, too. You start drafting an e-mail and you don't finish it before you accidentally push Send, especially if you have a few e-mail draft windows open at once. It's not the end of the world, but it's not the best practice at work to have to send another note to apologize for being too trigger happy. Even if it gives off just the slightest whiff of sloppiness, that's the kind of perception you *don't* want. The foolproof way to avoid this snafu is to get in the habit of adding in the e-mail address of the recipient *last*. If you're replying to a message, delete the recipient address before you start drafting it, and add it back later.

Quadruple-check before you "reply all." E-mails with a ton of people copied on them can be annoying, especially if everyone keeps hitting Reply All with reactions or things that aren't relevant to you and clog up your e-mail box. You might not be able to "be the change" here, but you can at least refuse to contribute to the e-mail thread disease by replying only to the person or people who *actually* need to know this information. AND check ten times to make sure you are not BCCed on an e-mail that you think you are CCed on instead. I've had employees put me on BCC strategically to just show me that something is done, but I'm "not supposed to be there." I've been too trigger-happy on my phone with replies that I've "replied all" to e-mails I'm BCCed on, and then it just gets awkward.

Also, there's really no need to reply all "Thanks!" As you know, I'm a big fan of saying thank you, but in this case all fifteen people copied on the e-mail don't need to know how grateful you are. Instead, why not pop your head in and say thank you to people in person instead of assaulting their in-boxes?

Don't babble. Being in the media, I get a lot of random e-mails, especially from publicists trying to pitch their clients. Having received a zillion of those e-mails over the years, I can tell you which ones I read and which ones I skip or relegate to my low-priority list.

WHAT I READ
- E-mails that get to the point, fast. Ideally no more than three sentences per paragraph and no more than two paragraphs for the initial e-mail.
- E-mails that say what the person wants quickly: a meeting, an interview, a Skype chat.
- E-mails that have all of the person's contact info at the bottom in their signature (everything *except* for a fax number . . . Who still has those anyway?).

WHAT I DON'T READ

- E-mails that make me keep scrolling and scrolling.
- E-mails with attachments. When you are sending someone an initial e-mail, attachments are almost a surefire way *not* to get a response. Why is a stranger making me open something? Um, delete. It's better to paraphrase whatever is in your attachment and say you would love to have a more detailed conversation about it or the chance to forward over more information. If you must send an attachment, make sure it's something that's actually useful to the recipient, not, say, a silly gif that's just going to be one more annoying thing to open, and eat up their e-mail storage.
- Anything that has a winky face from someone I don't know. I love, love, love me my emojis, but don't wink at me if you don't know me. It's weird, and I'm not into it.

The same rules apply to people in your office or anyone else who you're not introducing yourself to for the first time. Keep it simple and direct. TMI will get you SOL.

Chill with exclamation points. Oh, how I love me a good exclamation point! And, yes, admittedly I love more than one!!! But I try to limit them to one single one *per* e-mail at work. With your girlfriends, go exclamation point crazy, but keep it classy at work or you'll come across looking childish or immature. I KNOW you are excited by all the amazing work you are doing, but take a rule from my playbook and keep that excitement to yourself and show it with only one little but powerful exclamation point. (!!!)

Come up with YOUR sign-off. A ton of e-mails that come your way are signed "Best," or "Best Regards," or "Regards," or something like that, right? Well, all of those are fine. But I know you can be more original than that. Whatever you choose for your "signature" signature, just be consistent. My sign-off is always "Warmest, Nicole." It's my favorite one, and I'm owning it *every damn time* I sign a work-related e-mail. First off, it becomes something people expect from me. Plus, if it's not there and changes to "Best, Nicole," then people start to think I'm pissed and not thinking the "warmest" of them.

Get it ALL out. Take a beat before sending any e-mail; reread it from the beginning. As well written as it may be now, make sure you included *everything* you wanted to say. If you sent a list, let's say, of tasks or follow-up items, did you remember all of them? Did you give all details, including time (time zone, too, if relevant) and location, for a meeting? Sure, something else might come up that you may need to add to the list, or meeting specifics might change, but try to avoid the "Me, again! Forgot this one thing . . ." e-mail cloggers.

IT'S NOT THEM, IT'S YOU

Have you ever had e-mail remorse? "Why did I send that? Why didn't they write me back? Was it something I said?" Don't take it all personally. It's quite possible you have gotten lost in a busy person's e-mail chaos. I try to respond to any e-mail I get, but certainly some falls through the cracks. It happens. But sometimes the answer to the question "Was it something I said?" is *yes*.

The biggest culprit behind not getting a response is: being bor-ing. Don't be a Boring Bitch. Sending a generic e-mail saying that "it was great to meet you, let's keep in touch" is a snore of an e-mail and one that likely will yield radio silence. Instead, say something specific about *why* it was great to meet them and *why* you would like to stay in touch. Something like: "Hi, so-and-so, it was a pleasure to meet you. I loved your analogy about how computers were like old war gods, lots of rules and no mercy. I would love to continue our conversation about helping you find a research assistant. I think I have a solution. How does Monday between ten a.m. and twelve p.m. or after three p.m. work for you to jump on a fifteen-minute catch-up call?"

Why this works and is likely to get you a better response or a response at all:

1. You are being specific and showing that you were listening, and intently at that.
2. You offered to be helpful to them instead of vice versa (this is a hugely important secret to getting ahead in your career that I will talk about throughout the book).
3. You suggested *specific* times to chat. Leaving it open-ended is a recipe for it to never happen. Also, if you are available at *any time,* then it makes you look like you have nothing else important going on; even if you don't, don't come across that way.

MASS(ACRE) E-MAILS

I like to be as efficient as possible when I write follow-up e-mails to a lot of people I might have seen at a work function. So, generally, I write an e-mail template with the bare bones of what I'm trying to say, then personalize that for each person I'm sending it to, filling in specifics for each person.

So, I open up an e-mail draft window and write something like: "Hey, so-and-so, what a fun event at the game night at the pub last night. It was a pleasure to meet and chat. Would love to continue the conversation. Be well and in touch. Warmest, Nicole." (Yes, "be well and in touch" is my way of signing a note like this before my "signature" signature, and, yes, you can steal either one of those e-mail gems if you'd like!)

Now, even though this is template seems a bit boring, I make each one unique to the person I am addressing it to. Having a skeleton simply makes the process more efficient if you are shooting off five follow-ups in a row. However, *don't get too e-mail trigger-happy.* I've gotten myself into trouble when I cranked out these e-mails so fast that I forgot to change the name of the person I was sending to and/or forgot to change the personal tidbits I added about them. WHOOPS!

So don't make my mistake by copy-and-pasting the note so quickly that you forget to change the details. Check and double-check that you changed the name and added some personalization. I'm all about efficiency, until you get sloppy . . . and then it's just embarrassing.

NAIL YOUR BULK E-MAIL

You've probably both received or sent plenty of mass e-mails professionally or personally. Maybe you've used BCC in the past for blasts to everyone in your contacts about an event or asking them to support a cause. Those work . . . until they don't. Sometimes CC and BCC look similar, and then whammo: you find yourself in Reply All hell.

To avoid this mistake, try using the "mail merge" function found on many corporate e-mail systems, including Outlook, or one of the free (like SendinBlue) or paid (like Constant Contact or MailChimp) mass e-mail senders.

You could take some pointers from a friend of mine, Farnoosh Torabi, who sent out an e-mail to her list that I thought was pretty compelling with her tone and call to action. Farnoosh is a badass writer about money matters, not unlike myself, and she's as Boss Bitch as they come. Do I hear whispers about why I am promoting *another* woman doing something similar in my field in my book? Yeah, I am. Because confident women prop others up, not tear them down. So, as I was saying, here's one of her recent blasts:

Subject: Nicole, would love your help

Hi Nicole,

I hope you've been doing great since we last connected on my podcast.

Wanted to share that my new CNBC show *Follow the Leader* is finally on the air!

I got the insane chance to follow some of the world's top entrepreneurs for forty-eight hours. A new episode airs tonight with serial entrepreneur and online marketing pro Gary Vaynerchuck.

May I ask a favor?

We'd love some support on social media today to spread the word about the show. We're hoping for a ratings boost, as we're midway through the season. Every bit of support will go a long way.

If you're down, I've created some sample tweets/FB messages here. But feel free to write whatever you feel comfortable with.

Can't wait to watch @Farnoosh shadow serial entrepreneur @garyvee on #FollowtheLeader tonight. 10 p.m. ET/PT on CNBC!

Loving the new show #FollowtheLeader w/ my friend @Farnoosh. Tune in tonight for a fresh episode. 10 p.m. ET/PT on @CNBC

"Stop whining. Start hustling." Catch @Farnoosh shadowing @garyvee tonight on #followtheleader. @CNBC 10 p.m. ET/PT

And attaching a graphic for tonight's episode if you like including images with your tweets!

Thanks so much. I truly appreciate your help!

I love a lot of what Farnoosh has going on in this e-mail blast, which is essentially that it doesn't look like a blast. First, it's customized to say my name. Second, it has a personal first line. At first blush you are thinking: "Damn, this is an e-mail just for me!" Well, if you write a blast correctly, that's what your reader *should* be thinking. (In reality, this e-mail likely went out to *all* the people who were recently on her podcast.) Next, she gives her reader actionable, easy things to do that are basically already done for them. Last, her tone is spot-on for the audience of her friends and supporters. She's talking to people she already knows and who know her, so it's absolutely appropriate. And the attachment is okay, since it's not being sent to someone for the first time and it's part of the pre-chewed action points she is hoping you'll do on social media for her. Plus, she asks in such a lovely way, how *could* you say no?

FYI

Generally, the best days to send mass e-mails are Monday, Tuesday, and Wednesday. The logic behind that is that people tend to be more e-mail fatigued and burned out by the end of the week (not to mention, already beginning that steady slide into checked-out Fri-YAY) so they are more likely to press Delete. Typically, the best time to send bulk e-mails is around lunchtime, when people have more time to sift through their e-mail (but do a little research in your own industry for more specifics on the best timing). People often purge e-mail they got from the night before in the morning and are checked out in the late afternoon, so a little afternoon in-box delight is often the e-mail blast timing sweet spot.

E-INTRODUCING PEOPLE

E-mail introductions can be some of the most important e-mails you send in your career. If done properly and thoughtfully, your intro can create a ton of value for yourself and the two people you are connecting. If done too hastily, you can not only look bad but piss people off.

Yes, there is an art to the e-intro, but let me try to draw some lines for you to color within:

1. *Mutually beneficial.* Introducing people is only effective when it is beneficial for *both* of them. If it's super beneficial for one person and the other person is confused or annoyed by it, they'll be hating on you for doing it. Yes, yes, I know you wanted to be helpful. But as the saying goes, sometimes the road to hell is paved with good intentions.

2. *Have a pre-intro talk.* One of my biggest pet peeves with introductions is when the person doesn't brief both parties *before* making the intro and just assumes they both want it. A lot of times it works out fine and you get the green light. But every once in a while, one of the people says they are too busy or they are changing focus or whatever, and they don't care for the intro. In that case, you've saved yourself the potential hate from that person by doing it before asking.

3. *Put oomph into it.* The worst e-mail intros are the generic ones that go something like this: "Liz/Bob, you MUST know each other! I'll leave it to you two to take it from here." Whoa, whoa, wait, what?! This tells Liz and Bob zilch about the other person and zippo about why you are introducing them. Even if you quickly briefed them before the e-mail, perhaps they forgot and need a quickie reminder or would appreciate a little more color.

4. *Deets.* Make sure to give some specific and pertinent information

like full names and locations. Full names might sound formal, but if one person has only their first name in their e-mail (i.e., sabrina@start-up.com) or it's confusing to tell what their full name is (i.e., slogens@company.com—is that Sarbina L. Ogens or Sabrina Logens?), then it's tough for the other person to know what the other's last name is if they want to look them up, which is normal. Also, make sure to say what city each person is in. If one person is in LA and one person is in NYC, then it seems unlikely that they are getting together for coffee any time soon, or at least not without some coordination and a plane ticket. Instead, it would be best to suggest a call, in which case location is also important to determine the right time zones for the call to happen.

5. *Don't forward all side talk.* If you're the e-mail introducer, chances are you've had side e-mails with both people you are introducing to each other. As someone who has been on the receiving end of an introduction, I must admit that I've received some of those forwards that were probably not meant to be forwarded, either because they were inappropriate ("Yeah, I saw her picture . . . intro away!") or because it contained some confidential information about work between them ("A-okay on the intro . . . and by the way, I approved that $500 bonus for Mary Gold but rejected the one for Sari Smith"). If you are going to forward e-mails between yourself and the other person, make sure that everyone looks good and upstanding. When in doubt, edit it out.

Introductions and the relationships that stem from them can undoubtedly be among the most valuable currency you have in your career. Pay it forward to create goodwill. If you use care and caution, that introduction karma will come back to you in a big way.

DITCH THE EXCUSES

Shit happens that gets in the way of work. You get sick. Someone in your family gets sick. Your babysitter doesn't show up. Your car breaks down. Your dog dies. Whatever it is, it happens, and it sucks.

But it happens to all of us. We have to cancel or reschedule meetings or lunch dates or other work stuff on account of personal crap, and we have all had those things canceled or rescheduled on us, I'm sure, more than we'd like. When you're doing the canceling, though, for whatever personal reason, keep the explanation short and professional, avoiding TMI at all costs.

Let's do a little e-mail role-playing:

I had a personal emergency come up a couple of years ago that meant I had to reschedule a bunch of calls and appointments. I wondered, "Should I explain why I'm canceling?"

E-MAIL OPTION 1

"Hey, so-and-so, I'm so sorry, but my boyfriend-type dude got in a bad ski accident and I need to cancel. So sorry. Let me know when is good for you. I will totally make it up to you. Anytime, anywhere—it's on me! Thanks for understanding!! Nicole"

E-MAIL OPTION 2

"Hey, so-and-so, I unfortunately need to cancel our call today. Does next Tuesday at xx or xx work instead? Thanks, Nicole."

It took me about thirty seconds to decide on the second option. In a business setting, you don't need to explain a change of schedule, and you don't have to apologize for having an emergency. The aforementioned shit happens, people will deal, and the TMI and overly apologetic game makes you look weak and even unprofessional and juvenile.

DON'T SEND THE SNARKY E-MAIL

I'm sure reading that heading gives you flashbacks to the time that you impulsively pushed Send on a nasty e-mail you quickly regretted. Yes, it happens to the best of us. I've totally let my emotions get the best of me and chewed someone out on e-mail only to apologize with my digital tail between my legs the next day.

I get it: your blood can boil at annoying work stuff. And it's so, so easy to respond with something snippy and rash. E-mail or text gives us the chance to respond immediately, emotions and all, without the safeguard of social etiquette that comes with seeing someone face-to-face. But today, most communication does happen over e-mail, which means we are often left with our blood boiling behind our screens with no rational awareness of the repercussions of what we are saying (typing) in the heat of the moment.

The other problem with e-mail is that tone can be so easily misinterpreted. Let's say you get what might seem like an innocuous (to an outsider) e-mail from a supervisor late at night: "I need to see you first thing in the morning. I want to go over your deadlines and assign you something new."

Sounds like a normal note if you read it one way and sounds like an obnoxious note if you read it in your head another way, especially if you already feel overwhelmed, overworked, and underappreciated (oh, and by the way, if you have been drinking that night, those feelings are exacerbated, so do yourself a favor and sober up before even thinking about replying).

Because you are used to replying right away, you do, but you are pissed as hell, so you write back: "Okay, don't forget that I am swamped with seventeen of your other 'assignments.' Anyway, can someone else do some work around here for once? Thanks!"

I've been known to get passive-aggressive instead of outright mean when I'm mad. I used to think I could say something biting and then follow it up with a "Thanks!" and it would all be all right. Wrong. A passive-aggressive response is still a terrible response no matter if you write "XOXO" or say you'll give the person $100 at the end of it.

Instead of furiously hitting Send on that e-mail, do this instead:

1. *Chill.* I know it's easier said than done. But step the hell away. Go get a cup of coffee. Walk around the block. Have a cooling-off period.

2. *Write it nasty.* Write the craziest, nastiest, most awful e-mail back. Then . . . delete it. Don't forget to open up a new e-mail window for this *without* the recipient's address in the To box just in case of the accidentally (or accidentally on-purpose) slipped-finger Send. Get it out of your system and you're more likely to either forget it or say "fuck it" and write something less pissy and more work appropriate instead.

3. *Stop and wonder.* Ask yourself: "Is there a better way to respond to this than ripping this person a new asshole?" Could you say something like "I would love to chat about how to get this partnership back on track" instead of what you *really* want to say?

FYI

No, you can't recall e-mails you regret. Well, you technically *can* (with features on Outlook and Gmail), but all that does is send another e-mail "recalling" what you wrote but the damage is done because the first e-mail is still there and now you are drawing more attention to it.

Let's say all these precautions fail and you send the snarky e-mail anyway. Okay, it's done—don't down too many cocktails or pints of ice cream wallowing in it. You can deal with it in the morning. In person. Walk up to that supervisor's desk and say, "Hey, I was really stressed, and I let my emotions get the best of me. It won't happen again. I would love to update you on my current assignments and see how I can be helpful with the new one you mentioned."

If you took the low road, get up to the high one quickly. Offline.

ROCK YOUR BODY (LANGUAGE)

Obviously, you can communicate with your actual voice and over e-mail, but you can also communicate just as much if not more with your body language. And when it comes to making a good impression and getting your message across at work, watching your *P*s and *Q*s and mastering the art of body language goes a long way. Aside from the cliché sitting up straight and making eye contact, here are twelve less-obvious dos and don'ts to help you mind your manners in different business settings:

At Business Meetings Out of the Office

1. *Seat yourself.* Don't expect someone to pull your chair out for you; it's not appropriate in a business setting like it is on a date. (That is, I hope guys still do this on a date. Chivalry, anyone?)
2. *Hands off.* Whoever is the host of the meeting should put their hand out first to shake hands with others.

At Business Meals

1. *Be cost conscious.* Don't order the most expensive thing on the menu if you are the guest, even if you're *totally* craving it. You don't want to convey even the slightest suggestion that you are taking advantage. Also, steer clear of alcohol (for obvious reasons) and specials. When a waiter lists special menu items, they are usually 10–40% more expensive than items on the regular menu.
2. *Dessert, please.* If you are the one who called the meeting and the other person or people order dessert, then you should also order dessert. You don't want them to feel like they are making you wait for them. Same goes for appetizers. Even if you aren't hungry enough for two courses, just order a salad if they request a starter.
3. *No doggie bag.* I don't care how delicious your ravioli was, it's tacky to take anything to go, period.
4. *Who pays?* Whoever did the inviting. So if you called the meeting, you pay. If your guest insists on paying, say that the company is footing the bill and that will likely be the end of it. Even if the company isn't paying, you should pay and use it as a tax write-off.

Meeting New Work Folk

1. *Rise up!* If you are sitting while being introduced to someone, stand up, otherwise your presence is easier to be forgotten.

2. *Play handsy.* The higher-ranking or more senior person should initiate the handshake.

3. *Put it down.* Your cell phone, that is. You don't want to be tempted to be distracted, and you don't want the person you are meeting to think some text that you glanced down at your cell phone to see is more important than talking to them.

4. *Keep it straight.* If you tilt or cock your head, it can come across as looking weak or unconfident. Alternatively, it can sometimes be seen as too coy or flirty, which is not the vibe you want to give off.

5. *No, no, thank YOU.* Try to keep the thank-yous to a minimum. The more you say it, the needier you look. Keep it to one or two impactful thank-yous.

6. *Yes, yes, thank-you notes.* As you may remember from *Rich Bitch*, I need a thank-you-note intervention. I literally send a separate note (preferably handwritten but e-mailed if it needs to get there sooner) to everyone I meet. Like, seriously, everyone. I interviewed a mailman for a story once—boom, thank-you note. I might go overboard, but according to business etiquette experts (yes, those are a thing), you can't really go wrong by sending one.

One of the best ways to look like the strong, in-charge, and confident Boss Bitch that you are is to exude that vibe in all forms of communication at work. If you have some improvement to do on this front, it's all good. Maybe you fucked up an e-mail or you rubbed the right person the wrong way. That's okay. It happened. It's fixable. It's not the end of the world, even if it can feel that way.

Draw upon one of my other favorite quotes: "Everything will be okay in the end. If it's not okay, then it's not the end." And since you get to write your story, don't forget that you get to decide how it goes *and* how it ends.

BOTTOM LINE

Conventional Wisdom: Assertive women are overbearing.

The Real Deal: Hellz no. Don't scream. Don't be an asshole. But, don't be scared to be clear, assertive, and confident. And don't apologize unless you actually screwed up. People will respect you and what you have to say if you respect yourself.

Conventional Wisdom: Don't get too personal with businesspeople.

The Real Deal: Well, sure, don't let your freak flag fly, but keep it real with people at work. Don't be overly professional, "all work," and make it seem like you have a stick up your bum. Be human and honest; people will root for you at work if they get to know you on a personal level. Sure, you have to work hard, too, and can't rely only on connections, but people want to work with and for people they like. Seriously, don't you?

Conventional Wisdom: Sending e-mail is like texting—it's fine to make mistakes and send a lot of rapid-fire replies. People expect it.

The Real Deal: To some extent, yes. But not at the cost of clogging up people's e-mail boxes with knee-jerk responses to everything. And, as far as I know, texting doesn't have a BCC feature, so before you respond, check and check again to see if it was even supposed to be known you were on the e-mail in the first place!

BE A GOAL DIGGER

How to Get—and Crush—Your Dream Job

Forget this "gold digger" nonsense. We Boss Bitches are straight up *"goal* diggers." We don't need a trust fund or a man's cash to get ahead. We scoff at any notion of an "MRS" degree. We just need a clear, killer plan (and maybe some coffee, a topknot, and some Katy Perry jams) to achieve those goals the right way.

So roll up your tasteful work sleeves and let's get down to some serious *goal digging.* In Step 3 of "Being the Boss at Work," I'm going help you tackle the ins and outs of how to get a job, keep a job, move up in a job, and, if it happens (it's happened to me), handle getting let go—with class. Because, as I like to say, we Boss Bitches are: classy, sassy, and badassy.

HOW TO DIG FOR GOALS

There's no one way to move up the corporate ladder. In fact, it often feels more like a rope swing. And that's okay. Remember, this isn't your mama's career path; it's yours. And swinging will give you a better view than you'd get if you were stuck clinging to a ladder, anyway. Sure, it can also feel out of control and scary at times. So first things first: we need to figure out where we want that swing to take us.

SO, WHAT'S YOUR DREAM JOB, ANYWAY?

Before you get your dream job, you have to, hello, figure out what it is in the first place. You can't just say, "I want to be in communications." That's like saying, "I'm going to a party in Miami." Oh yeah? Well, there are a lot of parties happening every night in Miami—which one are you going to? What's the address? Who's gonna be there? Same goes for your dream job. You need to know the destination so you can figure out the best way to get moving in that direction. After all, if you don't know what your dream job *is*, how the hell are you going to land it?!

When you first start thinking about what those dream J.O.B.s might be, list *everything* you can possibly think of that you would be interested in or love doing. If you have only one role you want at one specific company, then I love your specificity and focus, but I would encourage you to cast a wider net, because chances are that exact position isn't a current option.

Just like in the wonderful world of online dating, the people who are most successful cast the widest net. Friends of mine who were frustrated by the lack of dates they were getting found husbands on dating apps only after they lifted *all* of the filters they had set to screen for everything they *thought* they were looking for. And guess what? Their dream guys turned out not to be the six-foot-blue-eyed-heart-surgeon-who-loves-hiking-and-the-Yankees-and-speaks-four-languages unicorns they first filtered for. But they were "their" guys, brown eyes and all. Think about broadening your search horizons in the same way when you are getting out into the job-hunting world, too. Start with a wider pool, then whatever comes your way that you really don't like, you can always swipe left, so to speak.

Whatever the reason for putting yourself "out there" professionally— you got laid off, you are looking for something new, or maybe you are looking for something part-time—be open-minded to all of your prospects. Think cause marketing sounds intriguing? Jot it down. Do you think being a day trader appears interesting and lucrative? Do friends say you are the best drink mixologist on this side of the Mississippi? Well, first, where's my invite? Second, write that down.

Then start exploring some of those options with the three *R*s (not including *rest* and *relaxation*, but nice try):

1. **Rummaging** through the "jobs" section of LinkedIn. Start searching the types of jobs you'd be interested in doing and check out the profiles of people who currently have those jobs to see what their trajectory has looked like.

2. **Roaming** around Glassdoor. Use this as a resource for finding jobs within specific industries in your area; you can even find out the typical salary and benefits offered for similar positions in your city, and read reviews from actual employees who have worked at each company.

3. **Researching** *exactly* what titles mean. Does "coordinator to the chief marketing officer of a nonprofit" sound cool? Read further down to the description. What does it say? "Coordinates scheduling and tasks for the vice presidents." That's probably code that you are going to essentially be Anne Hathaway's character in *The Devil Wears Prada*. If that sounds awesome to you, great. If not, move on.

Look at all the options for all the buckets on your list. Really, really analyze the description. And if you don't totally understand it or are "meh" about it, first ask an expert in that field for more insight, and if you still aren't jazzed, then keep going until you find something that gets you totally fired up.

THE BEST WAY TO GET A JOB

If you're crushing the networking game (which I'll talk much more about in the next step), then you should be hearing about jobs *before* they are listed on sites like Monster, CareerBuilder, or TheLadders. Why? First of all, employers of *listed* jobs usually get inundated with résumés up the wazoo, so good luck with that. And often, those posted jobs stay on the market a long time for a reason (just like houses you keep seeing month after month on house-hunting sites or guys on dating apps).

So don't wait around for your application to get noticed. Don't just sit and wait for the hirers looking at your résumé to call and take your professional breath away. Yes, still submit applications to the jobs on those sites that look interesting, but *also* tap your work tribe for *unlisted* opportunities as well. Those are typically the better, more coveted jobs anyway (that's why they keep them unlisted—they know it's a strong position and don't want to leave it open to just "anyone") and come to fruition faster because even just knowing about them means you have been "vetted" to some extent.

When you are hunting is the time to tap in to that network you've been building. After all, up until now you have just been planting seeds of goodwill—now it's now time to reap the fruits of what you've sown. Boss Bitches don't settle for sitting in the backseat of their lives in any capacity, especially not when cruising down a career path. Get in the driver's seat and check the traffic on multiple routes that get to your dream job so you can arrive there the fastest.

GETTING THE JOB

Don't assume employers will just magically know you're great—you have to show them. Yes, sure, this is what your résumé is for, but there's no chance I'm going to take the hard-earned money you spent on this book and bore you with lame advice about résumé formatting and fonts and all that jazz. Do a Google search for the best templates and don't get bogged down in what people say are the best fonts to land a job; that's crap.

What *I am* going to teach you is the *je ne sais quoi* for getting a job. That is, the little extras that make you stand out as the professional you are. The X factors that are going to get you plucked out of the million sans-serif résumés on an employer's desk—and then how to wow them when you get in the door.

When I was applying for my first job, I sent out literally hundreds of audition tapes and résumés to news stations around the country, starting with the smallest markets and working my way up to the national stations . . . I mean, why not, right? The worst thing they could say is no. And most did, but I felt good knowing I'd tried, even if it was a long shot.

My *je ne sais quoi*, which helped me to get noticed, was the little touches. Back in the day of VHS (damn, I'm old), applicants would send their tapes in generic black sleeves with a label affixed on which they'd handwritten their name. No, ma'am, not me. The first round of tapes I sent were packaged in red sleeves. It cost maybe a penny extra per sleeve, but it was well worth it to make my tape stand out. Then I had my labels professionally printed instead of handwriting them on the spine in—you guessed it—red, bold, all-caps font. With the next round of tapes, I got even fancier. I bought the hard cases like you'd get for a movie, with a clear sleeve around the box. I designed a slip (with my limited Photoshop skills) that had a red background (obviously) with my name and phone number front and center with pictures of me "in action" reporting from the field, and put it in the sleeve. The slip wrapped around the back of the case, where I listed the contents of the tape so viewers knew what to expect when they popped it in. Whether or not the news director liked what was on the tape, at least I got noticed. Once, a news director didn't have anything for me just then but kept my tape because he liked my attention to detail (and how *could* you so hastily dispose of such a lovely case?!) and called me a couple of years later to offer me a job. At that point I was already employed, but the callback proved my theory that my tape got me noticed *and* remembered.

And I didn't stop there. Most people would send a generic cover letter stating, "Here's who I am, and I've covered x, y, and z." But I wanted to be sure the stations I was applying to knew exactly what I could *bring* to the party. Hirers want to know what you can do for *them* and whether you are smart enough to think about how you can fill *their* needs before your own. So instead of bragging about how a-mazing I was, I did research on each market to see what was the latest news in the area and came up with three story ideas specifically for them. In other words, I wanted to show them, "Here's what I can do for *you*." And I can tell you from the callbacks I received, I was one of the only ones to think that way, and they appreciated it. Some station chiefs even "borrowed" those ideas, even though they didn't hire me, which I was flattered about . . . I guess.

CONFESSIONS OF A
BOSS BITCH

Getting in the Door

By the time I was a freshman in college, I already knew I wanted to be a news anchor. I was young and had no connections, but I was determined to find a way in. I set up an interview with the HR department at NBC in New York to apply for an internship. I knew they were looking for only juniors and seniors, but I applied anyway, thinking I at least had a fair chance of them making an exception if I showed the initiative and flew all the way there.

No dice. They shooed me away because I was too young. I don't like to take no for an answer, but how was I going to get around this age obstacle? Hmmm ... Think, Lapin, think. Well, I had one thing going for me: I still had the security badge for the famed 30 Rock building I was issued when I arrived for my appointment.

The only name I knew in the building was a consumer affairs reporter at the local New York NBC station, Asa Aarons, so I asked everyone I saw, "Where's Asa Aarons's desk?" I didn't even know what he looked like, just that he had red hair. Someone pointed me in the right direction, and I went straight over to him.

"Are you Asa Aarons?" I asked. He looked kinda startled that this whippersnapper was accosting him unannounced.

"Yes."

"Hi, I'm Nicole Lapin. I'm your summer intern," I said, and I stuck out my hand to shake his.

He said, "Oh, okay ..." Then he paused before saying: "I guess if you got yourself here through security and everything to come find my desk ... then I think you would make a pretty solid intern!"

And just like that, I got my first internship at the number one news station in the number one market in the country. That scenario could have gone *really* badly, with him calling security and me potentially getting locked up (okay, that's a stretch, but I could have gotten questioned or thrown out on the curb or something). Thankfully, I seemed unthreatening enough that that didn't happen. After all, the only weapon I'd carried in was my chutzpah.

From that experience I realized that you can learn the rules and play by them, or you can know the rules and then know when and how to break them. This was the perfect time to break them—and it worked.

NAILING THE INTERVIEW

Once you're in the door, you typically don't get the job on the spot like I did. In fact, that sitch at WNBC with Asa was quite cinematic, and nothing like it has ever even come close to happening again. For future jobs, I would endure months-long audition processes that were vetted by actual focus groups . . . talk about nerve-racking. Some of my interviews even came with tests. Quick: Can you name all the Supreme Court justices?! Yep, that's not a joke. That was seriously a question on a current-events test I once had to take for a job.

Luckily, most interviews, in most industries, are not so intense. Here are some ways to nail some of the most typical interview questions (that don't include current-events exams):

1. "Tell me about yourself." (Yes, I know this is not technically a question, but it's one of the first things most hirers say.)

Bad answer: Well, I went to school at XYZ university, then I got an internship at such-and-such company, then I got a job at another company, then I got another job, and now I'm looking for another. And I have a dog.

Why this is a bad answer: They see all this stuff on your résumé. Why are you reciting what they already see in front of them? And unless you see fifty dog photos in their office or you're interviewing for a doggy day care, assume they don't care what kind of pet you have.

Good answer: My passion for XYZ (the niche you have in the industry that you are interviewing for) started in college, where I found myself trying to solve these kinds of problems in my dorm room. Some of the findings there drove me to try to put those to the test in the real world, and company such-and-such was a hotbed of that type of work. Now I am looking to grow that knowledge base, which I know is an area you'd like to expand as well. I am here to learn what specific holes you might have in those areas and how I might be able to fill those gaps.

Why this is a good answer: My favorite phrase is "How can I be helpful?" It's something I often say not just in interviews, but at the end of all conversations. It reminds the other side that I want to be of service and am not there to brag about myself. In interviews, this answer also creates a story of your journey. It doesn't just regurgitate your résumé; it gives a narrative and a motivation behind your moves—past, present, and future.

2. "Who would you have dinner with, dead or alive?"

Bad answer: Gosh, that would be a big dinner party and definitely include the Dalai Lama, the president and the first lady, of course, and probably the Pope.

Why this is a bad answer: Ask one hundred people this same question, and I bet at least twenty-five of them will give this same exact answer. It's generic. Yeah, who *wouldn't* want to have dinner with any of these folks? No one. In any business. Stick to people relevant to your field and your passions, and show a little creativity, while you're at it.

Good answer: (If you're interviewing for a tech job.) I would love to meet Jennifer Fleiss and Jennifer Hyman, founders of Rent the Runway, tell them about the latest in XYZ (the technology that's related to the job you are interviewing for), and get their thoughts on how we might bring it to scale.

Why this is a good answer: You are staying industry specific and you are also giving color about *why* you would want to break bread with them and what you would talk about.

3. "Who do you look up to?"

Bad Answer: My mom.

Why this is a bad answer: I'm sure your mom is delightful, but she doesn't belong in the job interview. Unless you are interviewing for a job in an industry in which she has been a pioneer (in which case, lucky you that Boss Bitch–dom runs in the family!), save mama for your speech when accepting that first big award.

Good answer: (If you are interviewing for a job in finance, for example.) I look up to Carla Harris, who was one of the first female VPs on the Street (as in Wall Street). I admire her commitment to remain true to herself and her passions (she's an opera singer, too!) while winning clients over with her deep knowledge of international finance. She motivated me to find ways to let my personality and skill set drive my career forward and to always be innovating, which is a mission statement of this company.

Why this is a good answer: Again, this is an answer that needs to be industry specific. You should not just name the person but explain *why* you look up to her. Then bring your answer back to the mission of the company so that it shows you a) know what it is, and b) are striving to be the embodiment of that.

4. "What are your biggest weaknesses?"

Bad answer: I'm such a perfectionist it's scary.

Why this is a bad answer: What's scary is that almost everyone gives that exact answer to this question.

Good answer: My biggest weakness is that I get so focused on my work that I keep my head down too much. To combat that, I have been more mindful of reaching out to different groups within the company, especially one like this one that offers an open floor plan and an open-door policy. I've also really been able to build self-awareness of this issue, which I think is one of my biggest assets in learning and growing in this field.

Why this is a good answer: Everyone stutters when asked this question. You think you're going to kill your chance, you worry you are going to show them why you suck and they shouldn't hire you. You won't. The key to answering this question, aside from not saying you're a perfectionist, is to be open and honest but *pivot your answer to a strength* that ties into the company you are interviewing for. And you get big brownie points by playing up your self-awareness of your weakness, because that is a good quality of any employee. Plus, you can take this opportunity to express a desire to learn and to be a team player—both strong qualities for a candidate in any industry.

5. "Do you have any questions for me?"

Bad answer: Nope, you covered it all.

Why this is a bad answer: The worst answer to this question is no. The second worst is "How much does this job offer and what are the benefits or perks?" The first answer shows that you are not engaged in the company enough to go above and beyond to be inquisitive in a deeper way. The money question is just tacky and extremely off-putting. If you get the job, *that's* when you negotiate your salary, as we will talk about later in this step.

Good answer: I noticed that there is a burgeoning area of study in the XYZ area and that this company has started to explore it further. What are the plans moving forward for addressing this?

Why this is a good answer: Well, first, you show that you clearly did your homework on the company and took the time to craft a well-researched, well-thought-out answer to this question—because you *will* be asked it at the end of virtually every interview. Ideally, the XYZ you are steering the interviewer toward talking about with this question is an area of *your* expertise. In other words, you essentially want to plant the idea that you could help the company in building out this area. BIN-GO!

Remember, the biggest differentiator between the "bad" answers and the "good" ones is you. By that, I mean the bad answers are the ones where you mostly talk about *you*. This is not the time or place for sharing your entire life story. Remember, you are not on a date—you are at a job interview. The good answers are the ones where you talk mostly about how you will be able to help *them*. The "me, me, me" or "sell, sell, sell" will get you in the "no, no, no" pile fast.

PHONERS

Sometimes you will encounter a situation where the only option for the interview is a phone interview. I know you are so much better in person, especially after perfecting the stellar workplace communication rules you learned in the last step. But the phoner happens—especially if that employer is super slammed or if you are in a different city and there's no time or no money to fly you out.

Those two possibilities are important to keep in mind on this type of interview. If your interviewer is pressed for time (aka has a high-pressure job of their own), don't be long-winded to overcompensate for your lack of face time. The busier they are, the faster they are hoping to get to the point, so be pointed even if you have to rehearse "sound bites"— thoughtful bite-size answers that pack a punch—in advance.

If they can't schedule an in-person interview because they are pressed for time and need to hire immediately, you should also make sure to emphasize your time flexibility—which you should conveniently have a ton of if you're currently unemployed. If you *are* employed and *don't* have the time or flexibility, try to highlight the strong relationship you have with your current boss, who is a champion of your next moves, to assure your new boss that the transition process can be quick and easy.

If the reason they are doing a phoner is because they can't afford to fly you out, be mindful that this is a company that counts their pennies. During the course of the interview, try to incorporate your love for being scrappy and ways you've accomplished big things cheaply in the past. Emphasize the fact that you are super low maintenance at work (even if personally you are rather high maintenance).

A few other phone interview tips to keep in mind:

Answer the phone. This sounds silly, but it blows my mind how many people are in bad reception areas, or are in the other room, the car, or whatever, and need to call the interviewer back. That shows that you are unreliable off the bat.

Figure out who's calling who. I've had calls set on my calendar that say that so-and-so is supposed to call me to initiate the call. Every time there's confusion (they forget or think that I'm calling them), the call kicks off with a sour taste of incompetence in my mouth. To avoid this problem, you can also use FreeConferenceCall.com, or any of the other free conference-calling services out there, to set a dial-in; that way, you're *both* calling into the line.

Speak the lingo. Since you are using only your voice for this interview, make sure you speak knowledgeably and authoritatively. That means if you are interviewing in the advertising business, for example, you use their jargon—stuff like CPM* and SEO*—properly.

Exude confidence. Knowing your answers inside and out before you start will give you greater confidence to keep the conversation more, well, conversational. This way, the person on the other line will feel like they are just talking to a coworker (don't get *too* casual and veer too off topic or get too personal). Also, remember, the person you are interviewing with *wants* to hire you, I promise. It's because you are fabulous, of course, but also because if they are so slammed that they can't even make time for a face-to-face interview, trust me, they want to check the box that this position is filled so they can get on with the rest of their job—with you there to help!

FYI

According to recent research, 52% of Americans said they are unhappy in their jobs. So, either you or the person sitting next to you is counting down the hours till five o'clock so you can peace out. You don't want to be that girl. If it gets that bad, you have to plot to bounce. As our Boss Bitch favorite Audrey Hepburn said, "Happy girls are the prettiest." If things get ugly, plan your pretty escape toward happiness.

FOLLOW-UP NOTES AFTER THE INTERVIEW

This is a critical final step to the interview process that a lot of people muck up. Think of it as the text, e-mail, or call (or flowers!!) you get after a first date. Crucial, right? Without this, there is unlikely to be a second date. Well, interviewing is like speed dating. The follow-up sets the tone for whether or not there is something "*there*, there."

Immediately after a job interview, you should send something to this effect:

Hi Mr. Recruiter,
It was such a pleasure meeting you today. I loved hearing more about your endeavors in XYZ and how I could be helpful in growing that area of your business.
I think this is a mutually beneficial fit, and I look forward to continuing the conversation.
Warmest, Nicole
[+ my contact info]

It seems almost too simple, but it works. A thoughtful follow-up that stresses how you can be helpful to them and their company shows that you were listening and reminds them why you are the gal for the job. This will set you apart from the equally awesome candidate who did not think to follow up (or made the follow-up note all about how badly they wanted the job).

I'm old-school in a lot of ways, so I suggest e-mailing and handwriting the same note. Snail mail will take too long to reach your recruiter person in a timely manner, but it's a gesture that's still important. That's why I say send the same note via e-mail; that way, when they ultimately receive your handwritten note, you've already been hired and the note just reinforces their good decision to do that.

Now, what if . . . you don't get a reply to the thank-you e-mail? *C'est tragique!* No, it doesn't mean you didn't get the job, it just means that they are busy or still sorting through candidates, so you should poke them one more time with something like this:

Hi Mr. Recruiter,
Wonderful to meet you on [date] and talk about the opportunity at XYZ.
I am looking forward to discussing next steps. Is there anything I can do on my end to help the process along?

Thank you!
Warmest, Nicole
[+ my contact info]

The worst thing you can do is be passive-aggressive like "Hi, again, Mr. Recruiter" or "Me, again!" or "Haven't heard from you yet." Can all that stuff and just be professional and express exactly what you want to get across: that you are diligent, interested, and looking for a follow-up.

If you haven't heard from them after this, one last-ditch effort might be forwarding them the last note you sent with something like, "Just following up on this in case my message got lost in the e-mail shuffle." If still nada, assume they passed on you, because, as they say in Hollywood, "Don't call us, we'll call you." I pinkie swear, after two or three notes, if they wanted you, they would have called or e-mailed you. If they didn't, that's okay—dust off your shit-kickers and keep on kicking!

HOW TO THRIVE WHILE YOU STRIVE

Once you've got the job, a lot of people think, "Oh, that's the hard part—now I'm just going to coast." There's an assumption that if you just work hard enough and don't get in trouble, you'll be set. Boss Bitches know that's not true. It might be enough to keep the job, but it's not enough to thrive in it. To thrive, you have to stand out.

The most obvious but important way to stand out is . . . to be good. Actually, not just to be good—to be *great*. You don't need to be great at everything, and you don't even need to be great at something big, but you should be great at something that you can totally own. Find something at work to be the go-to person for: making gorgeous presentations, taking the most beautiful photos for the company website, or being proficient in Arabic. Whatever your thing is, you want to be known as the *only* person the office goes to when there is a presentation to be made, a photo to be taken, or an Arabic translation needed.

Thriving at your job comes when you feel confident in and sought after for your skill set. Do you still not think you've got something that unique to offer? Think again. We've all got something; it's up to you to identify it. Go ahead and blow your own damn mind. I dare you.

"DISRUPT," BUT DON'T BE DISRUPTIVE

While you shine with your skills, you can and should also shine with your ideas. One big buzz word in the business world that you should know if you don't already is "disrupt.*" Sometimes you'll hear it overused, but it's supposed to mean being so innovative in an industry that you shake up the status quo. Essentially, it's being a trailblazer with ideas that have never been seen in your industry before. So, for example, Uber disrupted the taxi and private driver industry. Airbnb disrupted the hotel industry. Netflix disrupted the movie rental business. It's basically saying, "Oh hell no to 'business as usual,' there's a new shake-shit-up sheriff in town!"

You're probably thinking, "Thaaaanks, Lapin. No big deal, just come up with a groundbreaking idea. I'll get right on that." I get it: that's easier said than done. But you don't have to found the next big tech company (although that would be cool . . . don't let me stop you) to disrupt your industry or even just your place of work. Ideas that disrupt can be as simple as figuring out a more efficient system of billing, a more cost-effective way of shipping, or a more streamlined method of disseminating assignments. Whatever it might be, rethink convention and start thinking for yourself.

That said, once you think of a disruptive new idea, it's important to present your ideas like a professional and not in a disruptive *way* (used in the traditional sense of causing havoc around you). The best way to do that is to do a little legwork to get everyone you work with, from your immediate team to senior management, on board.

The best method for doing this reminds me of the movie *Inception*, where Leonardo DiCaprio (swoon) plants ideas in people's minds so they think they are their own. So for you, that means that even if the idea stems from your own brilliant brain, you need to get others to feel like they're in on it and have a stake in it—maybe even like they helped come up with it—so they will want to help you. I'm all about getting shit done without the game-playing, but when you're working with an existing corporate structure you might need to play the game just a little bit to get the initial "buy-in"* from others. Here are some pointers:

Do due diligence. Identify the problem to be fixed. Why are you the best person to fix it? Which unique skills do you bring to the table, and what parts of making that idea a reality will you need from others? Which people and departments will you need to involve? Make sure you target someone from each of those areas to get on board.

Set an agenda. It's your idea, so you know the best way to present your findings. Once you've set meetings with the key players you are trying to win over, create a concise plan. If you are calling a meeting with more than one person, circulate that agenda ahead of time (you can even paste it right into the calendar invitation for the meeting). This way your team has a sense for what the meeting is about and can come prepared with ideas of their own—which you should obviously listen to and try to incorporate into yours.

Don't brag. Yes, I know this is the best idea in the history of the company and maybe even the world. But when you are presenting it, watch out for talking so much in the singular first person ("I") and start speaking with the plural ("we") instead. When pitching this or any idea of yours, remember that you're not pitching *yourself,* you are pitching the *value* your idea will add. It's still the same idea— you are just framing it in a way that shares the credit.

Provide examples. If you're looking to implement a new process, find examples from other departments or even other companies that have gone a similar route and been successful. Also prepare examples of processes that *haven't* worked so well, and what can be learned from them, so you can anticipate any pushback.

Set metrics for success. Don't just say: "I want to build our social media engagement." Um, great, but what does that mean? Assign an actual figure and deadline to any claims: "I plan to increase the likes on our Facebook page to ten thousand by the end of next quarter." Backing up your goals with metrics will give your team a sense of the scope of your idea, as well as actual, measurable goals to work toward.

Leave time for questions. If you are holding a meeting, build in an extra five minutes to the end of any strategic "buy-in" meeting for your disruptive idea to open up the floor for any additional questions. This will keep the rest of the meeting on track (boo on meetings that drag on), while demonstrating an openness to new ideas and others' opinions.

Branch out. Ask anyone you are talking to about your idea to suggest one to two other people who might be interested in learning more about it and set out to meet them. This has the added benefit of helping to expand your network, while leaving some of the legwork to those you've already met. Once they have a better sense of who you are and what you're working on, they'll be better equipped to be your "boots on the ground," ideally as an ambassador touting your genius to others at your company who might not know of you or who you haven't met yet.

If you've followed me on social media over the years, you know that I have my own take on the lyrics to Elton John's "Tiny Dancer" in my bio blurb: "Former LA Lady, Always the Seamstress for the Band." No, I'm not an actual seamstress, but I like to think of myself as someone who stitches teams and crews together in creative ways to complete a project. Think of yourself as the seamstress who "sews up" your idea, because if you don't, no one will.

SUREFIRE WAYS TO HAVE YOUR BOSS BITCH MENTALITY BACKFIRE (AND HOW TO AVOID THEM)

I know, I know, it's easy to get sucked into your plans for world domination and to start gunning for the corner office before you even *have* an office. Yes, I want you to always be forward-thinking, but only while remaining grounded in the present. If you rush it, or reach too high too soon and piss people off, they will bow out instead of buying in. That will make it harder for you to get shit done and thrive like you should.

I learned this the hard way in my broadcast days by trying to take on too much too early (I know what you're thinking: "Shocking, Lapin, shocking") and pushing corporate boundaries before I had the buy-in to do so. Here are a few of the mistakes I made—laugh at them if you must, as long as you learn from them so you don't repeat them:

Stop the press. During my early days at CNN, I accepted any and all press inquiries with enthusiasm. It wasn't that I wanted my face plastered all over the Internet and magazines (far from it, as you learned from my online photo-phobia), but rather that I wanted to boost my personal profile and brand in a substantive way, which I naively thought would be a win for the home team, since any press for me would expand CNN's profile in good ways, too. Right? Wrong. Maybe placement in my favorite vegan magazine was great for me, but not exactly on brand for CNN, the twenty-four-hour news juggernaut. Remember that even if you're a small fish in a big sea, you can still make waves—just be sure they don't go against the current of the ocean.

Twitter-gate. When I first took over the anchor desk at CNBC, I needed all the help I could get . . . which, as in many industries, meant finding a good intern. So I did what any good millennial would do: I took to Twitter to find one! I posted a little 140-character job description and actually got some great responses. There was just one two-character problem: HR. Apparently, human resources had a set procedure for recruiting and hiring interns, and going rogue to find one on Twitter was not part of that plan. URGH. I had the best intentions, but, by working outside of the existing structure without giving anyone the heads-up, I was quickly shut down, and I pissed people off in the process.

Work-work balance. When I started anchoring a show for Bloomberg, I was a work zombie. The show was based in San Francisco, and I was based in NYC, so every week I would take a red-eye back to NYC after doing the show on Friday, spend the weekend at home, and then fly back on Sunday to do it all over again. I tried to defy the space-time continuum by basically being in two places at once and squeeze more out of the day than was humanly possible. I tried to schedule shoots and interviews at any and all (odd) times possible.

It was only when I shared a production schedule I built out with my producer that I realized my faux pas. "Um, Lapin? I can't be shooting with you at nine p.m. on a Sunday. I have a kid." DOH. Just because I had no family and was fine with filling up my days with work and more work didn't mean everyone on my team was in the same situation (in fact, few were). If I wanted to go above and beyond, I'd need to enlist support when my team was willing and available, and be sensitive to the fact that not everyone wants to be working at all times.

Through making that "work-work balance" mistake (and losing a few allies as a result), I learned that there are two kinds of people in the professional world: those who work to live, and those who live to work. The "work to live" group are those who, if $1 billion were to magically appear in their bank accounts, would never work another day in their lives. Then there are the "live to work" people, who would take that unexpected $1 billion and found a company, form a charity, buy an alpaca farm, and who knows what else. While the work-to-lives are generally comfortable with the status quo, the live-to-works are happiest when they are pushing the envelope professionally and otherwise.

I'm not here to make a judgment call either way, but to make you aware that both types exist—and if you want to fill your twenty-four hours with work, work, work, then you'll need to find others with similarly aligned priorities. Not everyone thinks like you, and your idea of ambition is likely different from other people's. In my last example, my ambition was taking on more enterprising stories and interviews. That was *my* baby. My producer's ambition was to work hard by day and also have a family. That was *his* baby (literally). Neither priority is better or worse, just different—and the sooner you figure that out, the sooner you will stop running into walls with new ideas and instead find the support you need to fly over them. Don't forget that eagle mentality, and soar, bitch, soar!

YOU'LL NEVER GET A TITLE BY BEING ENTITLED

When I started as an intern, I made nada. As an entry-level reporter, I made minimum wage. In my next job I made less than 30K per year.

Yeah, so I can attest to the fact that a lot of entry-level jobs and internships pay squat. You might have to live with a bunch of roommates in a tiny apartment in a shitty part of town. You might rely on oatmeal as a viable meal . . . twice a day, with brown rice and black beans every night for dinner (yes, that felt fancier to me than ramen and cost the same . . . next to nothing). But you know what? That's okay! You're *supposed* to tough it out when you're starting out. It's not going to last forever. And not to sound like a crotchety grandma, but it *will* give you great perspective years from now when you look back on these impoverished-feeling days and you can appreciate how far you've traveled.

Pretty much everyone goes through this, so however irked you get by your financial constraints in the beginning, keep that shit to yourself. Remember, the vast majority of us in most industries pay our dues, so why should you be the exception? Do not, under any circumstances, do what a 25-year-old employee at Yelp did and write a public letter addressed to the head of the company complaining that she got paid so little, she couldn't afford her rent. Because guess what? You'll get fired, just like she did. Then you *really* won't be able to pay your rent.

Yes, some lucky people skip paying their "dues" to their industry, but most of us suck it up and pay up. If you're either just starting out in your career or trying to break into a new field, don't look down on entry-level jobs, even if you think they're "beneath" you (which, by the way, is a shitty notion you should ditch all together). Don't fall into the trap of thinking you're so special that you get to skip a level. That's not how it normally works, and if it does, isn't it better that it be a surprise than an expectation? Plus, you'll love and appreciate the top even more once you get there if you know what the climb feels like.

I think it's actually really helpful to start at the bottom so you can see how a company runs at all levels. Major talent agencies like CAA and William Morris Endeavor make everyone start in the mail room so they can see how the agency sausage is made, so to speak, regardless of their education level (I've seen some people with law degrees sorting mail down there), before moving up.

- Jeff Zucker, the president of CNN, started his career as a researcher for NBC Sports right out of college and worked his way up over the next twenty-five years until he was CEO of NBCUniversal.
- The president of CNN before Jeff, Jim Walton, started as an intern at CNN and worked his way to the helm of that company.
- Phyllis Grann, the first woman CEO in the book publishing business, started her career as Nelson Doubleday's secretary.

BECOME BFFS WITH ASSISTANTS

Every time I call someone and their assistant answers, I ask them about their day and find out more about them before asking to be put through to their boss. And, always, I address them by name when I call the next time. It's mind-boggling that people are actually dismissive and even mean to assistants, but I hear cringeworthy stories like this all the time.

So, a few pointers.

DON'T be a meanie to anyone.

DO know that meanie-ness gets back to their boss. Be an ass to an assistant who has the power to make scheduling either easy or hard for you, and you'll see karma bite you in your, well, ass.

DON'T forget that everyone moves up and around. The assistant you might have talked to a few years ago could end up being your colleague or even your superior before you know it. In short, the world is small, life is long, and memories are strong.

DO go out of your way to take an assistant out for a drink or stop by their desk to chat, and they will move mountains for you, and not just with short-term favors. Believe me, they'll never forget your kindness in the long run.

BEHIND CLOSED DOORS

They say that a true friend not only won't talk shit behind your back, but she'll defend you there, too. In the next step, we will focus on making more allies at work, but for now, let's talk about why you should care about what's said there.

The most important decisions of your career are made when you *aren't* in the room. Take that in for a second and think about it. Decisions about whether you are hired, promoted, or fired all happen when *you aren't there* to say anything in your defense.

So, what are they saying about you? Oh, to be a fly on the wall, right? Well, guess what? *You* control what they say, even in absentia. In a lot of cases, your managers aren't going to take a long time to discuss much about the specifics of what you've done or haven't done. Most likely, they will distill their thoughts into a sentence or two general statements; something like, "She's smart, hardworking, but frazzled with her tasks."

People at work are going to form a big-picture impression about you based on all kinds of data points and experiences about how you act. But guess who determines which data they complete their picture with? You. If you always take on too much work and always have a hyperventilating way about you, then, of course, they will say that. But if you're generally positive and upbeat and thoughtful, they'll say that, too. You don't have to be this way all the time for them to form this impression, but most of the time.

Remember: your actions determine what they say about you and whether or not they fight for you. So what do you want those adjectives to be? Do you want to be known as flaky, disorganized, and frazzled, or smart, thorough, and reliable?

The little things you do on a day-to-day basis won't make cameos (unless, of course, they are *really* bad) in the behind-closed-doors conversations, but those few words will, and they will follow you if you ever need a reference check. So what are yours, bitch?

CONFESSIONS OF A
BOSS BITCH

Riding Undercover

When I was working superhuman, early-morning hours, I had a black car pick me up every morning to take me to work. It sounds very fancy, but it was more out of safety and efficiency than anything else. I mean, there's no easy public transportation from Manhattan to New Jersey in the wee hours. Alternatively, would you trust yourself to drive from Manhattan to New Jersey at one a.m. in a car you don't have because you live in . . . Manhattan? Didn't think so.

As tired as I was, I would always talk to the drivers. They more than just got me to work safely, they were my pals. I often got them coffee because we were on the same wacky schedule and I knew they'd appreciate it (and, let's face it, it was in my interest for them to be fully caffeinated). We would often talk the whole ride . . . about sports, politics, relationships . . . whatever.

One day, my driver talked about other people he drove. I don't generally have the patience for gossip, but this discussion was fascinating to me on a career level. The driver told me who was mean to him and who was gracious and kind. Yes, he named names (although I would never repeat them).

The driver told me about a number of my colleagues who were unnecessarily rude to him and even snapped at him. Since it is the driver's job to stay cool, he just had to take the abuse and not say anything back. But he never forgot those assholes and their bad behavior. Nor, clearly, did he hesitate to tell other people about it.

Turns out I wasn't the only one this driver talked to about what people were *really* like in the car. One of my superiors had had a very similar conversation about who treated drivers well and who didn't. It was kind of like an *Undercover Boss* scenario where the boss didn't identify himself so as to find out the real deal about his employees (sneaky, right?).

Clearly, you shouldn't need justification for being kind, but remember it's not just about being sure to be nice to the work people you think "matter." It's about being nice to everyone you encounter, because just when you think no one is watching, they are.

One of my first mentors told me that if you really want to know about a person you are hiring, don't talk to the references they provided for you (you'll no doubt get a glowing review from the folks the potential hire suggests). Rather, if you want to see their true colors, it's much better to ask the security guard or the receptionist how the person treated them. He paraphrased a Rudyard Kipling poem in what may be the best career advice I've ever heard: "Walk with kings [queens] and carry the common touch."

SHOW ME THE MONEY

Now that you've proven that you're a badass at work and can manage the interpersonal currency of presenting your ideas and winning over your colleagues, it's time to start thinking about monitizing your badassery—by asking for and getting a raise.

The gender pay gap is one of the most hot-button issues of our time, so much so that celebrities have recently come out raising awareness of it in the film industry. But my take on the issue is this: Yes, pay inequality sucks. Yes, sexism sucks. But remember, you are the boss of your career, and this goes double when it comes to your salary. So instead of wallowing on how unfair the gender pay gap is (and it is), why not do something about it? Take a page from Boss Bitch actress Jennifer Lawrence, who, when she found out how much less she was being paid than "the lucky people with dicks," didn't get mad at the aforementioned people with dicks or the studios setting the pay. She said, "I got mad at myself. I failed as a negotiator."

J-Law is right. It was no one's fault but her own. She didn't ask and push for more. And she's not alone. Research shows that only 7% of women negotiate their starting salary, compared to 57% of men. Sit with that for a second. That stat is bananas and should make you just as pissed as I am reading it. So, as I said, the pay gap sucks. But the only person who can close the gap for you is *you*.

HOW MUCH DO PEOPLE MAKE, SERIOUSLY?

I recently spoke to a friend who was interviewing for a new job and she said, "You would be so proud of me. I asked for a ten percent raise!" And

I said, "Ten percent of what?" "Ten percent of what I was making at my old job," she said with a smile.

I was not smiling, though. Yes, I'm happy that my girlfriend is in the mind-set of asking for more, but I was not pleased that she asked for 10% more than her *old* job. Why? The first problem with that is that she offered up the exact amount of her old salary to her new employer; that is a no-no. The second problem is that she asked for the 10% before knowing what that position at the new company paid. My friend had made $80K at her old job and asked for $88K. Sounds like a nice bump until you learn that the person who held her new position before her was making $110K. What she should have done is, first, get *that* piece of information. Then get the offer, and then ask for 10% more of *that*, which is $121K. By not having *that* very important benchmark of what that position typically paid, she negotiated *against* herself—and cost herself $23K extra. Ouch.

Now, my sweet, wicked-smart friend knows a lot about a lot of things, but she didn't know the ins and outs of negotiating a salary. I mean, we don't learn this stuff in school. We learn about the bullshit Pythagorean theorem, but we don't learn basic business skills, which, of course, boggles my Boss Bitch mind. All she knew was that she needed to "negotiate," but she didn't know where to start. I don't blame her, and she shouldn't blame herself. After all, it's important to forgive yourself for not knowing what you haven't learned. And then learn it, grow, repeat. Hating on your former self for not previously knowing what you know now is a waste of time—time that should be spent putting that lesson into action.

Back to my friend. When I broke it to her that not finding out the going rate for her new job had cost her $23K, she responded, "Honestly, how *could* I ask someone what they make? It's so taboo and so awkward; *who* would tell me *that*?!" She's right. People are so weird about talking about their salary. In fact, I did a study with Nielsen that shows that women would rather admit their weight than their salary. Yes, neither subject is super fun to talk about. But it begs the question: What are we so guarded about?

When people ask me for advice about negotiating their salary, the first question I ask is: "What do you make?" Because how the hell am I supposed to help you if I don't know what I'm working with? The second question is "What do other people in your position make?" Because how can you know how you're stacking up if you don't know what your colleagues and peers are pulling in?

Unless your position is CEO of a publicly traded company, this information is probably hard to get. Why? Dirty little secret: the bosses don't want employees to share this information with one another because they know it could be used as leverage in negotiations.

Enter: *moi.* Yup, I'm the girl who is in a room with a bunch of women who work together and who has no shame throwing down the question of how much they make. And when I do? Crickets. Fucking crickets. Sometimes they hem and haw. And I don't let them get away with it. I ask them again and don't let up until I get an answer. They will happily talk to me about sex positions and bikini waxes, no problem, but salary?! Well, *that's* too taboo. Are you kidding me?

We all want to make more. We say we all want to help each other make more, but if that's really the case, then why the secrecy with the very thing that will help us do that? I'm asking my friends to tell me their salary because I want to make them feel empowered to rise up.

So here are some answers to the questions about *my salary* you might be wondering about. I'm not too chickenshit to put my money where my mouth is, and I encourage you to follow my lead. There's no reason that your salary should be a more closely guarded secret than your bikini wax of choice, so for the love of God, can we get to a place where we can have an open dialogue about it? Until then, I'll show you mine, if you vow to show yours to someone who could use the information—and then ask the same thing of them. So, here's what my salaries have been:

My first local small-market TV news job: minimum wage, which amounted to $7.50†/hour back then
My second local news job: $26K†

---

† Note, the dollar amounts listed here and on page 114 are hourly and yearly "gross" numbers, sans taxes, so this wasn't near my "net" take-home pay, which was less.

My third local news job: $32,500 (which I talked about negotiating up
   from $32,000 in *Rich Bitch*)
My job at CNN: started at $75K and moved up to about $85K by the
   time I left
My job at CNBC: started at $150K then moved up to about $175K by
   the time I left
My job at Bloomberg: $400K†
My CW show *Hatched*: $375K

See how easy that was? I didn't flinch writing down what I've made,
and if you want more specifics, then find me on social media, and I won't
flinch there, either. In Section 3, "Being the Boss of Your Own Business,"
I'll tell you how much my business made (and lost) as well as what my
other streams of income are.

If none of your peers or colleagues are Boss Bitch enough to come
clean about what they are making, below are some average salaries for
other professions. Remember that the salaries will vary according to the
type of company, the geographical area, and the experience level of the
person; if you want specifics, you have to ask around.

Here's a ballpark so you can get your head in the salary transparency
game:

Architect: $75,000
Publicist at boutique firm: $44,000
Graphic designer: $51,000
Accountant: $50,000
Software engineer: $95,000
Marketing: $60,000
Google research scientist: $145,000

---

† At this point I created a "loan-out"* S corp* (which I'll talk about in
Section 3), which essentially means I get paid through my company giving me
more tax love.

Surgeon: $274,000

Human resources: $60,000

Network TV production assistant: $40,000

Network TV producer: $138,000

Commercial pilot: $160,000

Again, NBD, right? The only questions I can't currently answer are: Why doesn't everyone just talk about it? You don't have to print it in a book like I did, but what's the harm in discussing it among friends? How will you know you're being compensated adequately if you don't know what others are pulling in? It's pretty hard to win if you don't know the current score of the game.

THE EASIEST WAY TO ASK FOR A RAISE AND GET IT

Asking for a raise can be a mind fuck. You might be thinking, "I'll get a raise as soon as my boss notices my extra-awesome work." No, you won't. In today's tough job economy, the hard work ethic you have and the going-above-and-beyond mentality simply aren't enough. So don't hold your breath, because you'll be holding it for a long time. Face it, your boss will *not* simply open the corporate coffers to you just to be nice. After all, they have their own job and salary to worry about. So, sorry, *your* salary isn't exactly top of mind for them. But it is for you . . . all day, every day, amirite?

It's time to get out of your own head. Hard work is just the baseline for keeping your job; the only way to get more compensation is to ask for it, whether it's for the first time or the second (because if you fail the first time, you keep at it, obviously). And having that chutzpah is what gets results. A recent study found that, of people who put themselves out there for a raise last year, three-quarters saw their paychecks go up.

The number one, two, and three most important things to do when asking for a raise is to get leverage. What is leverage? It is getting someone else to want you, and then using that to get what you want. In other words, the most surefire way to get your employer to pay you more is to first find *someone else* who will pay you more. Even if you don't want to jump ship, the mere fact that you *could* will put a fire in your current captain's belly.

That said, looking for leverage is a tricky line to toe while you currently have a job. Yes, leverage could fall into your lap by way of a cold call from another employer who has seen your stuff and wants you to come on board. Or it could come by way of a call from a headhunter* who is looking to fill a position for a company and wants to talk to you about it and gauge your interest.

If no one comes calling with an out-of-the-blue job offer, there's only one thing to do: go out and find one for yourself. But do it in a savvy way that doesn't piss off your current boss. Here's how to prevent that from happening:

1. *Keep your mouth shut.* This might seem obvious, but loose lips can sink ships cruising toward a raise. So to avoid a job shipwreck, don't tell coworkers; don't even hint at it a little over post-work drinks. Why? Because nothing loosens lips like cocktails, plus, you never know if there is a mole in there who might sabotage your plans because they themselves want to get ahead. Keeping it quiet also goes for posting on social media—that means no "Hey, any leads on a high-paying marketing job? Thanks!" on your Facebook or LinkedIn pages. And no posting your résumé on job boards. The goal is to make it seem like you are sought after, not desperate, because you're not. You already have a kick-ass job; you just want to gain leverage to get ahead in it.

2. *If you land an interview, ask the place you are interviewing with to keep mum, too.* You might assume this is obvious to them, but it probably isn't, so be straight up and tell them that you haven't had a discussion with your boss yet and to take a beat if possible on reference calls. If they *have* to do some checking, connect them with previous employers or coworkers in whom you can confide about this. Another benefit of being straightforward with the place you're interviewing with is that they will likely be more accommodating about scheduling interviews during off hours so that it doesn't disrupt your current work

flow. People ask for this kind of discretion all the time, so employers are used to it. But like everything else, if you don't ask, you don't get.

3. *Don't let your current work suffer.* The point of getting leverage is to get ahead and get more out of your job. If you slack, people will notice, which is the exact opposite of what you do want to happen.

4. *Be discreet.* This might also be obvious, but don't search for any of this job-hunting stuff on your work computer or phone. I'm not saying that Big Brother is all up in all of your business or that you have to pull a Katie Holmes burner phone situation; just be mindful. Also, don't start dressing differently. If you wear jeans and a blouse to work every day and you start showing up in a skirt-suit, people are going to start to wonder.

The point of leverage is to get your employer to put a bigger ring on it. But there's always the possibility that you could fall in love with someone else in the process. It might be as complicated as when the same thing happens romantically, but it happens—and it's often for the better. Keep this in mind and don't be disingenuous with potential employers just to make your current one jealous. Because if you really loved the one you had, there wouldn't be another.

In addition to leverage, keep these things in mind when going in for the big ask with your boss:

Timing is everything. Set yourself up for success by finding a good time to approach your boss. The day after the company releases a dismal earnings report? Probably not the best idea. After you've received a stellar performance review or praise from a client? GREAT time to make your move. Let your boss know that you want to speak with her "this week at her convenience," which accommodates her busy schedule while putting a solid deadline on the conversation.

Gather your evidence. Come prepared with specific examples of your stellar performance and positive feedback that you have received from colleagues and clients. You don't need an entire laundry list of all the awesome things you've done at work, just a few key examples that demonstrate the qualities of a superb employee, including professionalism, work ethic, creativity, and cooperation. If you work in an industry that's data related (most are), pull out a few key metrics to *demonstrate* how much of an impact you have had on the company. You know what they say: show, don't tell.

Put community first. It's important to respect your relationship with your boss and coworkers. Think of yourself not as a cog in the wheels of the company at large, but as a single moving part. By this I mean demonstrate how your work has positively impacted the company's performance. And don't ever, ever put a coworker down. This is not a competition. And this is not a game of "I'm better than so-and-so." Getting anywhere near that conversation makes you look whiny, childish, and petty. *You never look good trying to make someone else look bad.* You want to show them that you're a team player, and the position you play on the work field is valuable enough to warrant a raise. This is not about anyone but you.

Rehearse. Many people wing it when asking for a raise. This drives me nuts. Would you wing your lines if you were in a play? No. So why wouldn't you rehearse this conversation, which will be one of the most important performances of your career? Instead of writing down a list of why you are worthy of a raise (remember, no one deserves or is entitled to anything), write down a pitch of how and why you've *worked* for more recognition in the form of a raise. Practice this fifty times if you have to: in front of friends, your dog, the mirror—I don't care who as long as you practice. Be so confident and come so prepared with airtight, relevant examples that your boss won't have a choice other than to be as confident in you as you are in yourself. If it doesn't work this time, you at least set the stage for an encore later on—hopefully sooner than later.

Be prepared for them to call your bluff. It could happen. You walk in, tell your boss that you have another offer, and imply that if you don't get the raise you're asking for, you're gone. Well, it is possible that she'll say, "Well, then go for it" and show you the door. Hopefully this won't happen, especially if you are the indispensable Boss

Bitch I know you are, but it could, which is even more reason to be open and honest with everyone involved.

IT'S ABOUT MORE THAN MONEY, HONEY

Having a solid base salary is awesome—but it's not everything. In fact, while negotiating your salary is important—critical, even—it's just one piece of the puzzle. Think of your compensation as one big, delicious pie. Sure, your salary is a nice, hearty slice of that pie. But there are lots of other slices that are equally delicious, and asking for those things when you take a new job or role should be part of your approach, too.

For example, maybe you ask to be able to work from home one day per week. I have some friends who have done this because they have a dog or young child at home (hey, dog-walking and day care can really add up, especially if you live in an urban area). But I also know women who have asked for it as part of their overall productivity plan. A girlfriend of mine works in PR, and she works from home one day each week so she can knock out her pitch calls all day long without being interrupted by her colleagues. Another friend is a financial planner and she likes to use her day working from home to make house calls in her neighborhood and build up her local client base. Another woman I know is the lead designer for a home decor company; she negotiated working from home on Mondays to allow a travel buffer for weekend buying trips for home goods and fabrics.

I've said it before, and I'll say it yet again: Your time is your most valuable asset. Being in control of how you spend it can be more valuable to you than a small bump in base salary. The sooner you start looking at your compensation from work as not just your salary, but an overall package, the sooner you'll be able get the raise or perk you need most, and that might not necessarily be straight cash. Here are some more things you can and should negotiate for other than your base salary. Feeling shy? Keep in mind that you'll never get what you don't ask for:

A *better title*. Why be "associate marketing manager" when you can be "head of strategic marketing"? A new title can be just the thing to reflect all of the cool projects you're working on and to put a pep in your work step. Plus, a fancier-sounding title will help you down the road if and when you decide to look for a new job.

Transportation costs. Calculate the travel expenses you plan to incur each month and ask for a stipend to help ease this expense. Think of what you're spending in gas, bus fare, or even flights for work-related commitments, not to mention car maintenance and the opportunity cost lost by being behind the wheel instead of at your desk. If it means you'll be at work and meetings on time and safely, your company just might build this allowance into your contract, or at the very least help with pretax transportation, pay-per-mile gas reimbursement, or parking.

A *prime-time office.* You're going to be spending roughly one-quarter of your life in an office; might as well enjoy it! A recent study showed that comfy work spaces with ample ventilation and lots of natural light increase productivity by as much as 16%, and job satisfaction as much as 24%, while substantially cutting down on employees playing hooky. So ask for a nicer work space, with a real door or a window or close proximity to the break room. If you tend to get antsy, build in a budget for a standing desk or an ergonomic office chair. Depending on the level of your position, many employers will be happy to accommodate your office needs if it means getting the best work out of you.

A *wardrobe allowance.* If you're in a position where you're public-facing (not necessarily on air but visible, as in the case of public speaking or meeting with clients), ask for a yearly or quarterly clothing stipend to be built into your contract. You have to ask in the right way, though, with a clear, professional justification (not "I love Prada but I can't afford it!"). If you're going to be meeting with high-powered clients regularly, your company should want you to look your best; after all, you're representing their brand as well as your own.

Personal development. There are few better ways to ensure future job security than by continuing your education—on your employer's dime. From workshops to seminars and conferences and even a secondary degree, see if your employer will help you pay for additional education or certification within your industry. Many companies are willing to do this, since they view it as a direct investment back into the company. You can even ask for it retroactively while you're negotiating your benefits; ask for an extra monthly payment to use toward the student loans that made you such a valuable candidate to begin with. Worth a shot, and remember it's an automatic no if you don't ask!

Extra vacation days. Your boss will immediately want to know if there will be a gap in work flow if you ask for extra time off. Anticipate that pushback and assure them that you will monitor e-mail while you're away. You should also say that you will brief coworkers on the ins and outs of projects you have your hands on before you leave. I know I sound like a broken record talking about how time is so valuable, but think about it this way: getting an extra week off will yield the equivalent of a salary bump. Say there are two hundred business days per year. That means one vacation day is 0.5% of your salary (one divided by two hundred).

Health care. Chances are that big companies won't be able to budge on this much, but you might have some wiggle room if you work at a new start-up. If you work at a smaller company that doesn't provide health care, ask for a cash stipend so you can cover your own. If you already get one, ask for a bigger one. It's cheaper for the company than getting you full-on insurance, and you presumably won't be taking time off if you are healthy.

Your bills. Are you always on your cell phone for work? Ask your employer if they might consider covering your plan. Highlight all the work calls made on your personal phone and then present it to your employer, especially if those outnumber your personal calls. Do you work in media? Ask for your cable bill, newspaper, magazine, and/or online subscriptions to be covered if they aren't already. If you work in one of the many industries where you need to stay informed, being plugged in is part of your job.

An expense account. Do you have one? Do you want one? Come prepared for your negotiation with a list of all the additional business you could generate if you were able to take potential clients out to lunches or dinners. If you already have an expense account, but it's limited, ask for a bump in your cap. Make a case for how this will enable you to bring in more clients and thus money for the company. You'll be surprised about how easy it is to get a yes on this one, especially if you're in a larger company. Smart companies see paying for a few lattes or dinners as a good investment toward the amount they will make off your extra sweat equity. Also, if you already have an expense account and want the cap raised, present a list of who you've taken out that has resulted in money for the company. Showing your track record of success helps put you in a great position to get even more. Heck, if you were working for me and a $40 lunch with a client turned into $4,000 in business, I'd let you dine out every day!

Also, remember this: many of these perks for *you* are tax deductible for *them*. So, yes, they are hooking you up, but in a way they are hooking the company up by reducing their tax liability. It's a win-win, and don't you forget that when you confidently ask for one or more of the above.

ROLE-PLAYING FOR THE WIN

You might be thinking, "Okay, so, Lapin, what the heck do I rehearse? What *am* I supposed to say?"

I get this question all the time. What you should *not* say is this:

YOU: Hi, boss! I just wanted to pop in really quickly to run something past you . . .

BOSS: I only have a couple of minutes before my next call, but shoot.

YOU: I think I deserve a raise. It's been a few years since I got a bonus, and I've been working extra hard, so I think it's something I deserve at this juncture of my tenure here.

BOSS: You want a raise.

YOU: Yes? What do you think?

BOSS: I think we are all tightening our belts around here. Corporate is really cracking down. Can we talk about this in the next fiscal year?

YOU: I understand. Thank you so much for entertaining this pertinent subject matter with me. I appreciate your time.

Why this doesn't work: 1) You didn't schedule a meeting. When meetings are scheduled, it means this conversation is important. 2) What are these weird big words? When was the last time you used the words *juncture* and *tenure* in conversation? These not natural; they are lame and distracting. Stick to your normal vocab. 3) You have no clear examples of why you deserve the raise whatsoever. If someone pitched this to you, you would probably say no. So it's no surprise you got a no, too.

Instead, get into the mind-set that this is not about emotions; it's business. Go in with all the hard evidence (go crazy with charts, graphs . . . whatever!) that illustrates your work "input" that deserves the raise "output." Consider a conversation flow like this:

YOU: Hi, boss! Thank you for taking the time to sit down with me. I want to discuss my contributions to the company over the last year.

BOSS: Of course. You've been working on that XYZ project, right? How's it going?

YOU: That's right, I have been, and it's been going great. I've outlined the clients that came our way before I joined XYZ and charted them against what's coming in now. As you can see [show snazzy chart], clients have increased 40%, amounting to another $100,000 for the company.

BOSS: Impressive. Why do you think that is?

YOU: It's been a great team effort, of course, and macro tailwinds that are working in our favor. But I was able to assess which of these clients were directly related to my efforts, either by requesting me by name or via my direct contact. And the chart shows that 50% of that $100,000 is directly correlated to me and half of those clients have signed long-term deals, which will amount to hundreds of thousands of more dollars for the company in the years to come. With that momentum, I would like to propose a 60/40 split amounting to a $30,000 pay increase, which is an equal split of my direct cash inflow.

BOSS: The numbers are impressive, and I want to incentivize you to keep bringing in more clients. I would be able to give you a 40/60 split of your contribution, or $20,000 with an option to reopen this conversation when your number hits $75,000.

YOU: I appreciate the offer. I actually have a projection for when I should hit that number this year. With that said, how about a 50/50 of $25,000 raise and the option to reopen the conversation when I hit $100,000?

Then you're off to the negotiation races! Of course, what you should say specifically is up to you and depends on your skill set and the progress you've made within the company. But regardless of those details, the gist should be something to the effect of: "Here's how I have been able to add value to the company . . . and here's how I plan to help the company over the next year." You should also keep Plans A, B, and C in your mind, because if one ask is turned down, you want an alternate suggestion of another compensation perk at the ready.

How much you should ask for is also specific to your industry, your current salary, the salary of your coworkers (which is why you should dig into that first!), and the last time you got a bump in salary, if you've had one before. The general range you should stick to as your Plan A is 5–15% more than your current salary. Plan B should be some cash and some other form of compensation. Plan C should be all in alternative compensation.

Regardless of what you ask for, it's important to go in there with a plan. No, Dorothy, you can't just click your ruby slippers and make it happen; you have to prepare. Yes, all companies are struggling; who wants to give out extra money "just because"? So make the case, and if it doesn't happen this time, you've prepared your boss that this isn't the end of the conversation. Remember, if the pitch doesn't work this time, change the tactics, not the goal.

I'm obviously a numbers girl, so let me break down how important it is to get a raise.

- Let's say you get a $25,000† raise for one year.
- You invest that $25,000 (How? I go into this in depth in *Rich Bitch*).
- Let's say you get a 7% return (which isn't that aggressive).
- You let that money grow and compound (compounding interest* is your best financial friend when it works in your favor) over the next forty years.
- The amount of money that earns you is $350,000. Seriously. That's on top of your initial $25,000.

As you know by now, I hate the mandate from other financial experts that you should skip buying your morning latte in order to grow your wealth over time. Come on. That isn't your golden ticket to financial heaven. What is? Focusing on the big stuff, like getting a raise. That's the best way to get a substantial amount of money (while indulging in the little things like a latte) and letting your wealth grow, baby, grow.

GETTING YOUR ASS HANDED TO YOU WITH CLASS

You could follow every piece of advice in this book precisely and still get fired. Maybe you made a mistake you couldn't bounce back from or maybe it was beyond your control and you fell on the "restructuring" sword. Whatever the reason, it happens. And it sucks.

I'm not going to tell you that it doesn't. It sucks when it's because you did something wrong. It sucks when it's because you didn't do something wrong. It sucks when it's from a job you love. It's sucks when it's from a job you need. It just sucks.

What to remember when it does happen is that we've *all* been there. And sorry to say, if you haven't, you will be. So, while it's cool to eat cereal out of a big salad bowl in your sweats for a day, keep it to twenty-four hours

---

† If the $25,000 mark feels outside of your grasp. I'll calculate the compounding interest of $5,000 for you with the same return over the same amount of time . . . which comes out to $75,000 on top of your initial $5,000. Still a pretty sizable chunk of change.

of wallowing. After that, put on your big-girl undies and get on with it . . . your future, that is.

BIG GIRLS DON'T CRY

If getting fired happens to you, remember to Keep. It. Classy. That means as much as you might want to cry and throw a hissy fit, don't. In the single-stall bathroom, later? Fine. In the car on the way home, emo music blaring? Also fine. In front of your boss and staff who just let you go? Not okay. You may no longer have the gig, but you do have your dignity. Protect that shit.

This is the time to look forward, not back (after all, you're not going that way). When one of my talent agencies fired me because I "wasn't fitting into one clear lane," I wanted to remind them of all the awesome things I was doing and defend myself with my track record of success. Instead, I took a deep breath and said, "Thank you so much for all of your help in the last year. I am so grateful to have worked with you and for all that we've accomplished together. Life is long, the world is small, so I am sure we will meet again." Trust me, I *wanted* to say something else, but in the same way you want to argue with someone breaking up with you, there's really nothing you can say to someone if their mind is made up. In hindsight, I'm relieved that I kept it classy and let my steam out over margaritas with my girls instead of on that call, because, of course, I have already run into them again in business.

FYI

Even the biggest titans of business have gotten the boot in the past:

- J. K. Rowling got fired from her job at Amnesty International for secretly writing on her work computer.
- Madonna got fired from Dunkin' Donuts in the 1970s for squirting jelly filling on a customer. This is not a joke.

- Mark Cuban got fired from his job as a computer salesman in the 1980s. Since then, he's never worked for anyone else and has made more than $2 billion.
- Anna Wintour got fired from her first job at *Harper's Bazaar* because her shoots were "too edgy."
- Oprah got fired from WJZ-TV in Baltimore for being "too emotionally invested" in her stories.
- Walt Disney got fired from the *Kansas City Star* newspaper for—get this—lacking imagination and having no good ideas.

I could say, "Look who's laughing last," but I'm sure you already did.

One of my favorite firing stories of all time is that of Andrew Mason, the ex-CEO of Groupon. He wrote an e-mail to the company (which, of course, inevitably gets leaked by a colleague or even by the person themself) saying: "After four-and-a-half intense and wonderful years as CEO of Groupon, I've decided that I'd like to spend more time with my family. Just kidding: I was fired today." He didn't leave it at that, though, or it could have gone from being funny and honest to being perceived as being snarky fast. Instead, he was up front that the company wasn't doing well on his watch (the stock was in the pooper), and that the company deserved better saying, "As CEO, I'm accountable." He didn't sugarcoat the firing like a lot of people do with that lame line (which he poked fun at) "I've decided to spend more time with my family." Instead, he was honest: about his firing and why it happened. And FYI: he cofounded Groupon in his twenties and left in his early thirties. I'm pretty sure he's going to bounce back and be just fine. Handle your firing with dignity, and you can bounce back, too. Here's how:

Don't take to social media. Don't be like that Yelp girl I told you about who went online to write about how she was suffering *so much* living in San Francisco with roommates while working at a lower-level job at the coveted tech company when she thought she should be moving up quicker. Incredibly, even after she got fired for that, she still kept at it online. Now, do you think her next potential employer is going to take well to that kind of behavior? I'm not even sure what to advise her to do when she goes into interviews except to explain that she was young and foolish, she's learned XYZ from that experience, and she wants to contribute to a meaningful team. Even if it's not that extreme, I see too many people taking to social media to vent or say, "welp . . . got fired today. #theirloss." That shit comes back to bite you, so don't do it.

Don't be obnoxious. I know it's the absolute worst when security escorts people out of the building without notice so they can't use corporate e-mail after being let go. I've seen it happen, and it's hard for everyone. You have two choices in that situation: you can either walk out kicking and screaming or you can walk out with your head held high. Boss Bitches do the latter, because anything else will burn bridges, and you never know where the people you worked with will end up or who they know at jobs you might be looking at next.

Don't lie about it, but don't highlight it, either. When you interview for another job, your last one *will* come up, and when it does, you have to explain what happened. Be honest, but don't dwell. The best position to be in here is to have left the work breakup on good terms, having said something to the effect of (even if you're fuming at that moment), "I'm so grateful for my time here. Moving forward, I would still love to use you as a reference to help future employers understand all the positive progress I've helped create," to your (ex-)employer on the way out. If you leave on those terms, you should be golden if there's a reference check, which there most likely will be. If it's a little murkier than that, you should keep it honest but short and positive with the company you're interviewing with—something like, "We both came to the understanding that it was no longer a mutual fit," then pivot toward what *is* a better fit for you . . . their company.

Learn and grow. Did you really do something wrong to get fired? Did you show up late every day for a month? Did you "misplace" the $100 bill at the cash register? Did you piss off the company's top client? Whatever it is, don't be in denial. It might look like a silly reason in the scheme of things. And, you're right, if your boss were looking at the "big picture," maybe you wouldn't have gotten fired. But just because they weren't doesn't mean you shouldn't. Keep your eyes on *your* "big picture." Yes, it will likely be affected by this bump on your career road, but only you can decide how. Will it be the precursor of more bumps on the road that you can't swerve around? Or will it give you the momentum you need to speed over the bumps faster? I think you know which one I vote for.

Don't hold a grudge. Holding a grudge is just letting someone live rent-free in your head. And, Boss Bitches don't do "rent-free" anything. Let it go, Elsa, let it go.

Getting what you want out of your career, busting your ass to make it a success, and fighting to move up isn't easy. But remember, what comes easy won't last, and what lasts won't come easy. Boss Bitches do hard shit.

And when the shit hits the proverbial fan, as it inevitably will, go ahead, be emotional, cry it out (at home)—and then realize that champagne isn't served at pity parties and put a cork in it. Champagne is, however, appropriate at most other times, and I personally drink it whenever I can—not just on special occasions. Why? Because, as Pollyannaish as it sounds, I truly believe every day is a celebration. And you should, too. I also believe that once you change your mind-set, your goal-digging future will follow.

What I don't believe in is destiny. I don't buy for one second the idea that your future is somehow predetermined or written in the stars. *You* dig your goals. *You* make your destiny. And as the fictitious but still awesome Blair Waldorf said, "Destiny is for losers; it's just a stupid excuse to wait for things to happen instead of *making* them happen." Preach, Blair, preach.

It's time to make it happen for yourself, no matter how many times you feel like cracking. You are a diamond, my dear Boss Bitch; shine bright like one, and they cannot break you.

BOTTOM LINE

Conventional Wisdom: You'll get ahead by focusing on making contacts only with people in positions of power. There is no need to bother with people who can't "do" anything for you.

The Real Deal: Ew. Grosss. Drivers, bathroom attendants, assistants—all of the people you encounter not only deserve your attention as human beings, but you also never know how they might be helpful to you by finding you an appointment on a tight schedule or giving you some helpful inside scoop about a company. And then there is karma, bitch.

Conventional Wisdom: If I work hard to the point that I deserve a raise, my boss will give me one.

The Real Deal: Incorrectamundo! Working hard is a given these days; it's business as usual. Getting a raise *might* happen naturally, but most likely your employer isn't going to just open up the company's wallet for you unless you ask. And if you do, you will usually get yours. Studies have shown that the majority of people who ask for a raise get it. And of those people, about half get the amount they asked for. Sure, the rest get less, but it's still better than if they never asked at all. Here's my favorite stat: You miss 100% of chances you don't take. Don't be *that* stat.

Conventional Wisdom: I don't talk about my salary because it's taboo and not ladylike.

The Real Deal: Um, what's more ladylike than acting like, talking like, *and* being a boss?! The only way to get more compensation is to get a sense of what others in your job at your workplace or across your industry are making. Start by showing yours first and others will be more likely to follow suit, especially if they understand, like you do, that knowledge will empower both of you. Just like in real estate, where you check out comparable sales in the neighborhood to assess your home's value, you should do the same to assess your value in your work 'hood.

Conventional Wisdom: A nominal bump in salary isn't going to change my lifestyle much.

The Real Deal: Are you kidding me? What else is going to change your financial life? Nickel-and-diming yourself? Cutting out your morning latte? Clipping coupons?! Don't be "pound foolish and penny wise." Getting a raise, even a nominal one, will change your financial picture and future exponentially more than cutting out your morning latte. Yes, I may be the only financial expert that argues for your morning latte (you're welcome). It's symbolic of a small indulgence that keeps you financially on track and from "bingeing" on something bigger. So buy your damn latte, get a raise, then invest the "bump" in your paycheck so that it grows to severalfold your *entire* salary over time. [Insert fist bump here.]

Conventional Wisdom: Getting fired is the worst thing that could ever happen to me.

The Real Deal: It may not be fun when it happens, but in the long run, sometimes the only way to open new doors is to let the old ones hit you on the way out.

YOU BETTER (NET)WORK, BITCH

Making Friends While Making Moves

Every Boss Bitch needs backup. There's a popular Internet meme that says, "Behind every strong woman is herself." I like that one because it doesn't say that she's backed up by a man—but I like this one even better: "Behind every strong woman is a group of other strong women who have her back."

I'm sure you have a squad of friends that rivals T-Swift's. But you should also create a squad to have your back at work. Your work squad is different from your friend squad in that they don't need to know about your man drama but respect you and advocate for you when drama at the office happens, as it inevitably will. In Step 4 of "Being the Boss at Work," I will teach you how to network inside and outside of the office, cultivating advocates and mentors, so that your vibe attracts a tribe that will propel your career forward.

FORM YOUR WORK SQUAD

Whether you want to stay at your current job forever or you are secretly plotting to jump ship or start your own thing, the people in your network will be crucial every step of the way. Just as they say, "It takes a village to raise a child," it also takes a village to create a Boss Bitch: to help her, to inspire her, to criticize her (but in a helpful way), and to cheer her on.

A GUIDE TO OFFICE SISTERHOOD

While of course you want to be friendly to everyone at work, that doesn't mean you can (or should) be actual *friends* with everyone. Just like in your personal life, there will be people you're closer with, people who are acquaintances, and people (or maybe, one person) who you basically share a brain with. In other words, the hierarchy that exists within your female friendships exists within your office relationships, too. No matter whom you choose to be part of your tribe, it usually includes the following roles:

Work crush. Like your #wcw (that's "woman crush Wednesday," if you haven't been on Instagram in the last five years), this Boss Bitch is your she-ro. She is typically someone in a leadership or even an executive position, who you admire—both her work and her as a person—and aspire to be like someday. You may not have a close relationship (or any relationship at all), but that doesn't mean you can't observe her from afar, learn from her, and, hey, try to set a meeting with her to pick her brain (or smell her hair).

Spirit animal. Like your bestie in real life, this person is your career spirit animal, someone you dream big with and maybe would even consider starting a company with. You read each other's minds on a professional level, and likely a personal one as well, and share similar short- and long-term goals. You two are going places together.

After-hours buddy. Like a friend with whom you hang out a lot but who won't be a bridesmaid in your wedding. You grab lunch to discuss big projects together and go for drinks after a busy workday to talk about your boss, that demanding client, the cute guy on the fourth floor . . . whatever. She's a fan who will go to the mat for you and give you more love and leniency in the office because she likes you.

Office mate. Like an acquaintance you went to college with, you have an experience in common but don't know much about each other on a personal level. At work, these are the people who are cool with you but won't go out of their way to do anything particularly nice for you (or mean *to* you).

Haters. Does this one need further explanation? These are people who are constantly thinking about how (maybe even actively trying) to bring your ass down at any given opportunity. You should protect yourself and your tribe from them.

TURNING FRENEMIES INTO FRIENDS

We're human, and even we Boss Bitches can't be on top of our work game *every day.* Sometimes even the shiniest objects crack. And when that happens, you should take that work blunder into relationship rehab ASAP. Just like a sprain is easy to recover from if you treat it quickly, rubbing someone the wrong way is an easy thing to fix as long as you do it before it festers into full-on war.

Here are some tools for your work-relationship first-aid kit:

Praise them behind their back. If you really have a beef with someone, praising them to their face might feel too fake for you and come off too disingenuous to them. Instead, try to say something nice behind their back in a way that you know will ultimately get back to them.

Sample Scenario:
- You are annoyed with Sally. Sally is annoyed with you.
- Sally gives you RBF (resting bitch face) when she sees you.
- You can barely eke out a "Good morning, Sally!" so saying something more like, "Nice blouse, Sally!" might require a cocktail.
- You and Sally are working on the same project.
- You tell a coworker or even your supervisor that Sally is doing a great job and has contributed a lot to the project.
- That person tells Sally that you said that and gives her an "atta girl."
- Sally never gives you RBF again and says, "Good morning! Nice blouse!" Boom.

Research them. Okay, this doesn't mean going full-on *Single White Female,* but why not use some of the Instagram stalking skills that you use for potential love interests to learn more about your frenemy's hobbies and interests and use that for bonding purposes? The more you break the ice with them, the more these tidbits will help you swim yourself back into good graces. And learning more about them will likely soften your heart to seeing them as a person and not just a work foe, which will motivate you to make nice faster and hopefully more genuinely. This is a tactic used by high-powered CEOs all the time. Studies have shown that the best negotiators spend the most amount of time researching the people they are negotiating against and therefore get deals done in a fraction of the time. Knowing a potential enemy will make them a friend in no time . . . or at least in less time than others.

Be a sweetie. Say please and thank you. You don't have to be passive-aggressively sweet, but find something genuinely awesome that they did and either ask them for help with it or thank them for it. *Everyone,* even the nastiest of them, has good qualities. Find them. It will make it easier to win them back over if you start highlighting those good qualities for them (and for yourself). Did they come up with a cool e-mail signature with the company logo? Say, "Hey, I noticed that great new signature you have on your e-mail. Would you *please* show me how you did that?" People generally love sharing their opinions and teaching you things they are good at. Relish in the time they are relishing in themselves. Then, notice something they did that even in the slightest way helped you or your team. Did they bring cupcakes into a meeting? Say, "Hey, *thank you* for doing that! They were thoughtful and delicious." Pay the kindness forward and you'll get that karma coming back your way.

No matter what you aspire to be the boss of, people around you can be the biggest asset to you at work. Sure, sometimes these people will be real lemons. You can explain it in any way you want: "They're just jealous" or "They are trying to bring me down because I'm above them." But that mentality doesn't help you or solve the problem. Instead, make some fucking lemonade and drink it with your new friend (former frenemy).

FRIENDING YOUR WAY TO THE TOP

Chances are you actually work with some pretty cool people. I mean, your employer had good taste in hiring *you*, right? You might know some of your coworkers from meetings or in passing, but do you really *know* them to a level that they could have your back or vice versa? Getting to have-your-back status at work takes more than just a smile from across the table at a meeting—but not much more. Requesting a coffee "date" or "power lunch" at work can be the beginning of a beautiful corporate friendship. Here's how to get started:

1. *Think outside your (comfort) zone.* Take the initiative to set meetings with people outside of your department. Take the ten-thousand-foot view to identify who you might need to know down the road. For example, let's say you're currently a marketing associate at a medium-sized advertising agency, but you have your sights set on becoming creative director someday. Right now, you meet mostly with those on your immediate team: your marketing manager, design staff, project leader. But later on, as creative director, you'll need to work across multiple units like the one you're on now, plus legal, finance, communications, and others. So start making inroads in those other departments now, and when you are up for promotion in the future you'll already have some allies on your side who have your back.

2. *Meetings don't have to be a full-on affair, involve a formal calendar invite, or even be scheduled.* They can be the work equivalent of a spontaneous "meet-cute" in the movies. In line for lunch in the cafeteria? Talk to people in line. In the elevator? Strike up a quick convo with whoever gets on. You can do it: get off your phone, look up, say hi, and be present. You don't have to do this 24/7. I get it: we can all be shy or have off days. But on the rest of the days, chat with everyone. You never know who you are going to meet in the most random places.

3. *Face time is key.* Why? For starters, it's harder to be an asshole face-to-face. So don't e-mail and IM; walk down the hall. Make an ex-

cuse to meet people, even if it's just taking the long way around to the copy machine so you pass their office. Verbal communication, engaged body language, eye contact, using someone's name—all of this stuff makes for a better connection. And for the love of God, please try to put down your phone! Nobody wants to have a conversation with the top of your head. (My boss busted me for being heads down on my phone during a video conference with another office. I was trying to multitask and get shit done on my phone for the better of the teams on both sides of the video, but at that moment, the r-e-s-p-e-c-t was more valuable.)

4. *A girl's gotta eat.* You are going to need to eat lunch or grab a three p.m. coffee pick-me-up, so why not invite someone along, even if it's last-minute. "Hey, want to grab a coffee with me? I hear they are giving out free scones, too!" My homie Keith Ferrazzi wrote a great book on this very thing called *Never Eat Alone,* and you probably guessed the premise of the book: make every meal an opportunity to network. You'll get more brain food from the conversation than you'll get from anything you scarf down at your desk alone.

5. *Get committed.* Find something at work that you're passionate about, whether it's fund-raising for your company's running team, planning the annual all-staff spelling bee, or sitting on the advisory group for onboarding new interns. Participating in—or better yet, organizing—some extracurriculars at work will help you build relationships with a wider range of people outside your own department who have shared interests (remember, shared interests = deeper connections).

The key to successfully networking isn't going out and meeting every single person in your industry. That's just exhausting, and don't nobody have time for that. It's also wildly inefficient. Quality > Quantity. Be thoughtful. It's not about how many people you know. It's about building a network of trusted colleagues, targeting people who can help you and whom you can help in return.

RETHINK GIRLS' NIGHT

Lots of women shy away from budgeting because they fear it eliminates "fun." Um, not my kind of budgeting. I always advocate for fun (after all, if you go cold turkey on fun, you'll end up bingeing just like you would after a week on a zero-carb/zero-sugar/zero-yumminess food diet). All I care about is that you have your fun (financially) responsibly, so allocate 10–15% of your budget toward whatever kind of recreation your fun-loving heart desires. And, if you're like me, girls' night fits right into that category.

I have a group of Boss Bitch girlfriends (yes, you can sit with us!) who I get together with once a month for drinks. The twist is that each of us takes turns bringing one new friend who we think would be a beneficial professional contact for others in the group. For example, one of my friends owns and runs a concierge yoga service, which connects clients with certified private yoga instructors for practice in their home. I recently brought her with me to girls' night because 1) this expert liaison business model is huge right now and she's an expert in it; 2) all of my friends are super into wellness (even if I personally suck at yoga); and 3) she's positive, motivated, and fun—three perfect ingredients for someone *any* Boss Bitch would want in her corner.

The point here is not to blatantly pimp out your friends, but to connect people whom you believe in and want to help in a meaningful way. You never know how those relationships might flourish, professionally and otherwise. And if you're going to grab wine with the girls once a month anyway (or once a week, I won't judge), you might as well get some networking bang for your buck.

GET OUT AND (NET)WORK

Since I am a naturally reclusive person (this is not a joke), I've had to learn how to suck it up and put myself out there. It sounds like a paradox, but even though my numero uno passion in life is meeting new people and learning their stories, large group gatherings like industry events and conferences make my inner hermit extremely nervous. I've learned that in order to be my most relaxed, inquisitive, and outgoing self, it helps to strategize and plan ahead.

SCHMOOZING TIPS THAT DON'T SUCK

There are a ton of networking "tips" out there. Personally, a lot of them can feel icky. But I've tried 'em all, even the icky ones, and here are the ones that have been most successful:

1. *Be smart, not a smarty pants.* Be ready to be "on." Every time you walk into a room, you are presenting a valuable product: yourself. This means being polished inside and out. Do your homework on who is going to be at the event, whether it's a small dinner or a large conference. Make note of a few people you are most interested in speaking with and have a few relevant talking points ready ahead of time based on their interests and recent accomplishments (whatever you've found through a slightly more-than-cursory Google search). The trick to being strategic is not to come across as strategic at all. Don't read them their CV, and don't feel compelled to bring any of your talking points up if they don't fit or make sense (or seem stalker-ish). But if they do, you'll look smart and be memorable.

2. *Follow up.* There's no point in making a great new contact if you're going to shit the bed when it matters most: afterward. Always get contact information at the end of a good chat. Bring business cards (if you have them from work, great, but you can/should make your own, too) and also get her number or e-mail. At the end of the night (or when she walks away, if you think you'll forget), type in to your phone some of the details you gathered while you were chatting: the TV series she mentioned she's obsessed with; the difficulty she's had finding a dog-walker in her neighborhood; her partner's name. Then, when you send a follow-up note (which, of course, you should do within forty-eight hours of your first meeting), you can mention something with a personal touch, like "How did your husband Steve's birthday party turn out?" Better yet, find a way to be helpful!

"A friend suggested so-and-so dog-walker in your area; here's the contact information." These thoughtful tidbits will go a long way in making this new contact a more intimate acquaintance, while also subtly conveying your outstanding attention to detail.

3. *Take charge.* When you do ask for a "second date" with your new contact, suggest a specific time and place. No one likes the "Which restaurant do you like?" Ping-Pong match, and you always want to give the impression that your time is valuable . . . because it is! Even if you are totally wide-open, still suggest a couple of times and places; it's helpful, it's assertive, and it gives the impression that you're wildly busy. For example, say, "How's Tuesday at ten a.m. or three thirty p.m.?" instead of "Got any time next week?" Even if your schedule is clear, you 1) don't want to come across like you are and 2) should remember that your time is precious, too!

And while we're on the topic of following up, which you should *always* do no matter what, there is a right and wrong way to do it. Here are some follow-ups that suck:

Rambling. "Hey, Miss Executive at a firm I want to work at, I'm so excited to learn more about your company. When I was a little girl . . . yada, yada, yada. I was hoping to continue the conversation we were having about yada, yada, yada. It really had me soul-searching about yada, yada, yada. Oh, and I forgot to mention yada, yada, yada. Phew, that was a longer note that I expected because yada, yada, yada. If you're still reading, I hope to hear from you soon because yada, yada, yada." You can count on one thing: if you send this kind of e-mail, she's not still reading.

Being vain. "Hello there, Mr. Supervisor at a company that hosts panel events that I want to speak on, it was so great to meet you. Let me tell you how fabulous I am. I went to this fabulous school, my SATs were fabulous, my summa cum laude cap and gown were fabulous. I started working as an intern in these fabulous companies and worked long but fabulous nights, and now I am here at this fabulous job with this fabulous life I hope to talk about to your fabulous organization." Pass. If you were that fabulous, you wouldn't be so obnoxious. And if you were that important, you wouldn't be selling me to be on my panel; I'd be selling you. As Margaret Thatcher said, "Being powerful is like being a lady. If you have to tell people you are, you aren't."

Being dumb. "Hi, Mrs. Local Shop Owner, it was a pleasure to make your acquaintance. I would love to know what the mission of your business is, what you are currently selling, and where I can buy your goods to support your cause." Um, dummy, you can Google the company and find all the info there. Delete.

FIVE WAYS TO (NET)WORK THE ROOM

A networking event is only as good as the people who attend it . . . and that means *you*, sister. So, now that you're ready to hit the networking scene and make your industry your bitch, try these outside-the-box ways to get your soon-to-be contacts into the room:

1. *Be the hostess with the mostest.* Rather than attending networking events, where you are one of many and have to compete for other attendees' attention, host events of your own and make yourself the host everyone wants to chat with. Keep it classy and fun but also organized around an inclusive theme, like "women who work in digital" or "working women who are thinking about having kids" or whatever. If you don't have enough people in your existing network, look to sites like meetup.com to find other people in your area who are interested in the same things as you. Pick a topic, or browse those already on the site, then invite friends, colleagues, and their friends to join. As host, you'll be able to guide the conversation in a way that's useful for you and your guests. Pro tip: When you send the e-invite for the event, ask guests to RSVP with their updated contact information (e-mail, phone, and address). That way, instead of coming out of the evening with a few business cards, you'll already have full contact info from every guest in the room.

HOST A GAME NIGHT!

BITCH TIP

Because sometimes the best way to relax and reconnect with people in your broader circle of friends and colleagues is to be a kid again. One of my best girlfriends hosts Game Night once a month, complete with Pictionary, Monopoly, Scrabble, and a themed snack and drink menu. She caps the event at a certain number of people and sends out a message as it's nearing capacity (even if it isn't *actually*) to create a sense of urgency and get a good group of people there. After all, the FOMO is real! Then we gather at her apartment for some good, clean fun and sneak-attack networking.

2. *Sweatwork.* There's nothing like pumping some endorphins to make for a great bonding opportunity, which is why I love the current "sweatworking" craze. Instead of the usual coffee or drinks date, invite your colleague or contact to attend a fun workout class with you. Choose something a little "out there" so that it's new to the both of you, like an aerial yoga or cardio trampoline class. Learning something new together—and inevitably making fools of yourselves—is a great way to break the ice and get your creative juices flowing. Once you've sweated it out together, grab a juice or lunch nearby. Yes, in the process this person will likely see some mascara schmutz under your eyes (and maybe some pit stains, too), so get down with knowing that *now*, because there's nothing like sharing that realness to take any relationship up a notch.

3. *Think past the golf course.* Your game, your rules. Not into golf, happy hour, or other common schmoozy activities? Who cares! Find an activity that you love: it could be getting your nails done or taking a cooking class. Then, either meet people there or invite new contacts to participate in that activity with you. You are your most compelling, authentic self when you're in your own element, and that confidence makes for great networking no matter where you are.

4. *Get a winglady.* If you are introverted or not super comfortable in the typical networking event circuit, that's totally fine! Put yourself at ease by enlisting a networking winglady. It's easier to engage others in conversation as a tag-team effort instead of going it alone, which can be super daunting. This person isn't necessarily your bestie (in fact, it's probably best that she's *not*, because then you'll be tempted to just sit in a corner and talk to each other, which defeats the entire purpose) but someone with similar goals and values as you. Choose a friend or colleague who has skills that complement, but don't compete with, your own: for example, if you're an associate at a law firm and attending a networking event for legal professionals, go with a friend who works in business affairs. She'll understand the work and bring her own business perspectives to the table—while still allowing you to shine. Build in some time after the event to grab dinner or a drink with your winglady and discuss what you learned, then combine contacts for two times the impact. If you are looking for new wingwomen or just moved somewhere away from your ladies, try Bumble BFF, which works like the popular dating site but hooks you up with potential pals instead.

5. *Give back.* Volunteering for a cause you care about is a great way to meet other like-minded people from across all kinds of industries. You already have something in common (the cause you're rallying around) and can grow meaningful networking relationships from there. No, you don't have to drop a ton of money to be on the board or dominate the silent auction. Instead, donate your time and spend it doing double time making a difference in the world and getting to know your fellow volunteers. The more hands-on, the better. I still have professional contacts with whom I've bonded over the years while handing out clothes or delivering food.

NETWORKING NO-NOS

So, you're ready to be an eager networking beaver? Excellent. But don't let that zeal turn into royal F-ups. Here are some faux pas you should avoid so you don't end up on an episode of *Networking Gone Wrong*:

1. *Sporty events.* Unless you are Sporty Spice, don't sign up. You don't want a reputation for being the girl who sucked at softball and ruined the season for everyone else. Having a good rep and building a fan base is the point of all this networking jazz, so you don't want it to backfire and be forever known as the girl who dropped the ball . . . literally.

2. *Stuff you have to pay for.* If it's worth it, then cool. But membership fees for stuff you can get for free is not cool. Early on in my career I forked over a lot of money to join a particular women's group that was (and still is) super well respected. But I found myself struggling to pay the dues and ultimately opted for very similar versions of the group that were free.

3. *Getting sloppy drunk—or not drinking enough.* Getting shitfaced is never cool. But a drink (if you do indeed drink) to relax and have the social lubricant to introduce yourself to people can be helpful. Yes, I'm endorsing drinking lightly (if you are of age and not driving, of course). If you don't drink, then bring a friend who either does or is drunk on life (we all have a friend like that!).

CONFESSIONS OF A
BOSS BITCH

The Funniest and Most Mortifying Conversation I've Ever Had

I couldn't believe my luck when I finally met one of my work crushes (who I told you about in Step 1 of this section) while on vacation, on a boat, of all places. As the founder of Spanx and an all-around badass, Sara Blakely is my she-ro. I don't get nervous around most celebrities, but I'm not going to lie, meeting her heightened my nerves enough that I couldn't stop fidgeting with my hair tie. I had a million and a half questions in my head to ask her. I couldn't wait to ask her everything I ever wanted to know about her and her business and make her my new BFF.

We got to chatting over drinks, and she launched into a story about how much she loves diving.

"Oh, awesome," I said. "I used to love diving as a kid." (Okay, that was an exaggeration, but I'd tried diving at a local pool a few times, so I thought it was enough to sustain the conversation.)

"Yeah, my husband and I went diving by the cliffs the other day," she said.

"Wow, Sara, that's so brave of you. How long have you been diving? Cliff diving seems advanced?"

"Well," she said, "I got certified a couple of years ago at a public diving pool near me in Atlanta."

"Oh, certified—that's so fancy."

She looked at me like I had four heads and said, "You know you *have* to get certified to dive."

I obviously did not know that, but I guess that made sense if she was talking about diving off of scary cliffs. "Right, of course, you should have to be certified for safety. How high does that certification let you go?"

She said, "How deep, you mean?"

"Oh, sure, right . . ."

"It's about 130 feet," she said.

"Oh, that's so intense," I said, not really knowing what that meant but just trying to keep a casual conversation going that would end in us skipping down the beach holding hands. "You should be on *Diving with the Stars*!!"

"Isn't that a show about high diving?" she asked, probably thinking, "Get me the fuck out of this girl's presence now!"

"Yeah, you would be terrific! With all your experience jumping off cliffs and what not, you would totally crush it."

"Wait—what are you talking about? I was SCUBA diving near the cliffs."

I wanted to jump off a cliff at that very moment! This whole time she was talking about SCUBA diving, and I'd been trying to impress her with my knowledge of the triple lindy?! Needless to say, I was *beyond* mortified.

Once my face turned back from being red and my palms stopped sweating, I thought long and hard about WTF had happened here. We had been talking in circles, and it was all my fault because I didn't ask the question at the outset. It was that simple: "Wait, Sara, I'm lost—what are we talking about?" I'd been so impressed by her and intent on making her my BFF that I'd lost all semblance of common sense. It was like doodling your hypothetical married name in your notebook when you just started dating someone. The lesson? When you meet a potential professional bestie, slow down, think rationally, and don't picture your life together as work wifies before you've actually established the relationship. In an effort not to appear dumb, I'd only made myself look *more* so. Just ask the question and you'll have a better chance at happily ever after.

SETTING BOUNDARIES

Meeting new people is not a good thing, but a *great* thing—99% of the time, anyway. However, there are the rare times when it sucks. It's a high-class problem: you are SO popular. But with that popularity comes the necessity to keep up with everyone (at least to some extent), which can be real work. It also means fielding requests from the people you are meeting (or maybe who tracked you down like you did others) with whom you don't have the time or particular desire to stay in touch.

The more friends and acquaintances you make, the more inbound inquiries you'll get from them to "pick your brain." So, how do you respond to the things that that don't pass the "hell yes" test I told you about earlier in this section? Do you just say no? Do you simply ignore the request and ice them out? Clearly, neither of those options is right.

Here's a little e-mail role-playing to help you figure out what you should say when people who suck want to suck your brain juice (which, FYI, is really what it means most of the time when they offer to "take you out for coffee").

SCENARIO 1

E-mail from a person you met at a conference two years ago:

"Hey, Nicole, long time, no talk. Hope you're doing well. I would love to grab coffee and get your advice on something . . . When's a good time for you? Best, Veronica"

E-mail you might write back turning her down:

"Hi, Veronica, it's wonderful to hear from you. I am against the clock on several major deadlines, so I am unable to meet at this time. Is there something specific I can help you with or might you have a specific question I can noodle on for you? Warmest, Nicole"

By the way, if you happen to be the one reaching out to a person you met a couple of years ago, here's a better way to go:

"Hey, Veronica, I just saw your piece on Forbes. I was thrilled to see how much you've grown your company since we met at the Coolest Chick Conference two years ago. Since then, I've done a lot of thinking about your advice to transition into the cloud computing world. I currently have an interview with Johnny Sky at your former company set for May 1. I would love to get your thoughts on the best way to approach the interview as well as get a better understanding of how you see that company and its competitors positioning themselves in this sector. I know how crazy your schedule must be heading into review time, but I would love to buy you coffee before I go in to see Johnny. How's Wednesday or Thursday at the Java Jam below your building? Many thanks and looking forward to catching up. Warmest, Nicole."

Why this works:

- You show that you've been following her work since you met.
- You remind her of exactly where and when you met.
- You tell her exactly what you want to discuss with her.
- You show that you've already made progress on your own, so you are serious about the conversation. (And if you're hoping for her to put in a good word for you, you allow her to come to that conclusion on her own.)
- You've given her specific options and made it convenient for *her* to meet.

SCENARIO 2

E-mail from a person who wants to "brainstorm" with you:

> "Hey, Nicole, I have the BEST idea for a business. It's going to disrupt and crush it like the world has never seen. I can't talk about it on e-mail, but I would love to brainstorm with you since you've built something awesome and have 'been there.' Let me know when works! Thanks, Veronica."

E-mail you might write back turning them down:

> "Hi, Veronica, it's wonderful to hear from you. What an exciting time for you to start thinking of new entrepreneurial moves. I'd love to help you during this time of transition. As you know, I consult businesses for a living and am happy to send along my fee sheet to see what you might be comfortable with. Let me know if that's something you're interested in. Warmest, Nicole"

Why this works:

- If you get paid for your expertise, then don't give it out free of charge. If you owned a bakery, would you give muffins away for free? Didn't think so. Your time is money, so if this is a person you barely know, then politely remind her of this.
- Even if you don't get paid for your expertise, you've spent years developing and honing your business, mistakes and all. It's good to remind people (humbly) of the fact that you value what you've learned and accomplished, and they should, too. Don't let someone knocking on your door invite themselves in and take food out of your fridge.

BUILDING A BOSS BITCH NETWORK

As you become more and more of a powerhouse networker, the more and more you should be super selective about who you offer a permanent spot in your community to. In the beginning of your networking odyssey, it might be all about racking up numbers of contacts. But then, as the numbers mount (as they undoubtedly will), shift your focus toward thinking of building a more valuable *network* and not just *networking*.

"Wait a minute," you might be thinking. "Didn't we just talk about networking? Aren't networking and building a network the same thing?" No. "Networking" can become too transactionally focused if you fall into the trap of thinking, "How can I sell this person on something?" or "What can that person do for me?" Guess what? The relationships you generate from that mentality are almost certainly going to be superficial and short-lived.

"Building a network," on the other hand, is for the long term. Instead of being in the "sell, sell, sell" mode, you are in the "in it to win it" mindset. The people you ideally want in your network are those who are at a solid level in their career and still on the upswing. Personally, I love to build out my close network with people who are in different fields than I am. Maybe there is something to do professionally together, but it's most likely not immediately. What happens immediately is that we get to know each other and gain each other's trust. That's the most surefire way to ensure that successful people in your network go above and beyond for you if and when you need them to.

FYI

Celebrities might seem like they "have it all," but even the rich and famous get richer and more famous with the help of people in their network. Here are some A-listers and their corporate bedfellows:

Ashton Kutcher and Ron Conway. Ron is a legendary Silicon Valley investor who has put money into virtually every major successful tech company, from Google to Twitter. Ashton turned to him when he was starting to expand his business portfolio from acting to investing in major companies like Spotify and Airbnb.

Kobe Bryant and Mike Repole. When Kobe was getting ready to retire from his legendary basketball career, he wanted to venture into the business world. He called on Mike, who cofounded Vitamin Water, for help with his multimillion-dollar investment into the sports drink BodyArmor. Didya notice that Kobe had a BodyArmor towel around his neck during his insanely watched final game? That's some product placement after a Boss Bitch's heart.

I don't care what line of work you are in—whether you sell flowers or financial services—people always look to *people* before the products in business. That is, *you* are the primary product in any business. Does a person like you and what you stand for? If so, they are more likely to buy whatever it is you are selling—because it's *you* selling it.

Stronger personal ties build a foundation for stronger business ties. So, instead of focusing on your products when trying to know someone in business, focus on talking more about the most important product: you. That doesn't mean that you should be obnoxious, but share things that are important to you personally: your adventures, passions, and interests. Successful people know that they must build and cultivate a strong network long *before* they need it. That way, if they get let go from their job on Friday, they'll likely have another one lined up (or at least in the works) by Monday.

GIVE MORE THAN YOU GET AND YOU'LL GET MORE IN THE END

My biggest secret weapon in building meaningful business contacts is . . . help. No, I don't mean getting help from your new contact but offering to help them. Maybe you're still thinking, "I'm just starting out in my career. What could *I* possibly have to offer?" Um, a lot. Here are a few ideas for how to be helpful to someone older and/or more experienced than you are:

1. *Your time.* Offer to help out professionally or personally, whether it's assisting with a special work project or charity event or teaching

your colleagues to use Snapchat. Your time is extremely valuable not only to you but to someone who's lacking in the resource at the moment.

2. *Your contacts.* Crack open your own Rolodex (yes, I know no one has these anymore, but I'm speaking metaphorically here) and make a helpful introduction; after all, those contacts are currency! It can be a professional contact or a personal contact, like your favorite masseuse or a great accountant. But tailor your intro to the needs of that person. Are they in need of a deejay for their daughter's sweet sixteen party? Well, then your friend from growing up who happens to be a hot deejay in town is a *very* good contact to have.

3. *Your ideas.* Don't wait to be asked to help out; be the first to take a stab at it. If, for example, she mentioned having trouble with a project she's working on, *show, don't tell* how you can help. Put together a simple document with some of your ideas and send it along.

GET YOUR GIFT ON

I have a gift-giving problem. Yes, I could (and I do) have worse problems than this one, but I am addicted to giving gifts. I could write a book (*Gift Bitch,* anyone?!) about the crazy gifts I've concocted for people I've met or am keeping in touch with. Yes, there have been the plain vanilla gifts like flowers or cupcakes. But you better believe I have gotten pretty damn creative, too, like sending a housekeeper to my lawyer's mother's home in rural Texas because she told me Mama was overwhelmed with housekeeping postdivorce. Or the custom bathing suit I sent to Sara Blakely's office that said "Diving Queen Blakely" on it after my mortifying boat snafu. Needless to say, gifting is my so-called love language.

Gifts can go a long way to show just how thoughtful, observant, and resourceful you are. They don't need to be expensive, either. I have sent a glass of orange juice up to someone's hotel room who met me for drinks at the bar but had the sniffles. I've sent a $10 bottle of rosé to someone who had an iPhone case that said "On Wednesdays We Drink Rosé" (on the following

Wednesday, obviously). And, of course, always, always enclose a memorable note.

Don't have an assistant or much time to schlep around for this stuff? No worries, utilize the "share economy"* of apps, like Postmates and TaskRabbit, that do this stuff for you. They charge a nominal fee to be your personal messenger for virtually any errand you need to run. (BTW, in the first step of Section 3, I'll show you how to do those jobs yourself as a "side hustle"* if you want to make extra money.)

Or you could stockpile some quirky gifts so you have them at the ready. My girlfriend Randi Zuckerberg is a rock-star technology expert with her own radio show called *Dot Complicated*. She keeps a stack of I LIKE YOU note cards featuring the Facebook thumbs-up, since she worked as the marketing guru at Facebook for a long time. It fits her brand, it's fun and memorable, and it's easy for her to give out at a moment's notice. What's *not* to "like" about that gift-giving strategy?!

Giving gifts or cards or your time are all great gestures to show that you are a "giver" and not a "taker." People in leadership positions are wary of career "leeches" who are always looking to ask something of them. Position yourself in the opposite way and they will let their guard down and (hopefully) look to return the gesture.

CONFESSIONS OF A
BOSS BITCH

Help Me Help You Help Me

When I started my own business in 2011, I was beyond overwhelmed . . . and I needed a lot of support (emotionally and otherwise). My first instinct was to reach out to everyone I knew to see how they could help me get this business off the ground, a method that got me nowhere.

That's until I stopped asking for help, and started *offering* help instead. I realized that the better way to reach out to contacts from previous jobs and projects to learn more about what *they* were working on was to ask how I could be helpful to *them* and *their* business.

Here's the thing: people *are* eager to help, but they are more inclined to do it if it feels like it's on their terms. For example, I learned from one friend that she had a big corporate retreat coming up that involved hosting a panel with some bigwigs at her company. I thought, "Oh, like prepping for a big interview on TV! I know a thing or two about that." So I offered to help her prepare for the panel and hone her interview skills ... which led to a four-figure media consulting deal with her company. By being a friend first, I landed some serious business second.

FINDING A MENTOR

When I hold financial seminars or talks to help women get their financial shit together, the NUMBER ONE question I get asked is: "How do I find a mentor?"

I usually say that the best mentors* can be found in the most unlikely places. Then I cite some of my mentors who people think are quite random: like my wise dermatologist or my gregarious doorman. At first blush you might be thinking, "Lapin, have you lost your mentee mind? How could people in those professions help *you*?"

The answer is easy: collecting smart people in different, diverse fields will give you perspective on your career decisions and work issues that people within your field might miss. Sometimes an outsider's view is the best, most raw and honest one. For me, it's often not the advice I expect to hear but the advice that I *need* to hear. Collecting mentors in different fields is incredibly important to broaden your tunnel vision.

Equally important is to seek the opinions of others at different experience levels. If you have a contemporary as a mentor, you might ask, "What would you do or how would you handle this situation if you were me?" However, when asking someone who is older and has more experience, the question is a little different: "What has been your experience in situations like this?" Both questions yield valuable POVs that should be taken into consideration.

Another quality you want to diversify is general attitude. This might be tough to sniff out at first, but you don't want too many super-optimistic, glass-half-full people around you, just like you don't want too many Debbie Downer, glass-half-empty people around you. You want a mix so that you can make your own unbiased decisions for yourself.

Think of your mentors as being your own personal board of advisors. Look for diversity in industry, experience level, and attitude to create your own well-rounded, well-balanced career council.

FYI

A mentor doesn't necessarily have to be someone you know in person. She can be someone whose path or career or work ethic or vision you admire. Do some research about that person and find out how they got where they are, how they accomplished what they did. Think about how you could follow a similar path to achieve your own goals, keeping in mind that your journey will likely be a little different (after all, *you* are your own Boss Bitch).

Mentors who you follow from afar, like bloggers or journalists whose stuff you read on the regular, *can* become mentors in real life. All you have to do is . . . ask! You can probably find that person's contact information on their website or ping them on social media. Shoot them a note or tweet telling them you love their work, and let the relationship develop from there. But be genuine. I can tell you from personal experience as well as from being an author that I love, love, love hearing from people who *actually* read my stuff, not just say they read it. And I promise I (and any other author, for that matter) can tell the difference.

Now, never, ever ask outright if someone will be your mentor; it's a little creepy, especially if you don't actually know the person. I also think if you are someone's "mentor" or "mentee," you already know that's the relationship without the formal title. Usually, there's no "Hey, we've been hanging out a while now; can I call you my mentor?" conversation like the "Are we boyfriend/girlfriend?" one that happens with a guy you've been dating awhile. Plus, whether you call it mentorship or not, you're reaping the same important benefits of learning and growing as you would with some silly title-consummation discussion.

If you find yourself in the presence of a mentor-like figure, someone you are spending quality time with who you can learn and grow from, remember these things:

Don't waste your time with them asking about anything you could find with a quick online search. "What are the leading firms for digital cloud marketing?" WRONG. "From your experience, what differentiates Salesforce from the other digital cloud marketing companies like Adobe, IBM, Oracle, and HP?" RIGHT ON!

Be ready to embrace honest feedback. If you ask your mentor to look over a draft of something and they think it sucks, that tough love can be more valuable than hearing that it's great. If you ask your mentor if you should raise your hand for a job or an opportunity and they say no, then that's more of a gem of information than most anyone else will give you. In business it's much better to get a handle on your weaknesses than your strengths, so soak up all the constructive criticism you can get. Remember: we all have flaws, and we are all still flaw-some!

Ask tough questions of mentors you have within your own workplace. It might make you want to break out in hives to ask your mentor if they will openly support your pitch for XYZ when it's up for supervisor discussion (if they happen to be in a position of power). But do it anyway. Even if it's a no (in which case you should try to understand the reasoning and rationale behind that answer), it's more valuable to ask the straightforward question up front, between the two of you, than to be blindsided when they don't support you publicly because you *assumed* they would.

You are not the only one reaping benefits. I have helped guide the careers of a few women in their twenties, and guess what? I learned so much from *them*, especially about the trends of their generation, which is information that is way more accurate coming from a member of that group than in a questionable online trend story written by someone who's not even part of that generation.

You reserve the right to "break up" with a mentor. Even if you set a regular monthly meeting with one of your mentors, you can stop going at any time you don't think it's beneficial anymore. But don't just ghost them. Tell them that you think you'll put "breakfast club" (which is what I call my regular meetings with one of my mentors) on pause while you focus on XYZ. They and their valuable time will thank you.

Now you see why being a Boss Bitch is a team sport. You may think you can go it alone, but you'll do so much better winning the work game with killer teammates behind you. Success *is* easier and sweeter with others; start by getting the right bitches on your team, work with them, and then go in for the big career W.

BOTTOM LINE

Conventional Wisdom: The most successful people are self-made.

The Real Deal: No Boss Bitch is an island. There isn't a person on the planet who doesn't benefit from the help of someone else, whether they ask for it or not. You wouldn't even be able to get to work if it weren't for the engineers who designed the roads and the trains, the workers who laid the pavement and the rails. For me, I wouldn't have gotten where I am today without the farmers in Colombia who grow the coffee that makes my Boss Bitch motor hum every single day!

Conventional Wisdom: You don't have much to offer more experienced people.

The Real Deal: Nonsense! Your time and contacts are actually uniquely valuable to people who have been in business much longer than you. Think of networking as a giant game of connect the dots. If you can fulfill a more senior person's need by connecting her to someone she might not previously have had access to, you have provided her with value.

Conventional Wisdom: Industry gatherings and conventions are the best way to make contacts.

The Real Deal: Don't wait to be invited to an annual rubber chicken dinner. Get proactive and creative with your networking approach. Game night and sweatworking can be much more effective and authentic ways to expand your contact list than slapping on a name tag at another traditional networking event anyway.

THE VIEW FROM THE TOP

Owning Your Role in the Corner Office

You were thrown to the wolves and came out leading the pack. And now you're the badass in the corner office. Well, chances are that these days it's probably not a corner office per se; maybe it's *an* office (with an actual door!), or more likely a bigger cubicle in an open floorplan. Whatever the digs look like, you are there, and you are there for good reason.

And now that you are, it's time to apply your boss *mentality* to actually *being* the boss. So shut up that annoying voice in your head that's telling you that you aren't ready. No one is ever really ready for any big step in life, whether it's a boss title or anything else. Remember, dreams come in a few sizes too big so we can grow into them. So, let's grow, bitch!

Stop second-guessing yourself and start treating yourself like a boss, because once you do, you leave others no choice but to treat you like one, too. That's why in Step 5 of "Being the Boss at Work," I'll show you the most effective ways to make your voice heard while leading and inspiring a team who wants to work with you and for you. Get on top, girl. It's more fun up there, anyway.

I'M NOT BOSSY, I'M THE BOSS

You might be thinking, "Whoa, whoa, Lapin, we've been talking about being a 'boss' this whole time . . . so, now we are 'a Boss Bitch' *and* 'the boss'? Explain."

Yes, it seems a little meta. But, as you know, being a Boss Bitch is about taking charge of your life holistically: from your personal life, to your job, to your would-be business. Remember that we all go through lots of these different stages in our lives. We could be an intern then go work for a start-up then go back to corporate America at a higher rung of the proverbial ladder then take time off to have a kid then start our own business. Or we could start a business then sell it and go freelance for a few years before going back into the traditional workplace at entry level. You get the point. It's a different path for all of us and it can zig and zag and zag and zig among different positions, different jobs, and different industries. But *you* are the constant through all of the zigzagging. And as we've learned, it's important that you feel like a Boss Bitch no matter where you are and no matter what title you have: whether it is "assistant" or "vice president" or "senior vice president" or "founder" or "CEO."

For this step, I'm going to focus on what it's like to take that Boss Bitch mentality into a more senior role within someone else's company (we will talk about mastering that role in your own company in the next section). That senior role could be as a VP with a team of one assistant and two interns; it could be a director role where you have three or four direct reports; it could be a president role with twenty direct reports, or even a C-suite role with five hundred direct reports. Regardless of the title, being a boss at work for the sake of this step means that you have people who call you *boss* in the official sense, as in their supervisor or the person to whom they report directly.

Being in charge of a team or more than one team is a big job. It means you need to channel all your Boss Bitch–dom to lead and inspire other burgeoning Boss Bitches. It's a big responsibility, no doubt—but it's one that you can and will tackle with the same panache you bring to other areas of your life. First, it helps to know: What kind of boss are you, anyway?

WHAT'S YOUR BOSS STYLE?

1. When you notice an employee is going above and beyond her assignments and crushing it big-time, you:
   A. Give her more work because she obviously can handle it.
   B. Ask her what she envisions as her future in the company and see how you can help her get there, while telling her to take it down a notch so as to not make other, slower worker bees feel bad.
   C. Give her a high five!

2. When an employee calls out sick, you:
   A. Send her a list of assignments that she will need to make up and ask her to keep you posted on her progress.
   B. Ignore the call, letting it go to voice mail. Assume she is playing hooky and ask someone else to take over her assignments.
   C. Tell her to feel better and ask her if she wants your assistant to send some Airborne over.

3. When an employee is struggling with an assignment, you:
   A. Pull up a chair next to her and walk her through everything step by step.
   B. Give her a couple of general tips and send her on her way to complete the assignment.
   C. Sympathize with how hard it must be, offer to rub her shoulders to help her relax (half jokingly), or take her out for a drink after work (not jokingly).

4. You just found out you are going to have to lay people off, you:
   A. Call a large a meeting, allow for an open-mic discussion, and log feedback for yourself and HR.
   B. Call those people into your office the day before you have to let them go and send a note to your staff the next day, paraphrasing or forwarding the directive that has been bestowed upon you from above.

C. Hug it out and give everyone you have to let go your personal e-mail and cell phone number in case they ever need anything professionally or personally.

5. You just found out that no one is stepping up to help the intern, and she is just sitting in the corner occasionally fetching coffee, so you:
   A. Forward your staff the company policy on managing interns, plus a recent article about the importance of doing so.
   B. Let the intern figure it out for herself—after all, you had to do that! Or casually ask one of your trusted employees to keep an eye on her while allowing the employee to pass the buck to someone else if she doesn't have time.
   C. Take over the responsibility yourself! Get to know your intern personally, send a note to your staff with her bio, and ask which folks want to help mentor this fine young person.

6. While taking an extra vacation day to extend a holiday weekend, you:
   A. Are on e-mail 24/7, checking in with your number two morning, noon, and night.
   B. Take it easy, relax, hit the beach, and get a massage. Check in with your number two once per day just in case anything comes up.
   C. Buy everyone in the office trinkets and souvenirs.

7. When you hear about beef two employees are having, you:
   A. Send an e-mail to both of them separately saying you want to see them in your office today to get each side of the story. Then call a meeting with them together the next day, corroborating their stories based on your notes. Ask them to see past their differences and tell them that you would like to have this same meeting in a week with a positive outcome.
   B. Let them figure it out as the grown-ass people they are and

check in with them separately after a few days to see if all is good.

C. Take them out to lunch off-site and help them work it out over kale salad and a glass of rosé.

If you answered mostly As, well, then, you are a detail-oriented boss. If you feel the need to dot every *i* and cross every *t* personally, you might be a micromanager. There's nothing wrong with attention to detail. In fact, that attention to detail likely got you where you are in the first place. But good managers will stop short of micromanaging to help their teams to understand the big picture while empowering *them* to tackle the more minute details of the project on their own. Your team will never learn anything if you do everything for them, and likewise you'll never realize your full potential as a leader until you learn to let go a bit and delegate.

If you answered mostly Bs, you are a chill boss. You're happy to let staff take the reins on projects, only reporting to you when they're done. Rather than get involved with office drama, you're more of a hands-off, let-the-baby-cry-it-out kind of boss. I applaud you for maintaining your cool during the rat race, but be careful that your laid-back attitude doesn't come off as simply not caring. Regular check-ins with your employees, even biweekly, are a great way to foster your workplace relationships and answer any questions that might come up—and also to catch any mistakes or misguided enthusiasm before a project totally derails on your watch or, more accurately, while you *aren't* watching.

If you answered mostly Cs, you are a super-friendly boss. You go out to dinner with the gang, maybe knock back a few cocktails. You're known as being approachable (maybe too much so) and almost like a bestie. Be careful not to blur the lines too much, though; after all, you're still the Boss with a capital *B* and, as such, deserve respect. You don't want to get into a position where you need to extend negative feedback (or maybe even disciplinary action) and aren't taken seriously doing it. I'm all about being a good cop, but a balanced Boss Bitch knows when to be a bad cop, too.

This quiz is only intended to show you which type of boss you naturally *tend* to be—not the one you *have* to be. A huge part of being a manager is managing *yourself*: playing to your strengths as a leader while actively improving those less-stellar tendencies, like micromanaging or being overly familiar with colleagues. The whole point of assessment quizzes like this is to make you aware of these behaviors. And self-awareness is the best possible quality any boss could have. The best bosses are a combination of detailed, chill, and friendly—and continually seeking to improve themselves even as they inspire their team to do the same.

Whether or not you are someone who is naturally comfortable calling meetings to talk about assignments, plans, or personnel issues, don't worry: boss skills can be learned. If you don't already have the attributes most successful bosses have, then you've come to the right place to get them.

These traits are pretty easy to work on if you know what they are. If you don't want a bad boss rap, get your good boss R-A-P on:

Reliable. Good bosses are the go-to people when anyone has an issue. If I had a problem with my hair, I would call up Alli Webb, cofounder of Drybar, for blow-out advice. If you look at her Instagram, you'll see how she comes across as the girl who will literally show up at your door with a yellow blow-dryer. That's the "go-to" reliability you want as a boss.

Attention-getting (not attention-seeking). Can you imagine Coco Chanel raising her voice or talking over someone in a room to be heard? No—she wouldn't have had to, because she's Coco freakin' Chanel. When a good leader enters a room, all eyes are on her and all mouths are shut—waiting for hers to open.

Passionate. There aren't many things worse for a goal-digging worker bee than to have to deal with a boss who's bored with and doesn't care about their job. I know, *every* day isn't a-mazing. But when you are a boss, you sometimes have to put on your lip gloss and get stoked (like my girl Mindy Kaling says); others are counting on you.

FYI

Even when you are the boss of others at your job, you will almost certainly have your own boss as well. No matter how senior you are, you will have someone *more* senior than you to answer to, and they will likely have someone more senior than them. Yep, even CEOs have bosses: they're called the board of directors. If you don't have a person whom you report to directly, you'll probably have a partner, a board, a parent company, investors, and shareholders, especially if you're at a publicly traded company* but often when you work at a privately held business,* too. So keep in mind that no Boss Bitch takes the world by storm alone; you might be calling the shots, but that doesn't make you queen of the fucking universe.

GET "BOSS OFFICIAL" IN WRITING

Now that you have a souped-up business card, a fancy swivel chair, and a gigundo expense account, you likely want to keep it that way. After all, the point of taking on all these new responsibilities isn't to coast; it's to accomplish something new, different, and/or groundbreaking for your company. You want to level up and do *better* than what was done before you—and you want to encourage your staff to do the same. Well, that takes a hot minute. Think about it this way: it takes a mere thirteen hours to build a Toyota, but six months to build a Rolls-Royce. You obviously want to be the Rolls-Royce of bosses—but that's gonna take time, just like making the actual car does.

But what if your corporate overlords get impatient and start breathing down your neck for immediate results? To ensure that you don't get booted while you are trying to build something great, you'll want a contract. Your company didn't give you one? Well, you need to ask for one. Don't love the terms of the contract they gave you? Then go back and negotiate, like you learned how to do with your salary earlier in this section. Even if you are happy with the contract you have, you should still negotiate to make it even better. And when it comes time to sign on the dotted line, "Yep, looks like my contact information is right, and it includes the salary I agreed to" is *not* the right or adequate response.

To make sure that contract is working for you, you've got to get down with the details. Here's what to look for in your contract before you take the reins as capital-B Boss:

What does the description of your duties say? Don't assume that you know what's expected of you. Read through the list of duties carefully, because this is what you are legally bound to do, day in and day out. If something looks fishy, flag it. Also, make sure that the contract has a term, as in a beginning date and an end date; otherwise it's just a glorified offer letter.

What does your compensation look like? So they have your salary correct, wonderful. What about benefits? Is health insurance in there, stock options, and everything else that you discussed? If anything is missing or you want something like that expense account or vacation time specifically guaranteed so they can't "change their mind" once you're in the job, ask them to write it into the contract.

Is your contract exclusive? If it is, you won't be able to do any kind of other work, whether it's other part-time work or working for yourself on the side. If you already have something you are doing on the side and you want to "carve it out"* of the contract, then write that down to discuss with your new employer.

What does it say about termination and what happens if the happy marriage ends? There are usually three ways you can end your employee-employer relationship: 1) with cause, which means you messed something up that you were contractually obligated to do; 2) without cause, meaning you didn't do anything wrong but the company is "restructuring" (which is a fancy business term for letting people go); or 3) resignation, aka you peace out. When your relationship ends with cause, your employer doesn't typically need to give you anything, and your termination can take effect immediately. If your relationship ends without cause, you'll want it to outline your severance.

Is there an "at-will" clause?* "At-will" means that your employer can fire you at any time with or without a contract. So if the term says that it's three years, but there's at-will language that says after a certain number of days—say, sixty or ninety—they can terminate you for any reason, then the three years doesn't mean that much. If you are certain you want to stay for those three years, then ask if you can nix that at-will clause.

Even if you don't have a signature on a piece of paper, you will likely be protected by an "implied contract," which can be as simple as a conversation or an e-mail between you and someone higher up at the company saying something like, "You'll have a job here as long as your sales remain above XYZ." If you had such an e-mail or conversation and your sales hit XYZ and they fire you, you can argue it was "without cause." Other implied protections can likely be found in your employee handbook. "Um, who actually reads those?" you ask. Boss Bitches, that's who. Plus, if you're gonna enforce the rules (or break some) as the boss, you've gotta know what they are, first!

MACGUYVER IT

BITCH TIP

You don't need to be at a big company or get a lawyer involved to get something about your job in writing. The hesitation on the company's part is usually threefold: 1) they don't want to spend the legal money to put something on paper; 2) you don't make enough to justify the time or money it will take them to negotiate with you; 3) maybe they want the flexibility to let you go whenever.

If you understand those hesitations, you can proceed thoughtfully. It's always in your best interest to have a little certainty about a job before you start (especially if you have a family and/or are moving cities). So DIY and send a quick, friendly e-mail that casually includes all the important notes a contract would hit:

Dear NAME OF HIRER/BOSS,

I'm so excited to be starting on DATE. I am looking forward to TERM of great hard work as your POSITION. As part of the job I can't wait to do SERVICES. I appreciate your generous offer of SALARY AND PERKS. Thank

you so much for allowing WHATEVER SPECIFIC THING YOU DISCUSSED THAT'S IMPORTANT TO YOU. I am thrilled to be part of the team!
Warmest,
Nicole

And while verbal contracts are enforceable, when things go south (maybe you have to sue or take them to small claims court depending on the situation), people might have a "selective memory," so anything in writing is good to have just in case. Consider it a work prenup, and if it's the right marriage you'll never need it.

Reading dense contracts with a bunch of legalese is zero fun. If your contract is complex enough, you might want to get an outside lawyer to help you either take a closer look and/or negotiate it for you. (And BTW, the key word here is *outside*, because if you use the company's lawyer, at the end of the day, they're looking out for their [now your] employer and not you). They will usually take a hefty fee for doing this, or, in some cases (like in the entertainment industry), they will take a small percentage of your entire contract or signing bonus. If you don't want to shell out cash for a fancy lawyer, this might be the time to call in a favor. You have to have at least one JD in your tribe, right? If not, and you're working through your contract yourself, here's what to do with all the things you marked up:

1. *Communicate with your employer* (verbally at first) to get a sense of where they are coming from on the issues you identified. Be professional (as you always are) and listen to their concerns. Then, follow up in writing (e-mail is fine). Otherwise, it's your word against theirs, and the contract process drags on.
2. *Don't draw a line in the sand for everything.* There could be important "deal breakers" for you, but you are more likely to get your way on those if you demonstrate flexibility on most, if not all, things. There is no way an employer will acquiesce on *everything*, so provide options for a compromise.

3. *Don't accept crazy terms.* While you won't get everything you want, don't feel forced to sign something that's unacceptable. You can always walk away, which most employers will stop you from doing by throwing you another bone because, don't forget, they have put a lot of time, energy, and money into trying to hire the best person (you), and it's not in their best interest to let you walk away at the eleventh hour. But if you make the decision to play that card, make sure you mean it, because sometimes they *will* call your bluff.

There are loopholes and ways around employment contracts, for sure. Still, they are important for peace of mind and some job security. So while there is no guarantee they'll protect you from every possible future issue, if done right they will help you avoid nasty surprises later on.

BOSS BITCHES SHOULD BE SEEN *AND* HEARD

I often hear two business clichés that I absolutely hate: 1) "The best man for the job is . . ." and 2) "I just want a seat at the table."

Off the bat, please remove that first saying from your lexicon, because the best man for the job might be a woman. As for the second, ladies, you shouldn't aspire just to have a seat at the table; you should aspire—no, *demand*—to have a voice at that table, too.

BE RESPECTED AND LIKED

Get it out of your head right now that you have to come into your new office digs with stilettos swinging and ready to be the *bad* kind of bitch. Nope and nope. Research has shown that, on average, female managers are more engaged than male managers, which results in leading higher-performing work groups.* The takeaway: people like working for women and work harder for them.

I used to work for a guy who harped on me for being too bubbly, saying it's better to be "respected" than "liked." Well, look here, Mr. Bubble Crusher, it's not an "either/or" but a "both." You can and should be respected *and* liked.

I hate it when career experts come out and say, "Well, they don't need to be your pals, but if your team respects you they will work harder." Okay, maybe. But what if your team thinks you're rad *and* respects you?! To quote the great Dr. Seuss, "Oh, the places you'll go!" The truth is that people want to work with and for people they like; it's human nature to gravitate toward people we think are dabomb.com.

Don't rage against that human trait; instead, use it to your advantage in building a team that gets shit done. No matter what your company produces, whether it's a product or a service, you'll find that your people are your greatest asset—if (and this is a big if) you lead them the right way:

Get to know them. Stop talking and start listening, and ask your staff questions about themselves. We're talking more than first names and hometowns. Your new employees may be anxious about what the change in leadership (that is, *you*) will mean for them. Put their fears to rest by showing a genuine interest in learning more about them. Make one-on-one meetings more than a one-time thing. Don't fall into the trap of being overly nice up front and then disappearing until the annual review.

Remember that one size does not fit all. People are not all the same. Duh. If you truly get to know the people who work for you, you'll get better work from them. Knowing their individual strengths (and weaknesses), will help you assign tasks that match their particular skill sets.

Trust them. It's easy to fall into micromanaging when overseeing people you don't yet know, but it won't make you very popular *or* effective. Plus, you'll only be creating more work for yourself. Regular check-ins will allow you to ensure that progress is being made without being overbearing; plus, they will allow you to adjust course as needed to get to the desired goal even faster.

Don't make them drink from a fire hose. By this I mean: don't overwhelm your team. Just don't. I know being a boss is stressful, but don't give that frazzled energy off to your staff. Personally, I tend to have a one-sentence-e-mail problem. When I get busy, I tend to fire off notes to my people as they come to mind because otherwise I think I'll forget. That clogs up inboxes and increases the chance that one or more tasks will be overlooked because my employees are spending time trying to decode my last fifteen e-mails (composed of a few words each). My latest resolution was to organize all my thoughts into one e-mail before sending it to my team; that way, we're all organized with our own punch lists of tasks.

Instead of drinking from a fire hose, drink at a bar. Day to day, you want to keep a line between chummy and professional, but every once in a while, treat them to a fun outing for camaraderie and team-building. But watch that line between cool boss and "Why is she still here? This is awkward" boss. Perhaps you join for one round, then pay up front for a second for your team (always a classy move) while politely leaving the outing so they can unwind without you. You want to be involved enough in their personal lives that they see how much you care about them, but not be so up in their personal business that it detracts from your first role of being their boss.

CONFESSIONS OF A
BOSS BITCH

Skittles Safe Zone

Most bosses *say* they have an open-door policy, when in reality either their door is literally closed or they seem closed off to their underlings (or, in the worst cases, both). Not the good ones, though. One of my favorite bosses had not only an open door but also an open bowl of Skittles on her desk.

Sometimes I would sneak into her office for no other reason than to grab a handful of Skittles. She knew that a lot of people did that (free food goes over great in any office), which is why she left them there: as a way to encourage people to stop by. If I ever came in while she was on the phone, I would kind of hand gesture with the "Oh, don't mind me, I'm just grabbing a taste of the rainbow, NBD," and inevitably she would hand gesture back with the "Oh, no, come here, stay here while I'm on the phone." Obviously, I couldn't just eat and run. She would put her call on speakerphone and let me listen to the work call that was going on.

This was super cool because listening in behind the scenes of how she conducted herself and business was more valuable than any advice she could have given me. I learned so much from her just by listening (while trying to chew quietly).

As a boss, I'm sure she knew that even though she had an actual, bona fide open-door policy, employees were still nervous to walk in. What my boss crush did was simple but genius: she took the pressure off by making her desk look more inviting. The word got out that she had Skittles, and people came running. (I mean, seriously, you would think that people working in that office hadn't eaten in years, considering how ravenous they were for free food.)

So think of some ways to get people through *your* door. Whether it's a bowl of candy, a massage chair, or even bringing your dog to work on Fridays, anything you can do to encourage people to stop in when they don't need to is a great way to get to know your employees, and vice versa. In fact, I've found that many of my most teachable moments have come when an employee came into my office totally unplanned; in our mutually relaxed state, we're more easily able to shoot the shit—and share ideas.

This works even if you are not a boss but want to be one. There was actually a study conducted that showed that of the people who have candy or treats on their desk to entice people to come by and visit or chat, 90% are promoted. And who are we kidding? At the end of the day, everyone wins when candy is involved!

COMPLIMENTS ARE FREE, SO GIVE THEM AWAY

Remember the power of your words by recalling a time when you were on the receiving end of a compliment from a boss. Mark Twain said it best: "I can live for two months on a good compliment." And if it's the right one from the right person, it probably holds you over even longer.

Before you dish out a compliment to your team, be sure to keep the right tone with my "Five Ss" strategy. Make it:

1. Short
2. Sweet

3. Soon
4. Sincere
5. Specific

Here's how that fits into a five-S-powered compliment:

> "Good afternoon, Anna. I loved the newsletter you sent out yesterday with the highlights of the week. It was a great idea to have a weekly spotlight feature of a stellar employee. That's an excellent way to engage the team and also allow the higher-ups to see all that we are accomplishing. You did a wonderful job doing that in a creative way."

1. Short: This was just five sentences, including the "Good afternoon, Anna."
2. Sweet: "I loved . . ." "It was a great idea" . . . "You did a wonderful job"—all kind phrases.
3. Soon: You delivered the compliment to Anna the day after the newsletter was sent.
4. Sincere: Your attention to the detail of Anna's weekly spotlight feature shows that you are genuine, versus just a generic "good job."
5. Specific: You told her exactly what you liked and exactly why you liked it.

Continual feedback, good and bad, delivered in the right way will make your team excited about working for you and keep their many projects on track. Remember, your team on its own isn't the secret weapon to rocking your role in the corner office; how you grow them is.

RUN A TIGHT SHIP

Since time is money, especially when you're a boss, you need to get down with anything that makes you more efficient. Think of your time as a lawyer would: measured by billable hours. You only get twenty-four in a day—the same as the president, the first lady, and Beyoncé—so make 'em count! Boost your productivity and work smarter, not harder.

1. *Rethink multitasking.* We've all been guilty of trying to do way too many things at one time, which normally leads to a less-than-stellar performance across the board. Rethink it. Instead of breaking your train of thought while working on a presentation to jump over to shoot off a couple of e-mails, spend a chunk of time focusing on the presentation: no quick tab jumping or e-mailing allowed! If you are going to do two things at once, make one of them relatively brainless. Brainstorm while going for a run, folding laundry, etc. And prioritize! It's better to get your five most important tasks for the day done well, versus all fifteen items on your to-do list done poorly.

2. *Hire help.* Obviously, this applies as it fits within your company's budget. If it does, even the smallest investment can be a good investment in productivity. Paying $7 for a grocery delivery can be totally worth it if you are able to get additional work done during the time that it would take to drive through traffic to the store, shop, etc. Weigh the cost of getting it done yourself versus paying a nominal fee for someone else to do it—so you can keep working. Oftentimes, the cost will be less than your "billable hours" if you did it yourself.

3. *Maximize office efficiency.* Minimize distractions at the office as much as you can (easier said than done, I know). Make sure that meetings have clear agendas that are circulated to all attendees ahead of time, and reassess if you and your team really need to meet as often as you do. Don't worry about replying to every little e-mail, and set aside specific times to reply to those that warrant it (I like eleven a.m.–ish, after I've had a cup of coffee—or three—to read through the day's headlines and outline my intentions for the day). A handy pair of noise-canceling headphones can really help with your focus as well—whether you're actually listening to anything or not (I personally do not; the quiet just gets me in the zone).

4. *App-ly yourself.* You're probably just as glued to your smartphone as I am, so make it work harder for you! I like using apps like Slack to message my team in real time, whether we're at our desks or not; Evernote to keep lists/notes/links in one place (and synced across devices); and, of course, a shared team calendar. If you need a chunk of time with ZERO distractions, turn your phone on airplane mode and watch the world (and distracting e-mail alerts) disappear.

DON'T JUST BE A GOOD MANAGER, BE A GOOD LEADER

You're a boss. Check. You're a manager. Check. But are you a leader?

"What's the difference?" you might ask. I like thinking of it visually. A leader plays chess and not checkers. Even though I'm terrible at chess, I know that not all pieces are the same; each one has its own special moves and role as part of the strategy of the whole game. But in checkers, all the pieces are the same and interchangeable. A manager might look at her employees that way, as proverbial cogs in the work machine. No one likes to feel like that. Leaders, on the other hand, understand that each player and each move is unique, and play the game accordingly.

Here are some examples of how a good leader would handle various scenarios, versus someone who is just a good manager:

Manager: Does a lap around the office at 9:05 a.m. to see who hasn't shown up for work yet.

Leader: Starts her day off leading by example. She brings in coffee half an hour before start time and sits in the break room to meet with anyone who shows up then. This opportunity for face time and free caffeine energizes staff to show up early and raring to go—without being asked.

Manager: Administers tasks that need to be done to maintain status quo and keep the place running.

Leader: Innovates and develops new plans or tweaks and challenges old ones for the better.

Manager: Asks "how?" and "when?"

Leader: Asks "what?" and "how?"

Manager: Relies on control, capital, and systems already in place.

Leader: Relies on trust in other people—the "human capital."

UNDERCOVER BOSS, BITCH

As a boss, there's no excuse for not knowing what's up in all aspects of the business you oversee. If you want to know how something is *really* working (or not working), get on in there and see it for yourself.

Fred DeLuca, the founder of Subway (the sandwich chain), was a friend and mentor of mine. Before he passed away after a brave battle with cancer, I had the privilege of spending time getting to know him and how he became one of the most successful American entrepreneurs. I learned so much from watching how he ran his business as a global brand, not dissimilar from how he ran it as a stand-alone sandwich shop. For starters, he had all of his executives go "undercover" and visit their own sandwich franchises around the world. It was important to him that his senior leadership see the real product for themselves: how the sandwiches are made, how they taste, how fresh they are. (While he did this himself, too, he wasn't always able to get away with it because he became too recognizable from the company's commercials.) As an amazingly charismatic guy, when he did visit his franchises himself, he always wanted to talk to the employees: What did they like, and more important, dislike about their jobs? Did they have any suggestions to make it better? More effective? Hearing the real answers to these questions from the front lines helped them win the sandwich wars for decades.

Meanwhile, Sam Walton, the founder of Walmart, was known to make visits to the stores of his *competitors*. Once, he was actually arrested for trespassing when he was trying to figure out how far apart the aisles were spaced in a competitor's store. After his team bailed him out, they asked him why he didn't just go undercover at his *own* stores, to which he replied that he already knew what was happening there; he wanted to learn new tricks and tactics from the competition to make his stores even better.

Maybe Walton crossed a line by, you know, getting arrested, but the point is, many of the great bosses realize that they can't just look at numbers from behind a desk; they need to get out and see how things really look for themselves. The best ones know that they have to go in unannounced so nothing is sugarcoated and no one hands out rose-colored glasses. Too often in business the steering wheel loses the connection to the tires, so to speak. Going undercover to find the faulty parts is sometimes the best way to get the engine running and that car back in the fast lane.

Most successful CEOs see the value in doing this; that's how the CBS show *Undercover Boss* is able to book business rock stars season after season. I've spoken to a bunch of the bosses featured on the show, and they told me that they found the experience to be so invaluable that they kept going undercover, even after the cameras were gone, just to pulse check how the many facets of the company were *really* doing.

MAKE A MEA CULPA

If things don't go wrong every once in a while in business, then you're not doing enough. Most bosses deal with multiple things going wrong in the course of the day. And most likely, some of those things are their fault. Good leaders aren't bosses who don't fuck up; they are bosses who take responsibility for things when they do fuck up. And they will often fall on the sword for the whole team if something goes wrong on their watch.

Like on the NBC show *The Apprentice*, if someone on a challenge mucks something up, the "project manager" is the one who usually gets called into the boardroom to go up against Arnold and his firing squad. The bad bosses on that show—who almost always hear, "You're fired"—are the ones who throw members of their team under the bus. The bosses with staying power are the ones who stand in front of the bus to save their team, even if it means they risk getting flattened by it themselves.

In Step 2 of this section, we talked about *not* saying I'm sorry. Well, that was in reference to saying sorry for things that don't warrant an apology at all (like when someone else bumps into *you*!). But when you do something wrong at work (especially if you are the boss), you need to apologize—and you should try to do it quickly, and in person. And here's how:

1. *Say I'm sorry, and say it genuinely.* People can always tell when an apology is forced or inauthentic. Normally, I say to make things all about "you, you, you," in business. In this case, keep it all in the first person.

2. *Explain why you are sorry,* so that your team (or one employee in particular) knows why you are apologizing and can also understand why what you did was wrong.

3. *Suggest a solution* for handling a similar situation better next time. This allows you to project a forward-looking attitude and resiliency.

4. *Listen to the response.* The team or individual you are apologizing to was most likely hurt in one way or another. Even if it's hard to hear, listen to their anger and frustration. Let them vent a little; you were an asshole and they earned the right to respond.

5. *Say something to the effect of, "Thank you for giving me another chance,"* depending on what you did. When you mess up, you need to be as humble as can be. None of this "I'm the boss, so I can make mistakes without acknowledging or apologizing for them" crap.

6. *Don't do it again.* Live (work) and learn.

It's brave to apologize instead of turning a blind eye or making excuses. A good leader is brave, accountable, and yet *human*. No boss is superwoman—and realizing that is what will make you a super boss.

DEALING WITH DRAMA

Office politics are like taxes and PMS: they're gonna happen and they're gonna be a pain. A Boss Bitch knows how to throw punches and how to roll with them, and a Boss Bitch who is a good leader to boot will minimize the drama wherever possible and deal with it gracefully when it can't be avoided.

Before learning how to handle drama, it's important to know where it comes from and what it does to the effectiveness of a team. Drama usually starts with emotion and ends with conflict. Sometimes it can stem from a simple misunderstanding. Other times it can be more complicated.

Regardless, it produces nastiness that ranges from childish behavior to threats of sabotaging careers. All drama in the workplace strains productivity and effectiveness by hogging all of the office's attention when it should be going toward projects and impending deadlines.

It's also important to be able to tell the difference between run-of-the-mill office tension, which occurs naturally in any workplace, and drama, which needs to be nipped in the bud. If it's the latter, the best way to handle it starts with collaboration and ends with resolution. Easier said than done, I know. Luckily, drama queens and kings tend to fit certain archetypes, and as such are easy to spot. Here are some of the types of people who are involved in drama and how to handle them.

THE BULLY

Who they are: This person is a meanie who is intimidating another member of your staff somehow, whether verbally or over e-mail. Oftentimes, this aggressive, controlling behavior stems from their own insecurities and is an attempt to overcompensate for them.

How to handle them: Well, here's something they can be secure about: you are in charge, and this shit doesn't fly. Call them in and explain your zero-tolerance for this type of behavior. If it persists, you need to document it and send it even higher up the food chain before taking measures to fire the person if the behavior still doesn't stop.

THE VICTIM

Who they are: This person is at the receiving end of the Bully's wrath. Sometimes, this person is totally innocent, and the wrath they are receiving is unsubstantiated. But, oftentimes, while they might claim it's not their fault, they have played some antagonizing role in why they are getting hated on in the first place and/or why it's continuing.

How to handle them: Call this person in and express regret that they are dealing with this. But then get real. Sometimes a Victim has a mentality that they are *always* the Victim. Suss out the truth and remind them that they can't engage with the Bully or they're implicit in the drama as well.

THE GOSSIP

Who they are: A mean girl who usually rolls in a clique. They are usually a wannabe Bully or a Bully in disguise.

How to handle them: This might sound like seventh grade, but break them up. If they sit in cubes next to each other, move them apart. To BS in the break room is one thing, but you don't want any of the others to feel uncomfortable if it's in their face while they are working. If it gets to a point where it's affecting people's ability to do their job, then call the Gossip into your office. My favorite tactic is to repeat the gossip back to them in a nonconfrontational way and say that you're going to call that person in (the Victim) and get to the bottom of it. Confronting the Gossip with their gossip and challenging them to verify their story usually gets them to back off.

ABOVE-THE-FRAY EMPLOYEES

Who they are: These are the hardworking, drama-free people on your team who have no time or energy for this nonsense—but are at risk of getting sucked in.

How to handle them: Keeping them above the fray is your responsibility. You need to remind them that behaviors exhibited by the Bully and the Gossip are not acceptable and can result in serious consequences. Above-the-Fray Employees might get sucked into the drama vortex if they think there are no repercussions, so remind them that it's not okay.

The number one cure for the drama disease that plagues so many workplaces is to treat it before it spreads. Remember, negative people need drama like they need oxygen. Lead with positivity, and it will take their breath away.

MAYDAY! MAYDAY!

"A woman is like a teabag; you never know how strong it is until it's in hot water," said OG Boss Bitch Eleanor Roosevelt. Strong women (you) thrive in times of crisis and don't get burned by it. As a boss, you'll deal with crisis. You'll deal with choppy waters. And when you do, be a port in the storm for those who work with, below, and even sometimes above you.

Here's an example of a crisis and how you might navigate it as the true Boss Bitch you are:

Scenario: You just found out that your biggest client hates a proposal you gave them and you need to redo it by tomorrow morning—or they will find someone else.

What not to say #1: "This sucks. I have a work event I already committed to . . . you guys go to town, and I'll look over everything in the morning."

What not to say #2: "Heads down. Do not get up. If you need to leave, you better believe I'll remember it come bonus time!"

What to say instead: "Okay, guys, we've got this. First, let's break away and all think of two good ideas. Then, in one hour, let's convene in the conference room and we will vote on the best ideas and divide and conquer to show them what we've got!"

The idea here is to remain positive and level-headed. If you freak out, they'll freak out. Make a direct call to action with set steps so that your expectations are clearly defined. Then muster your best coach mentality to inspire them to hustle, and lead the team to victory.

Of course, every crisis is not created equal; nor is there a direct play-by-play you can follow, but here are some general principles that should guide you through the rocky work waters:

Look reality in the eye. Bosses who are good crisis managers live in reality, not fantasy. They see the crisis for what it is but don't freak out about it because they see the big picture. They are able to juggle all the moving parts by keeping a helicopter view.

Be good at multiple choice and fill-in-the-blank. Once Boss Bitches have identified a problem, they come up with different options to solve it. But they admit what they don't know and that their way might not be the best way—and seek alternate solutions from others.

Don't waste time playing the blame game. Of course, if a mistake is egregious or the problem is caused by a single person/unit, that requires addressing, but don't waste precious time and resources in that moment by pointing fingers. The best bosses are such good firefighters that they put out the fire before you even smell smoke.

Demonstrate decisiveness. Once you have a solution, taking ownership of it means being decisive. When Boss Bitches feel they have listened to the best advice available, they make a decision. Strong leaders will use a combination of real-time data along with their "gut" wisdom built on years of leadership experience. While we always want to make the right decision, strong Boss Bitch leaders do their best with the information they have, knowing that making an imperfect decision is better than making none at all.

BITCH TIP

THE NUMBERS BEHIND DECISION MAKING

We've all been there with our significant others or our girlfriends: "Where do you want to eat?" "No, where do *you* want to eat?" and this goes round and round until someone faints from low blood sugar. This is called decision paralysis. In your personal life, it can just leave you hangry, but in business you don't have time to waffle (mmm . . . waffles) over making a decision. Keep these theories in mind to make a decision quickly:

The 70–40 rule. If you have less than 40% of the information, you're likely to make the wrong decision. If you have 70% or more of the information and you wait too long to try and get more, it's too late—others have decided and moved on. Make the decision when you're someplace in between those two benchmarks.

The 70% rule. This rule is not from an economist but from a comedian, and I love it just the same. Louis C.K. says that if you think you want to do something with 70% certainty, then just do it. Something magical then happens when you make the decision: your decision looks better to you because you start owning it and discounting other options. Getting close to being 100% is unrealistic. Don't let the perfect be the enemy of the good.

As a boss, not all of your crises are work related. We all have personal issues; as a boss you suck up most of those because you have a team depending on you. But you can't expect the same from your employees. Your employees will have crises of their own that will affect their work; that's just life. There could be a death in the family, an injury, a breakup, an illness, a robbery, or another unforeseen terrible situation. When that happens, and it will, it's important to handle it with empathy and care while also making sure the important business is handled.

CONFESSIONS OF A
BOSS BITCH

Empathy, Not Sympathy

Don't make the mistake of a former boss of mine, who sent chocolate to an employee whose mother had died. The goodies were a well-intentioned pick-me-up, but an inappropriate one. It wasn't the employee's birthday or work anniversary—it was a major, crushing personal loss. It was a sympathy #fail on the boss's part when all the employee needed was some time and empathy to get back on her feet.

The best thing a boss did for me when I was going through a family crisis was explain to me the benefits the company had in place for a situation like mine. If you have an employee going through a crisis, look for perks within the company, such as child care, psychological services, or legal services, that might be helpful to them. As much as you want to help them yourself, there are likely to be services at the company that can do a better job. And after all, part of being a boss is about knowing what you don't know and delegating accordingly.

YOU CAN GO TO WORK OR YOU CAN BE THE BOSS

Part of being a great Boss Bitch boss is bringing a unique vision and direction to your role. But the other part is more straightforward and often less fun: hiring, reviewing, firing, and promoting. These boss-lady duties aren't the most glamorous, but they are inevitable. They come around before you know it and can be stressful. Remember, the option to stress out will always be there . . . it's up to you to choose another option. The one I prefer: throw your hair in a bun, crank up the Rihanna, and handle it.

HIRING

There's no 100% foolproof way to approach this. Of course, you want to look for qualifications necessary for the job: for instance, an administrative assistant should know basic office etiquette and, say, the Microsoft Office suite. If you're looking for a bookkeeper, obviously accounting experience and/or math training are key. There are going to be a lot of people with the hard skills you are looking for. However, there will *not* be a lot of people who have the soft skills to fit in with your company's mission and vibe. Here's how to suss that out pretty quickly.

Ask the right questions. Remember when we talked about how to answer common interview questions in Step 3 of this section? Well, now the tables have turned. Figure out which questions are important to you and to the company at large. Some unique ones could be: "What makes you get up in the morning and do what you do?" or "What's the biggest trend you see taking over the industry?" Don't ask questions that are *too* creative, like "What kind of animal would you be?" That's just weird.

Let them interview YOU. It's not only important to see how their mind works and the level of curiosity they have about your business, but you also want to be very up-front with them about the job and the workplace. You want them to *want* to work there and to know exactly what they are getting themselves into so you don't find yourself with a disgruntled employee (or ex-employee) six months later.

Call references. But take some of them with a grain of salt if the interviewee is the one providing the references (duh, why would anyone provide bad references for themselves?!). When you talk to the reference, ask them questions like: "What was it like to work with the candidate?" "Why did they leave?" "Would you rehire them?" Hiring the wrong person costs a company more than $50,000, according to a CareerBuilder survey. Checking the references they provided, or better yet, doing a little digging to find your own recon on them, will lessen that likelihood.

Check their social media. If you assume people present themselves a little better at work than they do on their Instagram, then you want them to have at least a respectable display there, otherwise you're getting a "little better" than trashy. Pass. Having good judgment is a key part of any job, and you can find out if they do—or don't— pretty fast on social media.

Tiebreaker. If you are still choosing between a few good candidates, consider giving them a homework assignment. This could be something they would be doing in their job, like putting together a comparative analysis of two operating systems but on a smaller scale. Some hirers do this but intentionally leave out a deadline so that they see how quickly a candidate gets the work done. Sneaky— but effective.

Hiring people who are natural fits for your vision and the vision of the company ensures the best chance of success for both. Trying to force a great person into a position that's not right for them is worse than finding a less great person who "gets it." If your company's mission is to ride a wave, then hire a surfer—don't train a cyclist. It will make your life easier to find like-minded people than to train people who aren't.

REVIEWING

Most bosses handle performance reviews annually and joke that review time is like a pap smear: it comes once a year whether you want it or not. I suggest treating reviews like changing the clock: do it twice a year, otherwise you're screwed. And while these times of year (ideally summer and holiday—making the pay review and performance review separate) are "formal" reviews, reviewing employees informally should happen throughout the year so that when the official review time rolls around, there are no surprises.

Dos and Don'ts of Reviews

DON'T *be phony baloney.* Genuine praise can motivate a team to work harder; so can genuine criticism. If you are too fake-nice with an employee to avoid conflict, they just feel blindsided if they don't get a raise or a promotion.

DO *serve a compliment sandwich.* Here's my recipe: I start with a compliment and end with a compliment. In between, I insert the zinger, i.e., what I think they need to improve on. It's not phony to compliment someone whom you are also constructively criticizing—as long as the compliment is true. (And yes, you can find good in even the worst employees.) A constructive way to motivate the improvement of the bad behavior is to relay optimism and respect.

DON'T *read from a script.* Rattling off letter or number grades makes for not only a boring review but employee confusion, too, as they are left wondering what the hell you really meant.

DO *have a conversation. A real one.* If you use number ratings, make sure to explain what they mean to each individual employee. Translate the scores into discussion about their strengths and weaknesses, with suggestions on how to improve them. This leaves them with clear direction about how to use that information to be a better employee.

DON'T *leave things open-ended.* The main reason for a review is to give marching orders for how someone who works for you can do better, right? So, what *are* those marching orders? If you aren't specific about what you want them to do, you are setting them up to fail.

DO *set goals.* Setting specific thirty-, sixty-, and ninety-day goals and then documenting them together will give you *and* the employee a road map for what's to come, with accountability for not getting there or veering off course.

GET IN ON THE REVIEWING PARTY, TOO

BITCH TIP

A popular tactic of a lot of the best bosses is to have their employees review *them* during review time. As a boss, you want to lead by example in all senses, including self-improvement. Allowing your direct reports to give you criticism and feedback will force you to try to incorporate their suggestions just like you are asking them to do with yours.

I love the idea of asking people to rank things from one to four, not one to five. Why? Because with one to four, there isn't that middle, noncommittal option of three, as there is when you offer a one-to-five scale. If you choose one, it's most negative; two is slightly negative; three is slightly positive; and four is positive. There is no neutral. Neutral doesn't help anyone get better. Real feedback does.

Come up with a list of questions and ask your employees to rank you from one to four by passing out something like this:

How well does your manager, Nicole Lapin, do the following on a scale of one to four, with four being the best:

- Communicates in meetings
- Admits mistakes
- Manages conflict
- Does not play favorites
- Inspires confidence
- Helps employees learn and grow

Just like it's hard to hear negative feedback in any sense—from a boss, from employees, from a spouse, from a mother-in-law—it's also the best way to truly learn and grow, *if* you take it to heart and interpret it constructively, of course.

After you collect your feedback, call a forum to discuss the criticism—but only if you know you can handle hearing it and can listen calmly and carefully to what your employees have to say about you. Not everyone will show up. After all, it's way easier to shit on someone when you aren't face-to-face (hello, Twitter trolls!). The things that might be said can be difficult to listen to, but that's the point. If you can listen to it and use it to become a better boss, then you are not only learning and growing but also showing your team how to listen to feedback to become better employees themselves.

FIRING

Ask any boss, and they'll tell you: the number one absolute suckiest part of being a boss is having to fire someone. Whether it's a layoff because business is slow or the company is reorganizing due to a merger or change in business priorities, or it's a firing for cause because the employee screwed up, just like breaking up, it's really hard to do.

How to do it as painlessly as possible:

1. *It's not you, it's not me, it's us.* Using the right lens to frame a firing discussion can make it an easier process for everyone. If you are firing without cause, explain why their gifts (and *everyone* has them) and the strengths of the company aren't a good fit. While it's tempting to explain their missteps and flaws, take the high road and err on the side of positivity instead.

2. *Rip off the Band-Aid.* There's an old adage, "Hire slowly, fire quickly." Don't let things drag out. It sucks to have someone work for you who doesn't provide value. But remember, it sucks for them to work for someone who doesn't appreciate them or the value they provide (and everyone provides value in the right environment). The faster you do it, the better it is for them to move on and find a place that does.

3. *Explain what happens next.* Logistically, let them know if they will be escorted out of the building. Will they have access to their e-mail? When will they get their final check? Where do they turn in their badge? What are you telling the staff? Are you able to provide any more severance than they expect, either from a contract or customary practices? Can you write a reference letter? Only do

it if it doesn't compromise your reputation. Try to cushion the blow with whatever resources you have to offer.

What to say:

While you should stay positive, no one wants to hear you be overly complimentary when they are getting fired, because all anyone remembers is that they weren't a complement to you or the company, and that's why they were given the boot.

Something to consider saying is, *"You have so many strong qualities, which is why I hired you. Right now the company needs to focus on XYZ. While I was hoping you would improve your XYZ qualities, it still doesn't seem to be sticking."*

It's important to explain the reason for the breakup and the desire to move forward amicably. If you can, offer some actionable feedback of a few things they can work on in their next job, while also reinforcing a few things they did really well and should continue to hone. If they are a fellow Boss Bitch, they will take it like a champ instead of crying or trying to explain themselves to get you to change your mind. If they go out kicking and screaming, though, it just reinforces your decision to let them go.

When to say it:

Face to face. No e-mails. No phone calls (unless you work in offices in totally different parts of the country). Look them in the eye like you would (should) during a breakup.

Early in the morning. You won't be able to focus on anything else and neither will they if they get a calendar invite for an ominous one-on-one meeting at three p.m.

Give them time to say good-bye. Some people will want to jet for the door or cry in the bathroom. Others will want to hug it out with their colleagues. If they want to do that and you think it's appropriate, then let them. Even if they want to give a little positive spin, and you feel okay with that, then let them at it if it softens the blow for their ego to save face.

PROMOTING

This part is way more fun than firing, but it's a decision to be taken just as seriously. Personally, I don't think people should get promoted on any set schedule: just because you've been in a job for two years doesn't automatically mean you get bumped up. Promotions must be deserved. That means that the person you decide to promote is not only really good at their current job, they also 1) have what it takes to do the next job up, and 2) actually *want* the next job. There are some people who are content to do the job they're already doing, and that's as far as they want to go. If 1 and 2 both prove true, then you should also think about if you will have to hire someone else (you know how to do that now!) to fill a vacancy left by a promotion. The time cost of doing that should weigh into your decision, too.

BITCH TIP

Having a hard time deciding who to promote? If you identify some front-runners, here's what you can do to see if they are really ready for prime time:

Ask for volunteers to head up a committee. Who steps up to take the job? Who stands out?

Suggest a new endeavor and ask them to spearhead it. How did it turn out? Could they handle the extra work and pressure?

Offer more training. Do they jump at the chance to learn more? Do they use those skills to step it up a notch in their current role?

The key to promoting within a company is that you are not just helping an employee to advance, but helping an employee who will advance your team. Anyone can feel whether or not they are being set up for success. If they feel like they can succeed, it often becomes a self-fulfilling prophecy.

So you've mastered being a Boss Bitch B.O.S.S. by being "Built on Self-Success" within another company. Yay you. But there may come a time when, once again, you ask yourself, "Is this *all* there is?" Maybe you've done everything at the helm of this company that you can or want to. Maybe you are ready to move laterally to another company, since there's no more room to grow at the one you're at now. These are high-class problems to have but ones that you'll continue to need to address for yourself as you identify and attack new opportunities.

Perhaps you see yourself next as being the boss of your own company, but maybe you think you're not ready. Well, sister, should I say it again? No one is ever really ready for anything big—just like you probably weren't totally ready to be a boss at this job. I hate people who say that when it's time to jump, "you just know." My response to that is, "Fuck you and fuck your clichés." I hate clichés. If you want to be in business for yourself, then now is as good a time as any. If not now, then *when*?

BOTTOM LINE

Conventional Wisdom: I'm not ready for this big job. I'm an impostor.

The Real Deal: We all suffer from this line of thinking so much that it actually has a name: "impostor syndrome." This essentially means that despite being totally qualified for something, you think you don't belong there or don't deserve it and are a total fraud. Who suffers from this most? Ironically, high-powered women. The cure? Getting comfortable with how awesome you are. Do this exercise: First, inhale confidence. Next, exhale doubt. Repeat as needed.

Conventional Wisdom: You have to be a bad bitch when you're a female boss.

The Real Deal: First of all, Boss Bitches know that you don't have to be the latter to be both. Boss Bitches are good bitches, like Glinda the Good Witch, not the Wicked Witch of the West (you know, the one who kidnaps Toto). Bad bitches are who you think of in the meanie sense, but just because we go by the same name doesn't mean we are the same. See, witches and bitches can be good or they can be bad. We are the good ones. We are the ones who are respected *and* liked. And we don't need to veer into bad-bitch territory to overcompensate for having a vagina.

Conventional Wisdom: "As a boss, I need to talk a lot so that my team knows what to do, even if that means raising my voice."

The Real Deal: Well, yes and no. First off, there's no planet on which screaming is cool. If you're angry, keep calm and handle it the way you would want it handled if you were on the other side. Yes, you need to give your team good direction through e-mails or meeting in person, but that doesn't mean going into a monologue. It means being clear and concise, which leaves time for one of the most important boss skills you can have: listening. After all, you have two ears and one mouth—so listen more than you talk.

SECTION

3

BEING THE BOSS OF YOUR OWN BUSINESS

EVERY DAY I'M (SIDE-)HUSTLIN'

How to Explore Your Passions and Make Extra Money
(Cue: Rick Ross's "Hustlin'")

E very Boss Bitch knows how to hustle. But do you know how to "side-hustle"? It's a popular phrase in today's work world because . . . it's a popular thing to do. A *side hustle* (noun) is something you do on the side of your "day job." *Side-hustling* (verb) is the act of getting your ass out there to make extra cash and see what else might be in store for your career.

A side hustle can serve many different purposes. It can be purely a moneymaking tool, but it can also let you delve into your passions with the hope of turning them into a full-time job. And the right side hustle will be *both*. In Step 1 of "Being the Boss of Your Own Business," I'll teach you how to find the best side hustle for you: one that will make you the most cash *and* help write your next career chapter.

THE DREAM IS FREE; THE HUSTLE IS SOLD SEPARATELY

Do you ever find yourself thinking, "I'm way too smart and skilled to not be making more money." Or do you ever stay up late at night thinking, "What if I could only . . ."? If you have these thoughts but aren't quite ready to burn your corporate bra and start your own thing, then you're the perfect candidate to be a side-hustler.

A side hustle can supplement your paycheck while also developing the talents that are dormant in your nine-to-five. If you are in it just for the money, more power to you, sister. But, in this case, you want to make sure you are leveraging a skill that's really marketable, because if it don't make dollars, then it don't make sense. But let's be honest: Boss Bitches aren't motivated by money alone.

Side hustles transform into new exciting and lucrative careers all the time; I'm speaking here from experience. That's because, after almost eighteen months of juggling my rapidly expanding production side hustle along with my day job as news anchor, I resigned from that full-time job to pursue my side hustle as my full-time career (the one I have now).

BE AN HONEST HUSTLER

Hustler used to have a negative connotation. But we Boss Bitches are taking the word back and owning it (just like we've done with the word *bitch*). So wear your hustler badge of honor with pride.

Make sure to give your employer a heads-up that you are going to do something on the side, especially if it competes with the job you are currently doing. You want it to be kosher with your primary gig; otherwise your side hustle will become your main hustle sooner than you expected.

Before you get too excited about the potential of more cash, remember: it's money you have to hustle for, hence the name. And you will pay for whatever extra money you get from your side hustle with extra stress (and probably less sleep) because the only thing more stressful (but also potentially more rewarding) than a full-time job is a job upon a job. Yes, you will likely have to give up binge-watching *House of Cards* and you will often be the last to get to the bar, and the first to leave. When it comes to social events and your free time, *no* will be your new favorite word. But while the struggle of the hustle is real, so is the upside, potentially leading to more rewarding business results than you ever imagined.

GOOD THINGS COME TO THOSE WHO HUSTLE

"Good things happen to people who wait." Um, no. The best way to get started is to quit talking and start doing. Let your hustle be louder than your mouth and your success will speak for itself.

Before we make some noise, here are the three biggest questions to ask yourself before starting to play the side-hustle game:

1. *What are you passionate about?* You probably have more than one interest outside of work that gets your Boss Bitch juices flowing. However, for the purpose of this exercise, focus on those passions that fit the following criteria: a) you are really good at it; b) it's a service or product that fills a void in the market; c) you can realistically make money at it. When starting this exercise, though, list *everything* out. Don't hold back. Do you like dancing? Talking on the phone? Start with the whole shebang and then methodically decide their payoff potential.

Just like we did with your personal brand, let's organize your side-hustle ideas to come up with an action plan. Here were my answers when I started the side hustle that would later become my production business:

I'm really good at . . .	research, networking, storytelling, keepin' it real
I see a need in the market for . . .	smart, easily digestible content in the finance space
I can see myself making money doing . . .	media training, production consulting, informative web videos

Now it's your turn:

I'm really good at . . .	
I see a need in the market for . . .	
I can see myself making money doing . . .	

2. *How much time do you have?* And can you realistically stick to a self-imposed schedule while also having a full-time hustle? Tackling your side hustle after a busy workday is going to require more than a little discipline. Look at the list of skills you made and now analyze the time you can devote to that hustle. Remember each skill will be different because some you can do on your own at night and others will be "client facing" during more normal hours or require transportation that will eat into your available time/week. How much money will you make? Is it worth your time?

Take the skills you listed above that look promising and put them through some more analysis. For example, let's say you have some sweet copyediting, yoga, Photoshop, tarot card skills, and makeup:

SKILL	TIME/WEEK AVAILABLE	$$ POTENTIAL	INITIAL INVESTMENT
Copyediting	6 hours	$50-250/week	$26 for updated AP Stylebook
Yoga	4 hours	$100-300/week	$200 for mats and a music player
Photoshop	6 hours	$50-250/week	$70 for updated Photoshop
Tarot cards	2 hours	$40-100/week	$20 for deck of tarot cards
Makeup	3 hours	$100-1000/week	$500 for makeup, brushes, carrying case

Copyediting and photo editing definitely are the best side-hustle bets for this particular Boss Bitch. Of those on her list, both have a low initial investment, allow work from home with few supplies, can yield good money for the hours put in, *and* could potentially turn into a career.

Now it's your turn to fill out the chart to see which of your potential side-hustle skills may be in your sweet spot. Remember, you are looking for the options with the most bang for the time you have to devote with the lowest initial investment (training, travel, setup, certification, supplies, gear, tools) to get going.

SKILL	TIME/WEEK AVAILABLE	$$ POTENTIAL	INITIAL INVESTMENT

Once you commit to a side hustle, you have to allocate the time you'll spend on your side gig with the same importance and urgency that you have for your regular job. Set goals for the number of hours you'll devote to it per week, so that even if you don't get to it every single day, you still net out to the same overall commitment and ensure you keep the hustle moving forward. These hours can't be the first thing to go when life gets hectic. If your side hustle is ever going to turn into your full-time hustle, the time you spend on it must be nonnegotiable; your new business endeavors depend on it to gain momentum.

3. *Is there potential to turn this into a long-term career?* When sorting through your side-hustle ideas, consider whether they have at least the *potential* to become a long-term career (you know, the kind that pays you enough to, like, live). Even if you never thought you'd switch careers, you might feel differently in six months or a year if you start crushing the

side-hustle game. And if (when) that happens, is it something you'd be down with doing 24/7?†

SKILL	SIDE HUSTLE	$$ POTENTIAL	IS IT A LONG-TERM CAREER?
Copyediting	Freelance editing	$10-50/hour	Strong portfolio could lead to staff position at magazine or publisher
Yoga	Yoga instructor	$20-100/hour	Maybe a good side hustle if you're really good at it, but likely not a career (unless you open your own studio!)
Photoshop	Freelance photo editing	$10-50/hour	Strong portfolio could lead to a full-time gig as a photo editor or graphic designer
Tarot cards	Reading tarot cards	$20-50/hour, if you're lucky	Fun party trick, but probably not a long-term career
Makeup	Freelance makeup artist	$20-200/hour	Build portfolio/website with pictures and testimonials that could lead to a full-time position with a studio or designer

† If you need some examples to get the wheels turning, check out the Side-Hustle Matrix at bossbitchbook.com.

Based on the answers above, it looks like this Boss Bitch has a few opportunities to make money. Makeup artistry, tarot cards, and yoga could be lucrative side hustles but have a tempered chance of turning into something more. The side-hustle sweet spot (where money and passion overlap) for her seems to be either copyediting or photo editing.

GET OTHERS TO HUSTLE FOR YOU

BITCH TIP

At this point, your contact list is likely longer than you think. All of those extracurricular hours spent networking with players in your industry like we talked about in the last section haven't been for nothing. Now is the time to tap into those contacts to gain traction for your hustle, recalling all of the times you've offered to help *them,* and letting them know that you're open for business. Be specific with your ask; your contacts are more likely to support you if you make it easy for them. For example, instead of just asking for "help," I'll ask my contacts for introductions to other specific high-powered people I know they know by offering them a sample e-mail that they can customize (but normally they just copy and paste) to introduce us:

Hey, XX!

I'm writing to tell you about my friend Nicole, who is growing a successful concierge photo editing service. I used it personally after my 30th birthday party and was so pleased with Nicole's work. I'll definitely be using her again! I thought you two should connect about XX thing that would be helpful to you. I'll let you and Nicole take it away.

All best,
XX

This allows them to make the intro or intros I wanted without much work (or thinking) on their part, they just have to fill in the XXs. It also ensures that you are getting the message *you* want across. It's the same idea as when your high school teachers were happy to give you letters of recommendation for the colleges you were applying to if you wrote the letter for them and they just signed it (oh, come on, you know this happened).

CONFESSIONS OF A
BOSS BITCH

My Surprise Side Hustle

Right before *Rich Bitch* came out, I made some fun T-shirts that said RICH BITCH on the front and MY FAVORITE POSITION IS CEO on the back. (I know, pretty clever, right??)

They were intended to be used as a marketing tool for my burgeoning brand, but it turns out they were a little unwieldy to schlep all over the country for my book tour, so I ended up with boxes of extras. I only needed one for myself for posterity, and the same for my friends. The rest were considered to be "closeouts," (aka the extra merchandise a retailer has), except for the fact that I wasn't selling them—I was just giving them away. But then it dawned on me: Why *wasn't* I selling them?!

So I did. I approached discount retailers like Bluefly to turn what was just cluttering up my apartment into cash. The added bonus: selling them was basically like free advertising for my brand, and it attached a market value to my giveaways.

I know what you're probably thinking, because you're thinking like a Boss Bitch by now: I should have done it the other way around, selling them and *then* giving them away. Shoulda, woulda, coulda. Of course, if I did it again, I would have planned better. But we don't always have the luxury of hindsight. It's never too late to come up with a creative side hustle.

I always tell aspiring Boss Bitch entrepreneurs that figuring out what you *don't* want is as important as figuring out what you do. Why? Because you got it out of your system. You tried it and you'll either a) appreciate your job more or b) come up with a new idea for a business you want to try next. Or both!

There was once a part of me that thought I wanted to be a clothing designer. Selling the T-shirts that I designed gave me a taste of that world. It was a world I could have fallen in love with, but I didn't. Instead, I could say, "Welp, been there, tried that," and be over it and never wondered, "What if?"

FYI

CELEB SIDE HUSTLE

Let's be serious. Despite what you might read in your favorite guilty pleasure rag, stars are not "just like us" day-to-day (I hate to break it to you, but, yes, those photos are staged). But when it comes to side-hustling, celebs sometimes *are* like us. Here are a few who have started a little something-something on the side:

- Beyoncé (bow down) has a vegan food delivery company.
- Jessica Biel owns Au Fudge, the restaurant and kid's hangout in Los Angeles.
- Ian Ziering (who will always be Steve Sanders from *Beverly Hills, 90210* no matter how many *Sharknado*es he stars in) owns a travel agency for high-end vacations.

IS IT A HOBBY OR A JOBBY?

Doing something extra on the side for cash can be grand, especially if you make a few grand, but it can also be something that grows into your long-term earning potential. That doesn't mean you have to pull a Jerry Maguire at your current job. In fact, testing out a business idea as a side hustle while you're still employed allows you to determine proof of concept* with fewer risks, because you have, hello, a job that pays you already.

So before you try to take your side hustle from being your recreation to your vocation, let's get serious about determining if it's really a jobby—or just a hobby?

QUIZ: IS YOUR IDEA A JOBBY OR JUST A HOBBY?

1. Is your hobby something that is a career for other people?
2. If yes, does that career make enough money that you could subsist on with a lifestyle similar to what you have now?
3. Do you have enough money for the costs it will take to turn the hobby into a career without taking on debt?
4. Are you confident that you can do the less exciting parts of the hobby when turning it into a business (e.g., sourcing, bookkeeping) day in and day out?
5. Are you someone who stays focused without getting distracted or antsy and easily bored?

If you answered yes to *all* of these questions, well, then keep exploring how to turn your hobby into a jobby.

If you answered no to most or all of these questions, then think twice or thrice about trying to make your thing into more than a hobby—or a side hustle.

Testing out your start-up idea via a side hustle not only gives you the cushion and safety net of a steady paycheck (because you will NOT make money in the beginning stages of your business, as I'll tell you all about in the next step), but it also gives you the time to plan your transition period if you find that you can't stop, won't stop until your hustle is your main gig.

Let's say you love baking cupcakes. You go home after work and you bake whenever you can. You are constantly bringing your yummy homemade confections to parties or making them for you family and for friends. You are obsessed with coming up with crazy flavor creations. You have your own custom apron that says "I'm a Baker, Bitch." When you're at work you have OCD: obsessive cupcake disorder. You dream about a day you can have your own cupcake shop and just bake all day, every day.

You're banking on that idea to make you bank. So you take your cupcake making up a notch. Instead of just giving your goodies to family and friends, you start charging for them. You make little fliers to post around town to find new customers—and soon those customers start finding you.

Boom—your orders are coming in hot! Soon enough, you are baking your ass off until two a.m. trying to fulfill all the orders while you still need to get up at seven a.m. to go to work. You start getting so many orders that you need to rent an outside facility with a bigger oven; you need to start sourcing bulk containers of flour and sugar because buying it the store is now too expensive. You start needing to do your own accounting because you have more expenses, plus now you need to budget everything from the ingredients to the facility to the delivery to the boxes and labels.

This is what it's like to start to turn your beloved hobby into a business. Understandably, now you are exhausted. You are emotionally and physically (and likely financially) wiped out. Now when you go bed at night, instead of dreaming about cupcakes, you dream about never having to look at another one again. It stopped being fun and started getting real. In all the dollar signs you doodled in cupcake frosting, you never accounted for the other work you now have to do! Urgh, accounting. Urgh, cleaning up the kitchen *again*. Turning your cupcake love into a business wasn't all it was baked up to be. You miss the days of making just five batches per week while dancing around your kitchen to '80s pop. So you throw in the industrial-grade towels and you're out of the cupcake business—for good. You officially got the cupcake fever out of your system and can focus more on your regular nine-to-five, content that you now know you like baking much better as a hobby than as a job.

This is a scenario a lot of women experience. In this case, no harm, no foul; thank goodness you still have that trusty old paycheck coming in every month. Now, imagine if instead of trying it out as a side hustle first, you had left your job to do this. That would really suck. But, because you busted your ass and stayed up until two a.m. every day trying to get a feel for what having a real cupcake business is like, you figured out that it wasn't for you *before* plunging headfirst into a vat of frosting. All that flour under your nails was worth it. You figured out that your love of cupcakes was a hobby and *not* a jobby. Testing a side-hustle business idea first is the best way to figure out if there's really *"there,* there." If there isn't, get out of the proverbial kitchen until you can take the heat. Half-baked makes for a terrible dessert and career.

However, say you realize you love every single aspect of your growing cupcakery and can subsist on four hours of sleep because you just want to leap out of bed in the morning and get your hands into some batter. Excellent! The next four steps in this section will show you how to effectively plan for building your cupcake empire.

PLAN YOUR ESCAPE CAREFULLY

If you find that you love your side gig and want to peace out of your nine-to-five and devote your 24/7 to turn it into something more, then planning a smooth exit is key to keep the relationships and goodwill you've worked so hard to create at your job intact. I've said this before, but it bears repeating: life is long and the world is small. You *will* run into people again and again in business in one way or another.

If you hastily quit your job for this new amazing thing and leave your employers in a lurch, you might get a bad rap. And if you fail at said new, amazing thing and you need to go back to your job or ask the people you screwed over for help, it will be quite a long tail you'll have to put between your legs. Trust me, I made this mistake when I started playing in the producing game while still working for CNBC. In hindsight, I left my day job at the network more hastily than I should have. As a result, I spent more time than I should have mending fences that wouldn't have needed mending if I had made a more graceful exit.

You might be thinking, "Lapin, why are you being so pessimistic? Can't you be positive and trust that this next big thing will crush it?!" No. I can't be. First, in business, it's best to keep low expectations—then beat them. And second, there are too many people with start-up stardust in their eyes who fuck this up because they are not thoughtful about it. You are not going to be that bitch, at least not on my watch.

In the next step, I'm going to set you up with the best tools out there to make sure you're not in the 80% of businesses that fail (yes, you read that right) because, my darling Boss Bitch, being a negative statistic is never cute. And neither are rose-colored glasses.

I'm being tough on you because I've been there. So I know that it's a long fall from head in the clouds to landing face-first on the ground. The closer you are to the ground, the easier it is to recover when you fall—and the more incredible the view is when you fly.

CONFESSIONS OF A
BOSS BITCH

WARNING: Writing a Book Is NOT a Side Hustle

I've never given birth before, but after I "gave birth to" my first book, I said, "Oh hell no, this shop is closed for business for a while" in the same way that I expect a lot of mothers probably feel after their first kid. Then they forget the pain and go for the second—and so did I.

Don't get me wrong: being an author is an honor and was a goal of mine for as long as I can remember. But it was far from easy. It started as something I dabbled in on the side and quickly took over all of my career focus and energy. By the time I signed my contract for *Rich Bitch*, I had three ex–book agents (yes, finding the right agent *is* like dating), four other rejected book proposals, and one other signed contract that I had to get out of after my new employer didn't approve. My decade-plus of false starts put me face-to-face with a harsh reality: getting a book sold, writing a book, and making a book successful is a full-time job.

Yes, there are aspects of writing a book that can be done "on the side." You hear about it all the time, right? Actors and celebs publish books while filming movies or launching products or doing other projects. But, news flash: actors usually have a lot of help and/or pay someone to write their book.

For the rest of us, let's keep it real: an idea for a book is not necessarily a good book. A proposal for a book is not necessarily a good book. And even a finished book is not necessarily a good book. And here's the shittiest part of all: a good book isn't necessarily a *successful* book.

I'm the number one proponent of having a book that expands your brand to a wider audience. It can be a good marketing tool. It's definitely a good platform, and, yes, it's something you can tell your grandkids about. But before you go down the book-writing road, Jane Austen, you have to know exactly what you're getting into. Here's the letter I wrote to my younger, pre-author self so you can learn from her mistakes:

Dear 20-year-old Nicole,

The book world sounds glamorous. It is not. There are a million books online, in stores, and in the library. But, for every million books there are, there are 99 million rejections. You will get rejected. A lot.

The first thing you should know is that you need to write a proposal—and it better be solid. As a first-time author, that proposal needs to include at least a few chapters. The proposal can't be based on a so-so concept. And even though you will try really hard, your first proposal will suck. The second proposal you will write will be for a quarter-century memoir, which was a good concept. A publisher will buy it, but that will be at the wrong time in your career. The third proposal you will write is going to be about decoding the *Wall Street Journal,* which will seem like a cool idea—until the *WSJ* sends you a cease and desist letter for potentially violating their trademark. The fourth proposal will be called *Making Bank* and will bill itself as a cooler finance book geared toward young men and women. It will go far through the pitching process—until the publisher who wants to buy it before the holidays is laid off by the new year, which will lead to the death of that book and your idea.

The second thing I want you to know is that you need an agent. The first agent you'll have is from a small firm in San Diego. She will be about your age at the time, young but hungry, and thus tell you that your first proposal is awesome—when it isn't. This won't work out, and when you sign on with the prestigious CAA, they will have a high-powered book agent who will take you on; he'll tell you to scrap the first concept and push you to dig deep into your personal history. He will go on to successfully sell that book, but by the time that first deal fizzles, he will have such big clients that he will no longer have time for you. You will then find a third agent who forgets to tell you that using a name including the *Wall Street Journal* is not, um, legal as a title. And so, after many fits and starts, you will take a hiatus from the frustrating world of books.

The third thing I want to tell you is that if you do get a chance at your first book and it sucks, you can forget about having a second one. So while you are pissed by all your misadventures until now, they will all happen . . . for a reason. They are a blessing in disguise, because they will safeguard you from publishing a shitty first book and instead lead you to the killer book you will pitch ten years after you start this process, one that will become the right content at the right time.

The fourth thing you need to know is that you won't make much money on your first book. (BTW, J. K. Rowling got $4,000 for her first book deal.) You will technically get a six-figure advance, but it will be in name only. After paying a 15% agent fee and hiring a badass promotional squad, you'll make less than mama Harry Potter . . . and that's not a J/K. Dear Nicole, you will also discover that you won't get that money all at once; the payments will be broken down in thirds, forcing you to keep scraping by while you write your book. And you will reinvest whatever little remaining money you earned (and then way more of your savings) into marketing and promoting the book so it sells and you get a second book deal.

The next thing I want you to know is that you will hit the *New York Times* bestseller list, and others. It will be the hardest thing you will ever do in your career. You will spend months and months figuring out how to get on the most podcasts, radio shows, and TV. You will bust your ass trying to get covered in every publication no matter how small or big the outlet. You will plumb the depths of your contact list to find friends to ask to promote your book on social media, buy books in bulk, and throw parties for you. You will spend every hour of every day promoting the shit out of it to anyone who will listen. But I promise you . . . as exhausting as it all sounds, you will find that in the end it will be worth it.

The last thing I want you to know is that when all the marketing hoopla subsides, people will, it turns out, continue to buy your book, but not because of that hoopla; rather, because you actually wrote a good book. When all the razzle-dazzle goes away, people buy books because their friends vouch for them. So make sure that for every other book you write (there will be others), it is chock-full of good content. And to do that right, it can't be a side hustle; you must treat it as if it is a full-time job.

You can do this, young Lapin, but it's not something you want to take lightly. You can show your grandkids any book you write and they will be proud of it, but if you show them a good one, *you'll* be proud.

XOXO,

Older, Wiser Lapin

If the "Jobby or Hobby?" quiz was your midterm, then here is your final exam. This is the final "Are you sure you want to go through with this?" It's a feeling similar to the one you get before going on a roller coaster:

1. Are you ready to create a solid plan for your business and define specific measures of success, not just the willy-nilly, pie-in-the-sky ones you've been dreaming about?
2. Are you prepared for the major time investment you'll need to transition into a business of your own?
3. Are you cool with growing your company slowly, so that you can invest more time (which is technically free) than money? (BTW: Craig Newmark, the founder of Craigslist, started that major company as a side hustle in 1995 . . . and it wasn't until 1999 that it became an actual business.)

If you've answered yes to *all* of these questions after slaying your side hustle, then you're ready to turn this thing into the main course of your career. You'll still be hustling when you do, obviously. That's the thing about success: It's a constant hustle. Success is never owned—it's rented, and rent is due every damn day. Oh, and there's no elevator; you gotta take the stairs. So, bitch, let's start climbing.

THE BOTTOM LINE

Conventional Wisdom: Side hustles don't typically make much money.

The Real Deal: That's actually right. Some won't change your life much financially. But many will, especially if you pick something that earns you a premium because you have a special skill. Also, think of the money (and heartache) you'll save if you test an idea on the side and learn that it's something you *don't* actually want to pursue as a full-time career. I think those experiences are the most valuable of them all.

Conventional Wisdom: I can't find something that I like to do that also makes money.

The Real Deal: Zero chance. You can make money doing virtually anything if you think about it and are creative enough. You can get paid for watching TV. That's not a joke.

Conventional Wisdom: If you're passionate about a business, failure is not an option.

The Real Deal: I almost spit out my latte writing that. Look at the stats: businesses fail many, many more times than they succeed. Something like nine out of ten new restaurants fail in the first year alone. To have the best chance of being in the exclusive club of successful businesses, test your idea first and temper your expectations. You will fail. And I like to say that success is walking from failure to failure with a big smile and a wicked sense of humor.

I'M NOT A BUSINESS(WO)MAN.
I'M A BUSINESS, (WO)MAN

Deciding Whether Your Own Business Is Viable

I t's time, Boss Bitch. You've gone from being the boss of you to being the boss at work to being the boss of your chosen side hustle, and now you're ready to get real about being the boss of your own business. To paraphrase the words of one of my favorite poets, Jay Z: "I'm not a business(wo)man, I'm a business, (wo)man." And now you can be, too.

In Step 2 of "Being the Boss of Your Own Business," I'm going to help you assess your skills, knowledge, and drive before you flex your business muscles. Consider this your initial weigh-in at the gym before you start getting in shape. If you lie about it at the outset and cheat your training, you're only cheating yourself. But if you take a good hard look at *exactly* what you're working with, you'll get on the *right* plan to get that rockin' bod (business) in no time.

LOOK BEFORE YOU LEAP, BITCH

Being an entrepreneur is like being a rock star these days. Kids idolize famous start-up founders instead of the athletes, musicians, and actors we used to look up to growing up. I can tell you from hanging out with (and even dating) some of them that today, these founders are indeed treated very much like the old-school rock stars. The bling, the access, the parties . . . the works.

It's all very seductive and alluring. It's natural to see that and want it, too . . . like now. But before we start flying in private jets in our minds, let's get off the ground. And to ensure the least turbulence during takeoff, first answer these questions, honestly:

1. Do you have the support you need? Are you in a position right now to be without extensive health insurance?
2. Do you have nine months to one year of savings in the bank?
3. Have you researched the field you want to go into? And have you talked to people in the field or others who have taken the leap?
4. Have you tried to do this on the side? (Don't tell me you skipped the previous chapter; if so, go back, girl!)
5. Do you have a business plan or clear pitch for the business?
6. Have you been thinking about this nonstop, been pleased with your part-time experience, and will never forgive yourself if you don't go all in?
7. Do you have enough contacts and items on your résumé in case you go back into the "normal" workforce? And are you keeping all of these materials updated?
8. Have you come to terms with the idea that you will have a precarious income and not be able to budget in the way you used to?
9. Have you stopped the pie-in-the-sky thinking and accepted the idea that you are going to fail at some point?
10. Do you have a robust support system—even if it is one person or one mentor?

If you answered no to any of these, then deplane and get to a yes before boarding Entrepreneur Air. But, if you answered yes to *all* of these questions, then buckle up and get ready to take off!

ARE YOU READY FOR THIS?

As you start to ascend, don't forget that you're not flying private yet. The climb to whatever level of entrepreneurial success you want is going to have a lot of turbulence. But you started this journey for a reason, right? You got to the point where you needed or craved a change. So get ready for what that actually means: *change*. Some for the better and some for, well, not the better. (You didn't expect hot towels and mimosas right away, did you?!)

Yes, some people get lucky. No, I can't help you get lucky (there are dating apps for that), but I *can* tell you that the harder you work, the luckier you get.

Part of that initial work is laying a good foundation for yourself for what's going to happen in different areas of your life—financially, physically, and emotionally—once you burn your corporate bra. That way, you're not left exposed (literally) out in the business world.

FINANCIALLY

The hardest part of any career change is rejiggering your budget (or as I like to affectionately call it, your "spending plan"). When you change jobs, you're likely making a different salary, so the rest of your financial picture will need adjusting. Your benefits are likely different, too, and that's okay—you just have to adjust accordingly.

When you're going off on your own, your budget won't be as reliable because your income (if you have any) hasn't been determined yet, or might not be consistent, and you may not even have comprehensive benefits. This is the part that freaks a lot of us out because we want to be able to plan not only for day-to-day expenses for ourselves and our family but also for big purchases and our futures. So, here's what to know about getting into a life of financial unknowns:

1. *Have one year of savings in the bank.* Having a precarious income can often cause more anxiety than a frustrating job does. The best way to quell that anxiety is to have enough money saved, ideally one full year of expenses, before you take the leap. Having enough

saved before you start your new endeavor will give you some cushion in case your timeline toward being cash flow* positive takes longer than you think.

2. *Scale back your lifestyle . . . at first.* In the beginning, you likely won't be making much money (or shouldn't be, since you typically want to reinvest most of what you make into the business), so it's important to try to tone down your lifestyle from the one you were living before. Once you get back to your "normal" budget, keep it steady there even if you're making more. Before you know what the pattern of your income will be (for instance, will it be cyclical? Will you make most of your money during the holidays and barely anything the rest of the year?), it's better to be as conservative as possible.

3. *Your $$—your business's $$.* In the beginning, at least, you are your business and your business is you, so your budget will be the business's budget. As is the nature of all businesses, this budget ebbs and flows *a lot*—and that's also okay as long as it's just ebbing and flowing and not crashing and burning.

4. *Look out for black swans.* The thing about going into business for yourself is that it's all uncharted territory. Even once you've made it through some squalls and think you're in calm waters, you never know when the next storm is going to hit. These rough waters could be the result of something you're doing/not doing; or they could be totally outside of your control like a shift within your sector (a global shortage of one of your ingredients or materials, for example), the economy at large (a housing crisis), or geopolitics (a terrorist attack). In business, things you can't predict or control, like the housing crisis and terrorism, are called "black swan"* events. Think of it like this: say you are the nice white swan in *Swan Lake* (or Natalie Portman's character in the movie *Black Swan*) just swimming around in your lake and doing everything right when all of a sudden the black swan (Mila Kunis's character) comes by and fucks it all up. You didn't know she even existed, but she does, and once she shows up, life on the lake will never be the same.

When you add the black swans that can affect your business to the cyclical patterns you learn to expect, you end up with a lot more questions than answers about your livelihood. If you can accept the questions as questions, then you'll be fine. But if you expect to have the answers right away, you'll start feeling financially paranoid and out of control, which is unlike the calm, cool Boss Bitch swan you really are.

PHYSICALLY

There was a reason why I asked you if you or your family has serious health issues before taking the leap into starting a business. That's because, when starting your own thing, your health insurance might not be set up right away, and even if it is, it might not be as robust as what you had before. Whether you have COBRA, which extends your previous health insurance policy for a limited time, or you get your own policy, the coverage will likely not be extensive. Plus, you will now be responsible for 100% of the cost.

If you are just starting out in a business and aren't bringing in a high income (yet!), you may qualify for subsidies under the Affordable Care Act ("Obamacare"), which would lower your premiums (what you pay out of pocket each month).

Keep in mind that under the Obamacare law, there are actually tax penalties for not having any health coverage. And even if it turns out that it technically "costs" less on a monthly basis to skip the insurance and pay the penalty, I wouldn't recommend it. Saving money is great but anything you "saved" will be depleted and then some if, God forbid, you actually have something serious happen to your health.

If you want to go for something super cheap just in case, you may also be able to purchase "catastrophic" coverage under Obamacare, which has a super-low premium, but only covers major medical issues (and you're still responsible to pay for things like doctors' visits, prescriptions, etc., out of pocket). Stay tuned, changes are definitely coming under the new president's administration.

Keeping yourself healthy is always important, but as an entrepreneur—because you are quite literally your business—your body is now one of your company's most precious assets! You'll be tempted to work to the point of exhaustion, but don't run yourself into the ground. Long days are impressive but are counterproductive if they make you sick. You are going to need a shit ton of energy to run your business, but you won't have that if you don't care for yourself first. And you're no good to those around you, who are depending on you, if you're down and out with the flu.

Remember: you took a leap into starting that business because you loved it and couldn't imagine your life doing anything else. But if you don't keep yourself healthy, you won't have the energy to put in the sweat equity you need to succeed. I know, I know, "Thannnnks, Mom."

EMOTIONALLY

If you didn't know this already, I hate to be the one to break this to you, but you are going to fail—at least at some things, some of the time. So, mentally, you've gotta be down with failure.

You are going to make mistakes. You might have a business card that says *CEO*, but you'll feel like you're at the bottom of the totem pole. And to deal with all of that emotionally, having a strong support system is not just important, it's critical.

You might have been a ball of nerves at your job before deciding to start your own thing, but that's in the rearview mirror now. The people who typically fail at their new business are the ones who act on a whim because they were overly frustrated with their job and full of wanderlust. Well, now that you have wandered over to the thing you lusted for, there is no more wandering if things get tough. You can't just up and quit because you're frustrated or because you're overworked or because you hate your boss. Luckily, now you *love* your boss (hello, it's you!).

SHOULD I WORK FROM HOME?
A COST VS. BENEFIT ANALYSIS

When you are starting a business, chances are you have a pretty long commute: thirty whole seconds to the living room. Awesome, you might be thinking! But while the ability to cozy up to your laptop in your pajamas every day might sound appealing, is working out of your home really worth it? It takes a lot of discipline to set the alarm for six and power through a full day's work when no one is physically there to watch over you and Netflix is just a click away. Plus, let's face it, working for twelve-hour stretches with no one but your cat around to talk to can get pretty lonely, fast.

So if you're someone who yearns for the collaborative energy of a group work setting or struggles with time management when left to your own devices, then working from home may not be a good choice for you (not to mention, your overall emotional well-being). But if you're a self-starter who likes to live and work by her own rules, then being the boss of your home office could make perfect sense—and maybe even save you some money.

In addition to sparing the cost of renting out an office or even an itty-bitty corner of a shared work space, you stand to save in the following ways by working from home:

Tax advantages. You might be able to deduct your utilities, cleaning supplies, and office supplies from your tax return—meaning less money to Uncle Sam at the end of the year and more money in your pocket. Same goes for all work-related tools (which you can always deduct for business no matter where you are working from) like your cell phone, Internet, trade books, and magazines . . . pretty much anything that you use for work (it could be paint if you're an artist, dog treats if you're an animal trainer, etc.).

Transportation savings. The average person spends around $10,000 per year driving to work, including gas, insurance, and maintenance. By avoiding that daily commute, you're adding years to the life of your car while saving money on gas and repairs. Depending on your needs and location (who needs or even wants a car in a place like NYC? Not me!), working from home could mean the ability to ditch your car altogether, sparing you not just the cost of commuting but insurance premiums, car payments, and parking. Pro tip: If you use services like Uber for business, sign up for their business program, which helps you keep track of your trips come tax time.

Family care. If you have a child or pet at home, you're going to save more money than you'd expect just by being there. Day-care costs in many cities are the equivalent of taking on another mortgage, and at $15–25 per walk, dog-walking fees really add up at the end of the month.

Let's be serious: When you go into business for yourself, location is overrated. All you really need is Wi-Fi and a dream.

CAN ANYONE BE THE BOSS OF A BUSINESS?

Yes. You don't have to be a hard-charging ballbuster to be the boss of your own business. In fact, nice girls make the best Boss Bitches.

You don't have to be loud to be heard. Soft-spokenness can be a deadly weapon in business. Nor do you have to be a barracuda. In fact, a lot of times it's better if you're not, because you create a positive work environment where people *want* to work for and with you. And their desire to go above and beyond the call of duty for you is invaluable when starting your own business. The more people you have hustling for and with you, the stronger your business becomes—and the sooner you will achieve success.

Generally, there are two types of Boss Bitches in this world: "creative-minded" and "money-minded." To determine which you are, ask yourself this basic question: "What do you expect from your business?" If you answered along the lines of producing something cool or making a social impact, then you are a more creative-minded boss. If your answer includes number-based goals and metrics for expansion, then you are a more money-minded boss.

Any good entrepreneur needs both the creative *and* the money mindsets in order to have a sound business brain overall. And while most of us do have both in some combination, it will never be fifty–fifty. See which one you are stronger at and focus on fleshing out the other. And while you are at it, take a look at the top five traits many successful entrepreneurs share and see if you have other weak links you might need to strengthen as well:

1. *Risk-taker.* When you hear that, you might think about getting drunk in Vegas and risking everything at the blackjack tables—but I'm talking about taking calculated risks, like when Barbara Corcoran turned a $1,000 loan into a monster real estate business bearing her name, which she eventually sold for $66 million. Barbara's initial risk wasn't a lot of money, but she went all in with it, betting on herself—a bet that ultimately worked. The best entrepreneurs don't start with a lot of money, but they also don't let that stand in their way of taking the smart risks needed to make their business work and grow.

2. *Multitasker.* In your previous life, you juggled a lot—we all do: family, work, relationship drama, seeing friends, doing errands. But when you run your own business, the multitasking game gets even more serious, because at the beginning you aren't just the CEO, you are also the accountant and the housekeeper and the marketing director. You wear all of the proverbial hats. Many of the great entrepreneurs have a swagger about them that oozes confidence; no matter what comes up, they've got this shit covered. They are masters at juggling competing deadlines and troubleshooting problems while keeping their eyes on the prize at all times.

3. *Self-awareness.* No matter how awesome you are, you don't know everything. The best thing you can do is admit it, then surround yourself with people who *do* know the things you don't.

4. *Tough cookie.* You've gotta be able to deal with disappointment like a champ. Things won't go your way. People you hire won't work out. The business will have hiccups. The best entrepreneurs look disappointment in the eye and keep going, quickly calculating a different path or permutation of action to plow ahead. According to high-flying (literally) founder of the Virgin Group, Richard Branson, "It is how a beginning entrepreneur deals with failure that sets

that person apart. In fact, failure is one of the secrets to success, since some of the best ideas arise from the ashes of a shuttered business." Failure is inevitable; how you deal with it is what will make or break you.

5. *Sizzle seller.* If you can't figure out a way to make people understand and want to buy your product, who will? Um, no one. The uncanny ability to "sell" is a common one among world-class entrepreneurs. As a judge (and the only female) on my show *Hatched* on the CW, I hear pitches from entrepreneurs every week. The number one thing that sets the entrepreneur apart is how they "sell" the product to me. If I don't get it, no one will. The best saleswomen entrepreneurs out there are so passionate about their product that they make you want to buy something you never thought you would want or need to buy. I bought reading glasses from an entrepreneur because the pitch was so good . . . and I have 20/20 vision!

Some of these traits are innate, and some are learned. Even if you naturally possess the qualities that make for an A+ entrepreneur, remember that you still have a lot to learn, and real-world experience is the best degree you can get. You'll be tested on your determination and passion all the time. And the more those things are tested, the more clear it will become: Do you want to go to the head of the class, or will you drop out?

SHOULD I GO INTO BUSINESS WITH A BESTIE?

You might think, "I have the smartest bestie ever. We finish each other's sentences. She's the right brain, I'm the left. We spend all of our time together, anyway. . . . Why not just go into business together?!" That sounds adorable, and a lot of times friends make for amazing business partners. Some of the most famous brands and business have been started by bestie cofounders, including Apple, eBay, and Procter & Gamble (which was actually started by two guys named William Procter and James Gamble). Makes sense—I mean, who knows you better than your BFF? And who could you possibly trust more than her?

If you're indeed a great complement to each other's skills, it could work smashingly. Here are three dynamic duos who have created killer businesses together:

> *Pamela Skaist-Levy and Gela Nash-Taylor,* copresidents and cofounders of Juicy Couture, said that going into business together was the best decision they ever made, because together their highs were even higher and their lows didn't feel as bad. They sold the famous velour jumpsuit company (I know you rocked those in five different colors in the early 2000s) for $195 million.
>
> *Carly Zakin and Danielle Weisberg,* cofounders of theSkimm, started their company because they didn't have time to read the news every day and felt out of the loop. These two roomies built the company to provide other busy women with a newsletter that breaks down all the news we need to know for the day in digestible chunks. And we all thank them for it.
>
> *Katie Rodan and Kathy Fields,* cofounders of Proactiv, started their business when they were dermatology residents at Stanford and suffering from acne. After experimenting for five years, they launched the company known for the infomercials that suck you in with the amazing before and after images. It is now the top-selling acne medication in America.

But—there's a *but.* For every successful bestie business duo out there, there are countless others who fail in business together (and often in friendship, too, because of it). I would hate for that to happen to you and your BFF, so here are a few things to avoid:

1. *Not making clear roles.* She does X, you do Y. Yes, a lot of times there's an "all hands on deck" situation, but otherwise, you can't conquer if you don't clearly divide. When there are simultaneous issues in different parts of your business (and there will be), you need to clearly outline who fights which fire. She takes care of sales issues, you handle the design ones. She deals with the pissed-off client, you figure out why the website keeps crashing. If there's too

much friction trying to resolve issues together, the next spark could quickly turn into a wildfire.

2. *Not getting it all in writing in advance.* It might feel icky, but please don't wait to draft a legal agreement that spells out not only which roles you have but what the plan is for equity* and taking on outside capital investment.* You need to make sure this is all discussed with a lawyer and with each other so there are no surprises later on.

3. *Not discussing long-term goals.* What happens if there's an option to sell the company? Merge the company? Do you have a potential exit strategy,* and how do you plan to execute it? You have to get on the same page with this well before D(decision)-day comes.

The biggest risk of starting a business with a friend is that money can be a source of strife, and ultimately it can lead to the end of both the business and the friendship. But, if done right, the biggest advantage of starting a business with a BFF is that you know each other really well, so there's no learning curve like there would be with someone new. Also, good friends don't let you do anything crazy . . . at least not alone. There's an African proverb that says: "If you want to go fast, go alone; if you want to go far, go together." So if you decide to go it together, more power to you; just be sure to be aware of all these potential pitfalls first.

SHOULD I GO INTO BUSINESS WITH A SIG-O?

Now, friends starting businesses together is one thing. Significant others going into business together is another story, one I'm less bullish on. Here are the pros and cons of diving into bed and work with the same person:

Pros
- You know and love each other unconditionally (I hope)
- You (should) have the same life goals
- If it works, you'll be a stronger team for it

Cons
- It's tough to keep your personal drama at home and vice versa
- Silent treatments and slammed doors don't work in business

- It can get messy figuring out how to divide expenses between business and personal

Just like when friends go into business together, communication is both your biggest strength and biggest weakness when tackling business with your romantic partner. This means going the extra mile to discuss what your roles within the business—as well as what your goals for the business—are. (BTW, creating equal roles wherever possible is better than one person having the subordinate one.) Whether the business venture is just for fun or to support your family's livelihood, being aligned is key to the success and longevity of the business *and* the relationship.

IT'S NEVER TOO LATE TO BE AN ENTREPRENEUR

I don't ever want to hear you say these words: "It's too late to become the Boss Bitch of my own business." Just look to these chicas before you who didn't let their age stop them:

Martha Stewart. When she was 30, having already worked as a model, Martha was still toiling in the trenches as a broker on Wall Street. She was 58 by the time her stock was traded there.

Julia Child. She didn't publish her first cookbook until she was pushing 40 and didn't land her cooking show until she was 51 (although she did have a cool job working for an American intelligence agency during WWII; that's right, she was basically a spy).

Vera Wang. She tried to make the Olympic figure-skating team (nope), then went for the editor in chief job at *Vogue* (nope again) before designing her first dress—at age 40.

Arianna Huffington. She was a BBC conservative commentator, an author, and an independent candidate for governor in the 2003 California recall election before becoming a liberal and founding the left-leaning *Huffington Post* in 2005 at the age of 54.

Forget your age. Live the life you always wanted. And remember, today is the youngest you'll ever be!

HERE'S YOUR MBA . . . YOU'RE WELCOME

You know my feelings generally about grad school from my discussion (rant) about it in the first section. But when it comes to getting an MBA, I'm torn. Can it help you get ahead in certain, more traditional companies? Yes. Do you *need* it for a start-up? Hell no. I probably could fill the rest of this book by naming all the famous founders who have built multibillion-dollar companies without even graduating from college, much less getting their MBA, but I'll list just a few for shits and giggles: Russell Simmons, Michael Dell, Ralph Lauren, Mark Zuckerberg. The list goes on and on for founders at the helm of companies like Twitter, Whole Foods, and so many more. I, for one, like to say I got my MBA at the school of hard knocks. It's a pretty awesome school—and, oh, by the way, I saved more than a hundred grand by going there instead.

I've always stood by the idea that on-the-job training is the best kind— and it works most of the time in just about any business. As a founder, though, you're going to need at least "101"-level knowledge of stuff like sales, marketing, and economics, and you'll need to learn how to speak the language of money, so you can feel empowered to engage in any business conversation that comes your way. And many, many will.

The good news is: those topics sound overwhelming, but they are not. By the time you finish this book, you'll understand the basics of what you really need to know about those subjects in a more practical and helpful way than a lot of what you would study in B-school. And it'll cost you a couple hundred grand less than said degree. You're welcome. Class is in session.

DO I NEED A BUSINESS PITCH OR A BUSINESS PLAN?

That's easy. You need both.

In Section 2, we talked about how to create an elevator pitch for your own brand. What does one of those look like when your brand is also your business? Well, for starters, you should follow the three Cs:

Conversational. Use your elevator pitch when talking to people with the goal of hooking them with something intriguing to kick off a deeper conversation. Good "hooks" paint the picture to help some-one visualize the concept quickly. A little (appropriate) humor goes a long way, too.

Concise. Yes, seriously, you should be able to recite this pitch in the time it takes you to ride an elevator with someone. Some venture capital firms even have elevator-ride simulations where entrepreneurs literally have to get their pitch out before the doors open.

Consistent. Get a good opening sentence or two, memorize it, and repeat it every damn time, while slightly tweaking the next line depending on who you are talking to. As you might remember from Step 1, mine is: "I'm Nicole Lapin, the financial expert you don't need a dictionary to understand." Then I say something specific to what I am pitching or selling like, "*Rich Bitch* is the first-ever financial book that swears." Come up with strong sound bites and have them at the ready.

Your elevator pitch is going to be the seed from which your business plan* blossoms. Here are the basic components of a typical one:

- An executive summary or mission statement, aka a somewhat more detailed version of your elevator pitch.
- An outline of the market you're in or planning to enter and how you plan to stand out in this field.
- What growth you've had so far and how you plan to grow in the future.
- Info about your management team, financial metrics, and projections.
- If you are asking for money, which I will talk about at length in the next step, your clear ask should be included.

The order of the elements is really up to you and what makes the most sense for your company. The purpose of the document is to provide a solid road map for you, your partners/employees, and future investors to know what this company is all about and where it's going.

FYI

The two Boss Bitch founders of Rent the Runway, Jennifer Fleiss and Jennifer Hyman, both went to business school . . . Hah-vard, in fact. So I asked them, "You went to business school—do you need a business plan? What does yours look like for RTR?" The Jennifers said maybe not—if you have a clear elevator pitch. Theirs was "the Netflix for fashion." Then they would adapt the rest depending on who they were pitching. The Jennifers just sold the sizzle and raised more than $100 million in investment using their verbal pitch as their go-to.

While all business plans are different and there's really no right way to do it, here's a very, very, very abridged example:

EXECUTIVE SUMMARY

Sabrina's Spray Tan (SST) is a premier mobile tanning service that caters to the high-end clientele of Austin, Texas.

Owners

SST is solely owned by Sabrina Smith. She has her PhD in spray tanning and is a national gold medalist of the Spray Tanners of America Awards.

Products and Services

SST offers an all-natural, organic, custom-blended patented spray tan solution with all spray tan sessions.

Market Analysis

The spray tan market has increased 2,000% in the last year in Austin, and SST is well positioned to take over a large share of that growth.

Strategy and Implementation

SST is looking to bottle their unique solution and hire two new employees to produce and sell it. SST is also going to be expanding its street team of expert tanners, hiring ten new SST technicians in the next year.

Financial Plan

SST is fully funded by Smith. In the last year of business, SST has grown 50% year on year* and has been cash-flow positive for the last five years. For her growth strategy, Smith is looking for $250,000 in funding;† in exchange, she will be offering 25% equity in SST.

A business plan is like any other major document you prepare in your educational or business life, whether that's your résumé or a term paper. The first time you do one, it's stressful, but it *does* indeed get easier. The key to them is getting across not just the goal of your business, but also how you will achieve that goal. After all, a goal without a plan is just a wish. And wishes are great . . . but they don't pay the bills!

FEELING CLUELESS? YOU'RE NOT ALONE

All this business-plan stuff sounds intimidating. That's why I included a whole freakin' dictionary of common business terms for you at the back of this book, because other dictionaries were pissing me off for being too un-necessarily complicated. Yes, there are a lot of weird business words and jargon, but, once you learn what they mean, it's all actually quite simple. Don't feel bad for not knowing what you didn't know before. And if you find you are beating yourself up a little, remember that you're not the only one who took a hot minute to learn the jargon:

> **Richard Branson,** one of the world's most famous entrepreneurs, who is now by some estimates worth $5 billion, didn't know the differ-ence between "net" or "gross" profits while he was already run-ning his business. He fessed up to it, and one of his colleagues tried to help him by literally drawing a sea, then drawing a fishing net in the sea and saying, "Well, Richard, the fish that are in the net, that's your profit at the end of the year, and what's outside is

---

† We will talk about funding soon—the ins and outs and whether or not you should take it at all—but this means that Sabrina is valuing her company at $1 million, because 25% of the company is $250,000.

your turnover." Branson said that once he learned the difference he started showing off by saying "net profit" and "gross profit" after not knowing the difference for the longest time.

Sara Blakely (who I will one day go "diving" with) admits that she didn't know what an "exit strategy" was while she was out to investors pitching her company. Though she is one of the world's few self-made female billionaires, she said that when they would inevitably ask, "What's your exit strategy?" she would think to herself, "What *are* they talking about?!" Being the Boss Bitch that she is, she would just answer, "To exit a room and look good doing it!" Though it was a smart and sassy way to respond, the suits were only trying to find out what her plans were to "exit," or "sell," her company.

The moral of these stories is that we are all shaking in our boots (stilettos) about this business lingo, including the best of the best. Plus, the lingo is always changing. I've talked to a ton of executives who get confused by business phrases all the time. So if you don't know what something means, no matter what stage you are in life or in the life of your business, just ask, because you're surely not the only one with that same question.

HAVING A LOT OF STUPID IDEAS IS SMART

I've had hundreds of terrible ideas. All good entrepreneurs have. And you will, too. But it's actually one of the best things that can happen. Why? Because it's a numbers game. The odds are stacked against entrepreneurs: only about one out of every thousand ideas is good, and the more bad ones you have and can identify, the closer you are to your good one.

What follows is a short list of some of the bad ideas I once had that never went anywhere because they were . . . bad. Maybe they could have been good with the right team or timing, but they made no sense for me at the time they came to me (likely in the middle of the night or in the shower). Regardless, I always wrote them down and sat with them to see if there was a nugget of goodness there. Here are the ones that didn't make the cut:

- Pink vodka
- A résumé builder site
- A stylish lockbox
- Designer desk accessories
- Boss Bitch cocktails (I'm going to revisit this one!)

I know, I know: your business idea is a-mazing. To you. It's your baby, and it's hard to give it up, at any stage. That's why you need to ask yourself, honestly, if it's any good before getting too far in, because the longer you wait, the more difficult it becomes to shut it down. Here's the ultimate question: Does the world need what you're offering? Just because you've thought through it a lot or even if you've already written a business plan doesn't mean it's a good idea.

Here are the five specific questions to ask yourself to see if your brainchild is a viable business idea or just a brain fart:

1. Is this a unique idea? Is there no or very little competition? (If you haven't found something similar, dig harder.)
2. Is there enough of the market share that I can grab? Is there "white space"* or opportunity for me and my idea to grow in the market?
3. Do I have the time to be laser focused on this idea to see it to success? (This shouldn't be one of a bunch of things you are trying at the same time.)
4. Will the demographic I'm targeting respond well to this?
5. Can it be profitable?

If you've answered yes to all of those questions, then you may be onto a good one. But ultimately you aren't the deciding vote. Which brings us to . . . the Queen Boss Bitch: the consumer.

CONFESSIONS OF A
BOSS BITCH

The Time I Not-So-Smartly Invented a Smartwatch

I had a genius idea. At least that's what I thought and so did the closest people around me. It was to create a smartwatch that tracked your spending throughout the day in the same way as a FitBit tracks your steps.

I saw the trend of wearables taking off, with the popularity of fitness trackers and the upcoming launch of the Apple Watch, and I wanted to get in on the action. There were ones for sleep and for steps but nothing for your money. I saw a massive opportunity to be the first to do that and the watch as another screen to reach my audience in a unique way.

I came up with the idea for a product and ran through a few names and trademarks (which we will talk about more in the next step). The first was WatchIt (like a watch that helps you watch your money . . . get it??). After some starts and stops, I ended up going with the name CASH; it was smart, simple, and not too cutesy. It said what the watch was intended to do: help you track the cash that you spend that often goes unnoticed or unaccounted for because it's in . . . cash. People told me it should have been an app instead of hardware, but at that time I was adamant that an actual watch was a physical reminder that you're on a financial diet just by wearing it.

I had been in business long enough to know that this wasn't a product that would go straight to the shelf of Best Buy, but I figured that if I could find a way to tell my story—and why budgeting like this was so important—that customers would come on board. The best way to do that, I decided, was to go on the Home Shopping Network (HSN), where I could describe the product to an actual audience. So, after going through the ranks at HSN, I flew down to their headquarters in St. Petersburg, Florida, to pitch it with a slide presentation I created. The room really liked it, and after a couple more meetings and calls, they gave me the greenlight! WOOT! Okay, so I had buy-in for my idea. But then . . . I had to make it a reality.

The thing I failed to keep in mind was that I wasn't just getting into the hardware business but also the software business; you can't track the money on a watch and just leave it at that. You then have to plug it into your computer to sync and have your data analyzed. Now, the software and hardware business are two of the hardest kinds of businesses to get into, and I knew approximately zero about both. I mean, I was just trying to invent the world's first-ever financial smartwatch. NBD—totally casual, right? But, with my great idea and a big buyer on board, I was determined to do it.

I hired a small staff: someone to design and manufacture the product and another to deal with shipping, customer service, and other logistics that I had also forgotten about. I didn't take outside money, so I deficit financed* it, which means I put my own money in with hopes to make it back and then some. The two guys I hired had a ton of experience in this area and were confident(ish) we could get this ready for our airdate in a few months, which is unheard-of for a product like this. And without stopping to think it through, we were on a mission of speed and cost-effectiveness. Needless to say, I was a victim of having too much speed but not enough direction—so I was just going nowhere *fast*.

Before I knew it, my team was in China looking at samples for the casing, for the straps (there are literally millions of options—I picked out gray stingray, white crocodile, and black rubber to make them interchangeable for all looks and outfits), plus a stylus, a box, lining for the box, the little pillow in the box . . . ahhhh! Then I worked with a software team to come up with an interface for when the watch is plugged in via USB to your computer. I customized a saying for each permutation in "my voice;" so, for example, if you were over budget on transportation, I would say something like "Girl, you *have* to quit Uber" or "Take the bus, bitch." All of this took hours and hours, and the bills kept mounting and mounting.

Despite all of the challenges, most of the launch plans seemed to be coming together. I shot promotional videos and went on a press tour in the lead-up to the big day. But beyond the buzz, the product itself almost fizzled the night before. HSN has a super-strict QA (quality assurance) policy of inspecting *everything* that goes on air. Hours before launch, the HSN team didn't approve the wall charger—and I was at the brink of my $250K investment going in the shitter just because of that damn charger (which was already in each box). I was not about to let that happen. So my team went through the five thousand boxes we had in the warehouse (we were going to "drop ship"** to customers, which just means ship it ourselves) and took out every single charger. It was take it out or get out—so we did what we needed to do.

I've been on TV for fifteen years, literally thousands of hours, and I've never had a more terrifying experience on the air than being live on HSN. It's a network that makes $3,000 per MINUTE, and if they aren't making that when you are on the air, they simply take you off and replace you with somebody who will. Plus, I was on in the evening (not that two a.m. graveyard slot that they start a lot of products out on), so there was even more pressure in "prime time." If that wasn't bad enough, there are crazy-intimidating graphs and charts on large flat-screen TVs blasting the real-time sales data on set. I don't even remember what I was saying while we were on camera; I just wanted to hear the host say, "We've sold out!" . . . But he didn't.

I got off the air and I wanted to throw up. I asked immediately: "How many did we sell?" My massive investment and my team were dependent upon what had happened in the last ten—no, actually, eight—minutes (I didn't even make it the full ten—a bad sign). They said, "You didn't sell out, and we need to calculate the web sales and the rest of the numbers before we can tell you for sure." Oh, and PS, everyone on the show that night sold out. Except for me.

Don't get me wrong, I sold a good number of CASH smartwatches that night. But it wasn't the blowout I was expecting. I flew home, and my adrenaline high totally crashed and left me feeling absolutely bummed. In the weeks that followed, we sent out all the orders and started brainstorming what to do with the rest. But then came the most devastating blow of all: the returns started coming in.

Before you can calculate real sales in any business, you have to account for returns, and my return rates were higher than I had predicted. "What is going on?!" my team and I wondered as we figured out how to proceed.

And the answer became so shockingly clear, it was embarrassing that I didn't know before: we didn't test it. We moved so quickly to make our deadline that we never put the product in the hands of a test group to work out all the kinks. It was buggy. Of course it was.

There were a million things in launching that product that I had needed to juggle, and misstepping with almost any one of them could have ruined the product at different stages. But not testing crushed the product in the end. I ended up using the first round of real customers as my test group, which you should never do with people who *pay* for your product. Their feedback was spot-on and helped me and my team iterate the website and the watch itself enormously. We focused on getting the product to a good place before even thinking about reordering anything.

But that time did come when I needed to strategize for the future of the company and the inventory we held. It was time to either throw more money at it to make it more user friendly to a mainstream audience or service the customers we already had and close it down. It was one of the harder decisions I made, but I needed to say, "No more—we are done."

In hindsight, my idea should have been an app instead of an ambitious foray into the crazy hardware and software worlds. But, of course, that's not my "am-bitch-ious" style. Yes, yes, we are all Monday-morning quarterbacks with what we "should have" done differently. But instead of replaying the game over and over again, I just wanted to admit I fumbled and move on. I failed with the endeavor, but at least I didn't fail at knowing when it was time to quit.

TESTING, TESTING, TESTING

The most important thing you should do before deciding if this can be a viable business is to get out of your own head and try it out with consumers. Before you launch anything, do the consumer research and market testing. Sometimes you think you know how this will go over and you are right, but other times you have no idea, and other times—as I learned the hard way—you are just plain wrong.

The idea that "ideas don't work unless you do" is true, but it's also true that ideas don't work if they just don't. To ensure that doesn't happen to you, here are a few ways to test your product without breaking the bank:

1. *Have an MVP.* Not "most valuable player" (that's you, duh), but "minimum viable product."* If you are selling a consumer good, create a small batch or at least a prototype cheaply and get it out into customers' hands. If you have a web-based product, create a quick and dirty site on Squarespace or WordPress or Shopify with an experimental landing page. Give out whatever you would be selling for free during this first round or "beta"-testing* period. Devour what people are saying. You can set up a SurveyMonkey questionnaire or Facebook pool, or make up your own method. Whatever you choose, make sure to follow up. Be annoying if you

have to. This initial consumer feedback is gold in defining and refining your product.

2. *Pulse check.* Any of the sites you used to set up your landing page will have an easy analytics tool, which helps you understand traffic to your site. Who's going there? How long are they staying? You can also create a small budget for Google AdWords for your product (the ads on the side of your browser). You can create an ad in literally two minutes and then see which "keywords"* get the most traction for you. The most important metric is your "conversion rate," or the number of folks who bought or signed up for your product after seeing the ad. This stat helps you understand how much money you will need to throw into advertising to "acquire" a new customer. The question there is: Is it worth it?

3. *Don't be a zombie.* As you are testing, clearly define what you want out of the test. What are your metrics for success? Did five people buy it? Were they just your family and friends? Don't be delusional about the feedback. Let's say you got fifty sign-ups—is that good or bad? You need perspective to analyze any stat or number. "Zombie companies"* are ones that keep trudging even when they look like death. Figure out first whether the numbers make sense for you to stay alive and thrive versus a dead woman walking.

4. *Be creative.* There are all kinds of out-of-the-box ways to get feedback about your product before throwing it out into the marketplace. For example, when the popular UK beverage company Innocent Drinks started out, they tested their product at a music festival. After people tried their smoothie, they could throw their cups in one of two bins—*yes* or *no*—underneath the question, "Should we give up our jobs to start this business?" At the end of the festival, the *yes* bin was overflowing. That was enough to have them leave their jobs and chase their smoothie dreams.

These principles are what make my show *Hatched* different from *Shark Tank*: We hear pitches from entrepreneurs and then test their products in a retail environment to see and analyze the consumer feedback before giving them our final decision. Sometimes the consumer feedback reiterates what I and my fellow judges thought all along, but sometimes it surprises me and the rest of the panel. We do it this way because we believe that we should no longer tell the consumer what she wants; instead, she tells us and her friends what she wants.

A product can be designed to the nines and have the most brilliant minds behind it, but if no one buys it, it's dead. And if people buy it but don't love it enough to tell their friends, it's on life support. But if people buy it and love it, then it's got a chance.

When the two founders of Airbnb started their company (as a side hustle to help pay their rent), they didn't just go out and throw everything behind their idea; they tested it first. They set up a basic website with pictures of their extra room, images of the air mattress they would be getting, and a promise of a cooked breakfast for anyone who rented. They had three air mattresses, so they listed it three times, and all three air mattresses sold out in minutes. This was the small-scale but successful start to the testing they did that proved they were onto something before rolling out the company in a big way.

If, after you analyze your testing, you realize that your product is either not resonating with consumers or the cost to get in front of new consumers is too high, then consider that a victory. It's a victory because you've just saved yourself months of time and money working on a product that wasn't worth much of either. If the feedback leaves you scratching your head and asking yourself, "What the hell *was* I smoking?!" look back at your list of ideas, create a business plan for another, and test again. Because the only thing Boss Bitches smoke is their competition.

KEEP YOUR FRIENDS CLOSE AND YOUR COMPETITION CLOSER

I get it: you've tested your product, and it's good. But the question now becomes: Is it better than what's *already* out there? You'd like to think so, sure. It's okay to enter a crowded market, but only if you know the crowd you're entering.

There will be competition, and if you don't find some, do a deeper search beyond the first couple pages of your Google search and use different keywords. Know how those businesses started, how well are they doing, and, if one failed, figure out why so you don't make the same mistake. If they do something differently from you, ask yourself and your team, "Is that a better way to do it?" The answer could be no, but you won't know if you don't know to ask the question.

Greats in all businesses study the competition vigilantly to get a leg up. The best professional athletes study tape of their opponents before games. In the last section we talked about Sam Walton, the founder of Walmart and Sam's Club, who studied his competition so well that he even got arrested. I should also mention that Mitchell Modell, the founder of the sports company Modell's, was charged with sneaking into the competitor Dick's Sporting Goods storeroom by posing as an executive from that company.

Okay, so these two examples probably cross the line, but if done right (and legally), there is no shame in creeping on your competition. It's not creepy, it's smart.

Go beyond a Google search. Google Trends lets you see general trends of the industry but also where people go after they leave your site. Set up Google Alerts for your competitors so you can track whenever there is an article posted on them. SpyFu lets you see which keywords and AdWords competitors are buying.

Read reviews. Go to Yelp or Citysearch or whatever review site would be most appropriate for your business and see what consumers are saying about your competitors. What do they dislike about that business and how can you do better?

Go to conventions and trade shows. If you have a business that would lend itself to a booth on a convention floor, go visit your competitors' booths. See what their products look like and how representatives from that company communicate their message and interact with customers.

Hiring and firing. If an employee from the competition leaves, take a look to see if they could be a fit for you to hire. Aside from being a good recruiting method, no one spills the beans quite like a peeved former employee. Also, check job postings to see the positions competitors are hiring for. You can learn a lot about a company's strategy and direction from those postings. Are they hiring someone for their web team? They will usually list what programs they will need someone to be proficient in so you can see which ones they use. Are they hiring a delivery driver? This probably means they are going to start or ramp up the delivery part of their business.

Ask customers directly. Whenever I judge a company on my show, I call their suppliers and ask them how that product is selling and what they think of it. This is perfectly ethical; I never misrepresent myself, though I've never actually had someone ask why I'm asking. You'll be amazed what people who answer the phones of your suppliers or competitors will tell you if you just ask.

Aside from your own intelligence (and *that's* hard to compete with), consumer and competitive intelligence are among the most important pieces of information you need to hone your business. This detective work might seem annoying to do on top of *everything* else you are doing, but you know what's more than annoying? When your competition smokes you.

ROLL LIKE A BOSS

A true Boss Bitch has laser-sharp self-awareness. She knows what she knows and doesn't, as well as what she has time for and doesn't. She has grown to accept her strengths and has the courage to change the things she can but also the wisdom to outsource the things she can't.

In the last step, we talked about how to leverage the "share economy"* to earn extra money by doing odd jobs. Here we are going to look at how to use some of those services to save time. And since you know by now that time is your most valuable asset, especially when launching a business, you'll agree that the small fees for these services are pretty much always worth it.

BE YOUR MOST EFFICIENT SELF

Think about yourself in terms of how much you're worth on an hourly basis, even if it's just dividing your weekly paycheck by the hours you work. If you don't know, just use forty (even though you probably work more than forty hours per week) to get your "hourly rate." Then take a look at how much it would cost you to outsource some things on your daily to-do list. My hunch is that outsourcing is worth it from a cost *and* sanity perspective.

SHIPPING

Shyp. This is one of my favs. You take a picture of what you are shipping, and a magical Shyp mate (my name for them, not theirs) comes over and packs it up and deals with it for you for just 5 bucks. Adios, waiting in line and dealing with packing tape and boxes.

TRANSCRIPTION SERVICES

GMR Transcription. With the app Easy2Transcribe, you can dictate your letters, memos, reports, or life story right into your phone, upload the file, and a few hours later they will e-mail you a transcript for a little more than a buck a page. Why type when you can transcribe?

FOOD

FreshDirect or *Instacart.* Do your weekly grocery shopping for your home or office (or home office) online instead of having to go to the store and deal with crowds and lines. Just order it, and you'll get it delivered in the specific window you choose.

RESEARCH ASSISTANT

Fancy Hands. You can hire administrative assistants for approximately $5 per task for up to twenty minutes. They may not get you coffee, but they'll do anything that requires a phone and the Internet.

TRAVEL SERVICES

Ask Sunday. This is a great service that gives you a virtual assistant to deal with travel itineraries (although they can do other things, too). How frustrating can it be to search for flights and deal with complicated business travel, especially when you are on a budget? Answer: very. For $8–$15 an hour, depending on the plan you purchase, you can kiss your frustration buh-bye.

FYI

MEET PARETO

In business there is something called the Pareto principle. It's known as the 80-20 rule in that it says 20% of what you put into a business is responsible for 80% of the results. So that could mean that only 20% of your staff could be responsible for 80% of your output. Or, it could mean that 80% of your productivity could come from only 20% of your time at work. I'm introducing you to an economist named Vilfredo Pareto to remind you that input doesn't equal output. So, do less, work smarter, and dominate more.

Six Small Business Spending Hacks

1. *Get a business card.* A credit card, that is. There are great perks out there like a 0% introductory APR,* free employee cards, and, in some cases, savings on business-related expenses and rewards for your office expenses.

2. *Let Apple hook you up.* As a business owner, you can sign up for a free business account that gives you access to Apple's Business Experts, who are on call for you 24/7. Put you and your employees on the same account, and once you hit a certain amount you get discounts . . . yes, basically one of the only ways to purchase an Apple product at less than full price.

3. *Be a discount shipper.* USPS is the cheapest option for small businesses for sure (BTW: UPS happens to be slightly more expensive than FedEx). The next time you are shipping for your business, ask for a "media discount." You don't need to actually be in the media

to take advantage of this; you just need to be mailing books, scripts, printed objectives, or test materials.

4. *Get legal on the cheap.* LegalZoom has changed the industry with affordable, easy solutions for previously annoying and costly legal efforts. Lawtender is a newer site that bills itself as "justice with a twist," where you can post your legal request and have it bid on by lawyers who want to take you on for a fraction of the going price.

5. *Trade business services.* Maybe you can design a website with your eyes closed, but you suck at math and need accounting work done, desperately. Instead of paying someone (there's nothing more annoying than having to pay someone to help you pay someone), find a business match and barter on a site like BizXchange. There's a hefty onetime fee of 800 bucks, and it costs $15/month, but it gives you access to a great business barter marketplace that, if used to its fullest, will pay the fees many times over. IMS, ITEX, and TradeJa are similar options. A caveat to remember here is that you have to report the fair market value of these services to the IRS on a 1099-B form.

6. *Go virtual.* Think artificial intelligence is weird sci-fi futuristic stuff? It's not. It's happening, and big-deal business folk are getting on board. Sites like assistant.ai or x.ai or "Viv" (by the Siri creators) will give you a virtual assistant who can schedule your appointments (they can even be programmed to automatically know your preferred meeting times and lunch spots), send out e-mails on your behalf (in your voice), and take care of other annoying stuff that your time is too valuable to bother with. Skeptical? I've tested this out, and it works I'd say about 95% of the time, and because these "AI" assistants are in their early phases, they're only going to get more reliable and sophisticated down the road. It's a little freaky when you think about it, but what will keep you with it is the fact that the price is right: free!

The first few years of owning my business sucked more than they were great. So I know from experience that there's going to be that sucky time for every budding entrepreneur. There are growing pains, there are adjustments, and there's a whole stretch of newly poured pavement to pound.

But that's what being an entrepreneur is all about: living a few years of your life hustling like most people won't so that you can spend the rest of your life living like most people can't.

BOTTOM LINE

Conventional Wisdom: Friends make terrible business partners.

The Real Deal: Not necessarily. Friends know you better than anyone. If you complement each other's strengths and weaknesses and address all the serious stuff up front, you could make one sassy and strong dynamic duo.

Conventional Wisdom: I need to go to business school to start a business.

The Real Deal: As if! Many of the best entrepreneurs didn't even make it out of college, much less go to business school. A few of the female founders we talked about in this step happened to go to Harvard Business School, but I can tell you from talking to them myself that they learned a million times more on the job and from friends and mentors than they ever learned in the classroom.

Conventional Wisdom: If I want to start a business, I need a business plan.

The Real Deal: Yes and no. Sometimes an "elevator pitch" for your company will suffice. Other times, especially when raising money (as we will talk about more in the next step), you will need a formal pitch and/or presentation. It's better to have both on hand, but for most occasions, a catchy, spot-on verbal pitch is what you'll use.

Conventional Wisdom: You need luck to succeed in business.

The Real Deal: I would never turn down a little luck, but I would argue that some luck is within your control. The more you keep at it, the luckier you tend to get. It's not necessarily better to be lucky than good, as the saying goes. It's easier, for sure. And if you do happen to be luckier than you are good, just make sure to be nicer than you are lucky!

HOW THE HECK DO YOU START A BUSINESS, ANYWAY?!

The Nuts and Bolts of Getting Your Gig Off the Ground

When people ask me how I went from covering business to being in business, I respond: "I went job hunting, hired myself, and never looked back." But just because I haven't looked back yet doesn't mean I'll never change my mind. I'm not planning to, but if I do, I'll be better at anything I attempt in the future for having conceived, birthed, and raised a business. And you will be, too.

I have girlfriends who have given birth to babies and businesses around the same time and, without a doubt, they always say that the business is the harder birth (even sans epidural). We are all just figuring it out as we go, often looking around for the adult to take care of things before realizing that, um, that's *us*. And despite the research we do in advance, we still consult YouTube videos for our "How the heck do we do *that*?!" questions. Consider this to be the business edition of *What to Expect When You're Expecting*. In Step 3 of "Being the Boss of Your Own Business," I'll teach you how to raise your business baby.

CHECK YOUR VITALS

Boss Bitches pay attention to every little detail because we know that little changes lead to big results. We know that success is only the sum of its parts. And each part is made up of smaller parts. So, before going all out with your business materials—including business cards—think long and hard about what everything on there says about you.

THE NAME GAME

What's in a name? A lot. Just like you stress over the name of your kid, you should be equally thoughtful about the name of your business. Here are some things to consider when picking a name:

Go *dictionary diving*. When the founders of Twitter were thinking of a name, they literally opened up the dictionary. They found *twitter*, which is defined as "to give a call consisting of repeated light tremulous sounds." They thought this was the perfect word for what they were trying to create: an ecosystem where people could communicate with short little bursts of sound and information. Most people think that Google is a made-up word. In fact, the founders used a creative spelling of the word *googol*, which means "a number that is equal to one followed by one hundred zeros and expressed as 10^{100}." The idea was to connote in just one word the massive breadth and scope they wanted their search engine to have.

Go *ahead, invent a language*. If you can't find a name that you like in the dictionary, consider making up a word, like Xerox or Kodak. The thing to keep in mind here is that since these are not actual words, there's no sentiment attached except the one you create through advertising and marketing that consumers relate to. If you don't want to or don't have the money to do this right, steer toward something that's already out there.

Go *halfsies with make-believe*. Can't think of a made-up name and don't want to go with a boring one? Then smoosh two together, like Acura and Compaq did. *Acu* is the root segment of *precise* in many languages, but Acura isn't its own word, it's just an extension of that. In the same way, Compaq came from the word *compact*. And think about all of the start-ups out there ending in *-ly*, *-ify*, and *-able* (like Bitly, Spotify, and Giftable).

Is it sticky? In business speak, "stickiness"* refers to how memorable the name is with consumers. The best names are those that you don't have to write down to remember, even after you hear them for the first time. When you're picking your name, test this out with a group by setting a meeting and throwing out potential names. The ones the group remembers without looking at their notes are your winners.

Is it visual? The founder of the equipment company Caterpillar came up with the name after hearing someone describe his tractors as "crawling like a caterpillar." He loved that visual, and so was born the name of one of America's most iconic companies.

Shorties but goodies. Studies have shown that briefer is better when it comes to company names. Nike, Apple, Facebook, Pixar, and eBay all have two syllables. Long names are harder to remember and harder for people to tell their friends about, which is the best (and cheapest!) marketing you can get.

Like anything else in business, if the name doesn't work, change it. Nissan used to be Datsun; Xerox used to be the Halloid Company; LG was shortened from Lucky-Goldstar. If you picked something that isn't resonating, pick something else; the longer you wait, the more brand equity you are putting behind a bad name that you'll likely change later anyway.

After you've narrowed down your favorite names to about five that you've tested and love, then do a trademark search through the US Patent and Trademark Office (USPTO). Chances are, you aren't the only one to come up with that name (but you might be the only one in your vertical to have it, which makes all the difference in the world). You don't have to trademark your name, but you might run into issues if someone else says they registered for the trademark and you are using it, leading to a mountain of legal fees and other hell. I would know.

CONFESSIONS OF A
BOSS BITCH

The Recessionista Wars

I started my media company in 2011, at the end of the so-called Great Recession. I left hard-core business news, where my primary audience was old, rich, white guys (BTW, I'm not stereotyping here—that's exactly what the Nielsen ratings showed), and I wanted to start reaching an audience of young women who didn't seek out money news (but who needed it the most).

I thought Recessionista was the perfect name for one of the digital properties in my media company. I paid a few grand for the domain Recessionista.com, hired a trademark law firm to secure the mark for the site, started creating original video content, and built out tools like an Easy Peasy Expense Tracker. It felt like the whole thing was just that—easy peasy—until it wasn't.

I heard from a woman, let's call her . . . Hary Mall. In fact, everyone I knew heard from this woman. She had a small shopping blog that I had never heard of, and she was calling herself "The Recessionista." This woman apparently registered for a different kind of web media site (as I would soon learn, there are a ton of different subcategories that you can apply for). Hary freaked the fuck out that I had something similar, even though her "Recessionista" blog was about shopping and my "Recessionista" site was about sneak-attack money advice and tools.

The fact that our content was totally different didn't matter to her. This lady sent mean letters to everyone she could find on my website, harassed me on social media (like really crazy, mean stuff that I never responded to until now, and I'm just waiting for her Twitter rant when she reads this), and then started suing me. I was happy to each have our own Recessionista thang, but she was not backing down.

So I didn't, either. But because I had a really good law firm (code for *super expensive*), I was paying tens of thousands of dollars defending myself against this lady on a Lapin destruction mission. The thing about the legal system is that you must defend yourself from even the most bogus claims or you automatically lose. This went on for a couple of years. She didn't want to settle and peacefully coexist on the expansive interwebs. Nope, everywhere I turned, there was Hary Mall harassing me in some way.

Thankfully, time and economic trends worked in my favor. As my first book was coming out, and the recession was long in our rearview mirror (phew!), I expanded my money and content offerings online, folding Recessionista.com and the *Rich Bitch* brand into my website, nicolelapin.com. It wasn't because of the blog lady, but because the times had changed, and what I felt was important changed. I wanted my brand to be aspirational—not just about saving money, but about helping people earn and make money. However, I can tell you that not having to deal with Hary Mall any longer was a huge bonus.

I tell you this cautionary tale because trademark spats can get ugly, no matter how carefully you set yourself up and "lawyer up." And sometimes the best plan is not a plan at all, but a pivot.*

Getting your trademark squared away from the outset will save you exponentially more money, not to mention hassle, down the road. Initial searches cost about 300 bucks from an online shop like the Trademark Company. Keep in mind that when you are searching for your name, there are multiple categories under which the name can be registered.* For my hellish Recessionista example, I learned that Recessionista was registered by multiple people and companies in different areas than media blogs, like clothing and spirits. (Cheers to you, Hary Mall . . . the only one from another category I ever heard from!)

In the end, it was a teachable moment reminding me that sometimes, even when you cover all of your bases, there are haters out there who are simply out to get you. *Fluctuat nec mergitur.* That's (roughly) Latin for: "Boss Bitches are tossed by the waves but do not sink."

PROTECT YOUR BABY

Aside from thinking about trademarks, you have to be on top of your copyright game if you have an actual product, like written works (poems, articles, books), music, movies, or visual designs (like wallpaper or jewelry).

An application for a single work will cost about $35, and you can start the process on copyright.gov.

If you don't have those types of products but invented something (okay, smarty-pants), then you need to get a patent. Make sure, though, that you really did come up with it. If it's not original or if there's something similar that has been patented, then you need to prove that yours is different and better. These applications start on the US Patent Office's website. Be prepared because they'll get super detailed, asking you to present drawings and schematics of your invention. They can also get pricey. Depending on the invention, prices range from $100 to $3,000 to secure your patent, not including the price of lawyers if you can't figure it out for yourself.

Let's recap, because I know these terms might sound similar. And that's because they *are* all similar in that they are designed to protect your intellectual property:

- *Trademark* is for a brand (the little ™ on the top right if you're claiming the rights to that product or idea, or the *R* with a circle [®] if you've actually gone ahead and formally registered the trademark).
- *Copyright* is for a work or idea (the little *c* in a circle [©]).
- *Patent* is for an invention (this one gets a badass patent stamp).

Be clear on what you are applying for, since all of them fall under a different government office, and trust me, you don't want to spend a bunch of money only to realize you're wandering around the wrong office and need to start over.

BITCH TIP

MAKE IT OFFICIAL

If you are doing business, you'll likely need a general business license that you can get for a flat fee at your city clerk's office. If your business requires special licenses to operate, make sure you have those, too. Here are the most common ones that do:

Type of Operation	Type of License
Retail	Resale
Restaurant	Liquor, Health Permits (some states require Resale)
Spas and Salons	Operational License
Hair, Nail, Massage Technicians	Cosmetology License

Don't assume anything when you start your shop. Every business and every city is different, so check the laws out thoroughly before you start taking money. An entrepreneur friend of mine assumed it would be cool to offer a yoga class in the park. "Why would I need a license or permit?" he thought. "It's a park, after all." Turned out he was wrong; a mistake that ended up in a downward-facing dog of a citation that wiped out his earnings for a whole quarter.

GET ALL THE EXTENSIONS

If you are registering your domain name, go ahead and spring for as many extensions and variations as possible. For example, this means not just securing nicolelapin.com but also nicolelapin.org, nicolelapin.net, nicolelapin.tv, etc. You never know if your competitor or a squatter is sitting on a domain that could be valuable to you and your search results.

In college, a girl in one of my broadcast classes was such a hater of mine that she went out of her way to buy the domain www.nicolelapin sucks.com. Who *does* that?! I know, but this is not a joke. (I'm not going to lie, part of me would love to tell you her name, but I will take the high road here, as Boss Bitches do.) So I went online to do a WHOis lookup to verify who owned the domain—and it was indeed her. I looked at what else she owned, and she did *not* own her own name + *sucks*. Shockingly, it was quite cheap—so I bought it. Not to actually use (like I said, keep it classy) but just to remind her not to throw stones when you live in a glass house.

Online sabotage happens all the time. You'll likely be the target of it, and when you are, remember: don't get even, get leverage against the stone thrower.

LOCATION, LOCATION, LOCATION

The real estate adage holds true when thinking about your first "head-quarters," too. Maybe you started with a home office (as every good, scrappy entrepreneur does) and now you're ready to expand a bit. Like anything else on your business card, be thoughtful about the address by being on the lookout for these three things:

1. *Research the backstory of the area.* Is it up-and-coming? Does it look like it's overpriced and has a lot of vacancies, meaning rents should be coming down? What's the socioeconomic makeup? Does it match that of your customers, if you are a consumer-facing business? Is it conveniently located for all of your future employees to get to work without stress? Is there a day-care center nearby for employees with kids? Are there coffee shops or restaurants where your employees can go or where you can take clients?

2. *Traffic.* Does the area have a lot of foot traffic? If you have a café, are there businesses whose employees could walk there for lunch? If you're a boutique, are there tourists who walk by? Additionally, is there parking? I'm from LA, and there are plenty of times when I just don't go into a store if there's no parking. Free parking for customers is ideal; also look out for space for trucks to make conve-nient deliveries.

3. *What does the space offer?* A lot of older buildings don't have the tech-tastic stuff you'll need to run a modern company, like enough

electrical outlets or . . . air-conditioning! But they might have old-world charm, like fireplaces or exposed brick, if that's the aesthetic you're looking for. Check which utilities are included and get an average from the building of the previous tenant's bills so you can prepare yourself for those on top of the rent. You should also ask if there's a janitorial service or you have to pay for that as well. Also find out why the previous tenant left. Did their business not do well in that space? Why or why not?

> **BITCH TIP**
>
> If you own or conduct business in a commercial real estate location, you will likely need to pay property tax to your state. If you lease the property, check your lease to determine whether you or the owner is liable for those taxes. States also collect property tax for business assets, such as vehicles and even computer equipment, so make sure you know exactly what you're gonna be on the hook for.

Can't afford a new office but need to get out of your house? Try renting an executive office space. Companies like Regus and WeWork have locations all over. You can rent a nice, swank office per usage (like if you need to meet with clients and you don't want them coming to your house). A lot of these setups have a receptionist who can answer your calls to make it *seem* like you're in an office, and doormen to accept deliveries and welcome guests on your behalf. Or, if you aren't looking for office space but still want that office-like feel, try a virtual phone service like Grasshopper, which gives you all the features of an office receptionist and calling features while you're just chillin' in your jammies. "Hello, this is Fake It Till You Make It, how can I help you?"

Before you push out your business baby, you've gotta make sure you have the right elements in place for its debut into the world to be a success. Strong branding and legal protections are like oxygen to your foundling business. So before you move on, are your vitals in check?

Boss Bitch Vitals Checklist

Yes   No

        Domain name registration

        Corresponding social media handles

        Business license (for the cities in which you're
           doing business)

        Permits and special certifications

        Trademark, copyright, or patents

HOW STRUCTURED ARE YOU?

The structure of a business is like the fit of your clothes: it can be as tight or as loose as you make it. When it comes to the legal structure of a business, none of these options go out of style—but you're going to need to stick with it for a while, so make sure it looks good on you.

SOLE PROPRIETORSHIP

A sole proprietorship is the easiest structure to set up. If the business is made up of you, yourself, and you, then this is likely the best route for you at this time. You don't need to file formal paperwork to get this going (which is why it's also the easiest to change when you do get employees). Any profit your company makes goes on your personal tax return.

Pros

    Free setup.

    Easy-ish tax returns. Just fill out a Schedule C* and a 1040, which is straightforward compared to any other structure. You are not required to but should pay an "estimated" amount every quarter so you're not stuck with a ginormous bill at the end of the year. If you want to DIY this, try a program like TurboTax Home & Business (which is slightly souped up from the regular one) or Quicken Premier (same deal) or check with an accountant.

Can offset earnings from all sources with losses you have in this business. Let's say you have a nail spa but you also walk dogs, and you lose a ton of money on the former but make bank on the latter. You can make the income from dog-walking decrease on your tax return because of all the losses on your nail spa. Having your income decrease means you save more in the taxes you pay, and may even result in a nice refund come tax time.

Cons

Might be tough to raise money because you don't look as "legit."

The business doesn't live on if something happens to you. Since you are the business, you can't pass it on.

You are on the hook for your company. If you go bankrupt or get sued, your personal money outside of the business could be at risk.

A sole proprietorship is ideal for a consultant who doesn't have a lot of risk of being sued or getting shut down. If, however, you're looking to set up a contracting company, you might want something more structured to better protect you.

BITCH TIP

REFUNDS ARE STILL FUNDS

If you own your own business as a sole proprietorship, you might get a tax refund back at the end of the year for all of those business expenses you wrote off. Just remember: it's not free money; it's YOUR hard-earned money coming back to you! So treat it that way. Put those funds into your retirement account, or better yet, reinvest them in your company. Have you been in sore need of a new printer for your home office, or jonesing to take a coding class to stay on top of the latest techniques? Your refund is a great way to "treat" yourself and your business . . . responsibly.

PARTNERSHIP

A partnership* is something you should look at if you have two or more people working for the business. There are two kinds of partnerships: general and limited. Let's say you start a business with two of your friends. In a "general partnership," all three of you are equally responsible for everything. So if one of your partners maxes out your business credit card, you are all responsible for the debt. If, however, you have a "limited partnership," where you are the main person in the business and two of your friends have a role but aren't doing the heavy day-to-day lifting, then that means that you are on the hook for the aforementioned credit card debt, while they are protected up to the amount they invested in the business (so keep an eye on your business credit card statements!). Pro tip: If you have this structure, require the signatures of all partners when writing checks just in case.

Pros

Low-cost, easy way to create business structure.

Some tax advantages when reporting the profits and losses of the business on your personal tax return.

Makes raising money easy because there's a simple delineation of shared financials among the partners with a simple path for additional employees to become partners.

Cons

You share profits with partners even if they are slacking.

You are personally responsible for the actions and debts of the whole partnership.

There are typically more spats among the partners about who is doing more or less because the business is technically shared regardless of who pulls their weight.

This structure is common in the real estate industry. But, as with any structure (and especially if it's between friends), you should get everything in writing first so that it's all spelled out and agreed to before you start working together. You should have a lawyer review this agreement as well.

Another variation on this structure is a "joint venture," which is basically the same thing (legally) as a partnership but has a set expiration date. This can be a nice option for collaborations, like if you're a clothing designer and your super-chic interior decorator friend wants to partner up on a limited-edition home decor line.

LLC (LIMITED LIABILITY COMPANY)

An LLC is a hybrid between a sole proprietorship and a corporation (which I'll tell you about in just a sec). If you own your own business, you also have the option to form an LLC by yourself. That means that you still pay taxes on your personal return, but you are protected against any issues with the business. If you are starting a business with partners, then you can also form an LLC, which gives you more personal protection. That means the "members" of the LLC share the profits and losses based on their percentage of ownership in the business but file personal tax returns.

Pros

Relatively easy for the protection it offers you. Can be set up in a couple of hours (way less time than a corporation), and you get an EIN number or a tax ID for your business. You'll need to register for this on the IRS website or have an attorney or accountant do it for you.

Personal protection against issues with the company (you are only on the hook for up to the amount you invested).

Better chance of raising money because you look more "legit."

Cons

While it's not as expensive as forming a corporation, it can still be pricey (between $1–2K to set up), and you also have to report the formation of the LLC in a few business journals (random but true).

You need to pay the self-employment tax on your income.

If one "member" peaces out, it could bring down the entire structure.

Liability protection is not absolute (i.e., it does not protect you against gross negligence, a fancy way of saying "when someone else on your team royally effs something up or just checks out of the business altogether").

The limited liability cousin to the LLC (limited liability company) is the LLP (limited liability partnership). The LLP (a hybrid between a partnership and a corporation) offers another layer of protection against other members of the company. So if a member of the group maxes out the credit card, they would be responsible in an LLP, whereas the group would be responsible in an LLC. This structure is best suited for companies who are not sure how much they will grow over the first few years.

REBEL WITH A CLAUSE

BITCH TIP

Aside from getting legal services on the cheap like we talked about earlier in this section, there are other sites, like the Company Corporation and BizFilings, that can help you to structure your business on the cheap. I also suggest reaching out to alums and friends of friends who are lawyers who can help with this kind of business structuring. A lot of times they will do it pro bono for you as an investment in helping you succeed in the future.

S CORPORATION, OR S CORP

An S corp* is the first step into the corporate world. It means that you are now a "corporation"—which sounds exciting except for the fact that you now have to do what a lot of corporations do, like pay payroll taxes and maybe form a board of directors.

Pros

You aren't double taxed like in a C corp (which I'll tell you about next), where the business is not taxed itself but "passed through" to your personal return. Instead, you might even *get* extra tax credits. Since you and the business are separate, you can sell your "shares" in the business without impacting the seaworthiness of the company, unlike in a limited liability situation.

You can have up to one hundred employees in this structure, which gives you the protection and the flexibility to grow.

Cons

Costly to set up with much more regulation, and will most likely require a lawyer and/or an accountant to make sure it's registered properly.

There is a lot more financial reporting that needs to be done, which is likely too much to handle if you are just starting out.

There can't be any foreign ownership. Yes, Canada and Mexico included.

This is the structure I personally have for my production company. It works for my company because it allows us to grow knowing that we likely won't top the one-hundred-employee mark and won't be raising significant amounts of money for the business.

SIGN ON THE PIXELATED LINE

Paperwork for setting up the legal structure and formation of your company can get aggressive. I personally am offended by using a scanner for a signature. Instead, my company said sayonara to them and signs all important documents with Docusign and SignEasy, which let you sign paperwork from your phone on the go. We also snap photos of important docs with TurboScan, which lets you save them as PDFs for easy e-mailing.

C CORPORATION, OR C CORP

This is the big gun in the corporate structure world. Most major companies, especially the public ones, are C corps.* The company itself is the one on the hook for any legal action or debt incurred by employees; that's because a C corp is essentially an entity on its own that can sue and be sued. We talked about the idea of double taxation above. With a C corp, that means that the money going into the company is taxed *and* the money you get is taxed.

Pros

Employees' personal assets are protected.

Ability to IPO (initial public offering*) and/or raise significant capital, because the structure is more accommodating to different ownership structures.

Benefits and stockholder options can be a draw to top-notch employees.

Cons

Taxes, requirements, and fees are most hefty and complex. Set aside at least a few thousand dollars just for the initial setup.

It's easy to go from an LLC or S corp to a C corp, but if you change back to an S corp, you have to wait a few years before restructuring.

High operational costs, including taxes for employee compensation (which means sending out W2s). Other structures typically leave employees to handle taxes on their own.

FYI

When entertainers or high-net-worth folks get paid, the checks don't usually go to them directly. Instead, many actors, musicians, writers, and the like get paid through a "loan-out" corporation. Why? 1) Because it limits liability if someone goes after you, and 2) it puts you in a preferred tax bracket. It's an arrangement where the person is technically an employee of that company (it can be an LLC, S, or C corp) and the one writing the check is doing business with that company in exchange for it "loaning out" your services. So when Kim Kardashian gets paid, the check goes to "Kimsaprincess, Inc." And when Mindy Kaling gets paid, it goes to "Kaling International."

.

Before setting up a C corp, make sure you're on a clear business path. If you are a start-up that is positioning itself for rapid growth, then a C corp could be right for you. Many major investors prefer this structure because of its ability to offer different kinds of stock (common and preferred), which is very important if you go public, but some investors even have restrictions about investing in any company that's *not* a C corp.

BITCH TIP

KEY (WO)MAN INSURANCE

This is actually just an insurance policy—a life insurance policy—on the "key woman" in the organization, aka the Boss Bitch. If your company should fold without you at the helm, then it's a good idea to get a life insurance policy on which the business pays the premiums and names the company as the beneficiary should, God forbid, something happen to you.

This way, even if you die (sorry not sorry, Boss Bitches need to think about this stuff), your investors and debt will be repaid and your employees can still collect their severance pay. If you have a partner or senior members of your executive team whose roles in the company are similarly integral to the survival of the business, it might be wise to take out policies for them as well. It's good business for you and those who are dependent on you (aka, your work family).

BTW, just being generally one of a kind doesn't qualify you for this type of insurance. Be super honest with yourself: Do you have nontransferable skills that no one else could replicate were you to be gone? Have you masterminded a corporate structure that won't stand without you leading it? If the answer is yes, then YES—you are a key woman and as such should insure the shit out of yourself.

BE YOUR OWN BEST CFO

When you're starting out, you are probably going to be all the executive positions of a company rolled into one: chief executive officer, chief marketing officer, chief operating officer . . . and the less fun ones, like chief financial officer and chief revenue officer.

If accounting freaks you out to the point of hyperventilating . . . you're not alone. But there's nothing to be freaked out about when you keep it simple. Consider these FAQs your cheat sheet for Accounting 101:

Q: Um, what's accounting?

A: Accounting tracks what goes out (expenses) and what comes in (income).

Q: What do I do first?

A: Set up a separate business account. This is very important, since in the early days you are likely comingling your personal and business funds.

Q: Do I need software?

A: It would help. Software like QuickBooks, Xero, and Peachtree can make the tracking easy and painless for you. Otherwise, make friends with Excel.

Q: Why am I doing this?

A: The goal is basic: your income should be higher than your expenses, and the only way to know that is by keeping track of yo' money. If your income *is* higher than your expenses, that means you are making a profit, which every business obviously needs for long-term success.

While you're at it, here are some seemingly complicated metrics that are actually a cinch to track:

*Gross margin.** You calculate this by subtracting the cost it takes to make something from the revenue you make on it (that's your margin, which is basically how much something is marked up). Then you divide that by the revenue. This gives you a percentage that tells you how much you make on every dollar. So if your gross margin is 25%, then you are making a quarter before any overhead, salaries, etc., are paid out. You want this number to be *as high as possible*. If your gross margin is low, you can adjust prices or volume to try to boost it up to get more money in the company's pocket after all expenses are accounted for.

Let's use Sabrina's Spray Tan from the business plan example:

SST Costs (tanning solution):	$5,000
SST Revenue:	$35,000
SST Gross Margin:	$35,000 − $5,000 = $30,000
	$30,000/$35,000 = 0.85 or 85% gross margin

This is a great gross margin. Stuff like spray tanning, cosmetics, vitamins, etc., typically have high gross margins. (Yes, it's maddening to think how little your favorite moisturizer actually costs to make versus how much you pay for it, but I digress . . .)

*Net margin.** Remember, *gross* just refers to the whole shebang, and *net* refers to what you take in. So net margin is gross margin after all the stuff like overhead and salaries are paid for (subtract your expenses and costs from your revenue and divide it by your revenue). This tells you how much your company is actually pocketing. Again, the higher the better!

Let's see how this plays out for Sabrina's Spray Tan:

SST Expenses (marketing, overhead, salary):	$15,000
SST Costs (tanning solution):	$5,000
SST Revenue:	$35,000
SST Net Margin:	$35,000 − $15,000 − $5,000 = $15,000
	$15,000/$35,000 = 0.42 or 42% net margin

This means that Sabrina is pocketing 42 cents for every dollar that comes in, which is a great net margin.

When you are first starting out, your main focus should be on getting customers and making money. The accounting stuff should be easy. Once you have more of both (customers and money), bring on a professional accountant—but don't get scared or bogged down by the financial terminology in the beginning stages of running your business. In the next step, I'll talk about how those professionals can help you plan your financial and tax goals. For now, here are a couple of other key things to watch for when looking at your books:

*Know your "fixed" and "variable" costs.** Something that's *fixed* is just what it sounds like it is: it doesn't change, like your rent. *Variable* just means that it changes. Be mindful of this to make sure you don't think you have less or more money than you actually do. Typical variable costs are things like your Amazon Web Services usage or a utility bill.

*Find your concentration.** In business, *concentration* means how much of your business is dependent on a particular client or partner. You don't want to depend on too few clients or partners for your business to stay afloat. It's expressed as a percentage, and you want to keep it as low as possible.

No one is going to care more about your budding young business than you, and no one else is going to take the time to do your homework for you. So put the legwork in to make sure you have a, well, leg up on the competition. You want to be able to take care of not just employee one (aka, YOU) but employees two, three, and four, and maybe someday four hundred!

VENTURING FOR CAPITAL

The first investment you'll make in starting your new business is an emotional one, and it often starts by simply saying, "I'm doing this." But depending on what *this* is, there is almost always an initial financial investment, as well. You know by now that my numero uno suggestion is to be as scrappy as you can with your business for as long as possible. But you might get to a point where you simply cannot take the next step—whether it's hiring or purchasing necessary equipment or inventory—without an infusion of cold, hard cash. Then, and only then, should you think about letting go of your bootstraps.

Here are the three main sources of your business you can tap for cash:

1. *Your equity.* Either money you've saved or sweat equity you are putting into the company by working your butt off doing jobs yourself that you could have otherwise paid someone else to do.

2. *Debt.* Charging business costs to a credit card, borrowing money from a bank, using a short-term lender, or asking a peer or a family member for cash.
3. *Company equity.* Giving up a portion of your company in exchange for money.

The last option is a popular and, don't get me wrong, *sexy* idea for entrepreneurs. It seems like "raising money" just goes along with starting a company, like *Shark Tank* tells you it does. The reality outside of reality TV is that raising money *can* be a part of "raising" a start-up, but it can just as easily not be. Taking money from someone in exchange for giving them part of your company means they can now call the shots, too. That's not the typical Boss Bitch style.

HOW TO RAISE MONEY WITHOUT KNOWING MARK CUBAN

So, you don't have Mark in your phone's favorites. Instead of trying to get money from him or the other "sharks," listen to his advice: "Sweat equity is the most valuable equity there is. Know your business and industry better than anyone else in the world. Love what you do or don't do it."

That's correct, even Mr. Shark Tank himself says that equity of any other kind (money) isn't as important as your sweat effort. So before you venture into venture funding, try these Boss Bitch money-raising tips first:

Boss Bitch money-raising option #1. Save up. This one should be obvious, but you'd be amazed how few people think to put money aside in advance of launching their own business. Future investors will want to see that you have skin in the game, too.

Boss Bitch money-raising option #2. Get a grant. Finding and getting a grant isn't the easiest thing, but who are you to shy away from a little challenge? If you can secure one, it's money that's yours, not borrowed from an investor. Depending on your business niche and demographics, there are various government grants available to you. Check out grants .gov to get started. There are also specific grants for women on the Minority Business Development Agency website.

Boss Bitch money-raising option #3. Enter a contest. There are a growing number of contests that offer big prizes to encourage innovation. Two notable ones to consider are the PITCH: Women 2.0 start-up contest and the Amazon Web Services Start-Up Challenge.

Boss Bitch money-raising option #4. Microloans aren't just for helping to end poverty in developing countries; there are plenty of micro-lenders willing to help out entrepreneurs back at home, as well. The nonprofit ACCION offers small business loans from $200 to $750K. You can also check with the Small Business Administration* (SBA) at SBA .gov for guidance to funding for businesses in your area.

Boss Bitch money-raising option #5. Peer-to-peer lending has become increasingly popular, although it's been around in the traditional sense for quite some time. Websites like Lending Club and Kabbage allow virtual peers to lend you money if they believe in your start-up idea.

Boss Bitch money-raising option #6. Crowdfunding* is one of the more buzzy ways to raise money. Kickstarter and Indiegogo have made raising money a thing of the online crowd. Some of the stuff on these sites is a little oddball, but there are awesome success stories like GoldieBlox, which produces toys and games for girls to encourage them to take an interest in engineering, which came out of a Kickstarter campaign (and raised $300K!).

Boss Bitch money-raising option #7. Swiping the plastic. Be afraid, be very afraid. Financing a business with a credit card is not my favorite option because, for starters, the interest rate is higher than you'd get on an old-school business loan. But some people have made a successful go of it. Kevin Smith financed his first cult hit movie, *Clerks*, with $2K in cash and $25K in credit card debt, and the movie raked in a little over $3 million. Not blockbuster money, but still a pretty good return on his investment.

Boss Bitch money-raising option #8. Creative PO (purchase order) financing. If you have a consumer product business (food, toys, etc.), one of the most common problems is financing a purchase order from a re-tailer. Yes, it might sound like "high-class problems" to struggle to keep up with so much demand, but not being able to fulfill those orders and deliver your product is bad. PO financing companies will help you make good on that order. Typically, these financing options have minimum requirements and interest rates of about 2–5%.

Boss Bitch money-raising option #9. Invoice factoring. This is basically an advance payment for your AR (accounts receivable). Anything in AR means that it's money that's been promised to you but not paid yet. Say you've delivered a product to a customer and invoiced them for it, but they haven't paid or the due date hasn't arrived. This is an advance or a loan of that money you're expecting. The cost is about 1.5–4% per month.

Boss Bitch money-raising option #10. Friends and family. I know it can feel icky to ask the people who are closest to you for money, but if you just need a little push to get going with your business, consider money from a family or friend as an IOU. Just remember that sometimes you have to decide which means more to you: the relationship or the money.

These options can be temporary loans or infusions of cash to keep you going. They are helpful tools for getting money when you need it quickly, but they are not options to lean on regularly.

Popular media has led us to believe that giving up equity is a simple way to get a fatty check for a company. And who *doesn't* want a fatty check?! You.

Yes, that's right, I said it. Don't take a big fatty check until you have to. Try everything you can to get your business off the ground before fundraising, because once you take someone else's money, they own a part of your business.

It sounds like free money: "I'll give you fifty thousand dollars for fifty percent of your company." At first blush, it looks like you're just getting $50K for a portion of your company; you might think, "Well, without that money, the company is nothing, so it's a no-brainer" or "Fifty percent of nothing is nothing, so they only get something if I do." But here's what it really means: a) by taking that money, you're now formally valuing your company at $100K (if 50% of your company is $50K, then 100% is $100K), and b) you have a 50% partner now. So, no, giving up equity is not free money, because once you take it, you're not the only one in charge (which was one of the "freeing" reasons you started your own thing in the first place).

CONFESSIONS OF A
BOSS BITCH

Hatching a Business, Baby

My show *Hatched* airs every week for fifty-two weeks per year (each of the original twenty-six episodes airs twice). So I get to meet twenty-six awesome entrepreneurs every season.

They all have their own amazing stories. The kids are, for sure, the cutest. But the most impressive entrepreneur I met was a woman named Rana. She started a company called "Edoughble"—it's edible cookie dough! Get it? The name is awesome, and she came to us with a delicious product that backs it up.

The day Rana pitched our panel, she was nine months pregnant. In fact, it was her due date. But she stood in front of us under the bright lights and pitched her heart out.

The next day, she gave birth. And the following day, she came back for our decision about whether or not to fund her product.

Rana was the embodiment of an entrepreneurial spirit. She did everything herself to grow her business baby and couldn't go a day without thinking about it, even from the delivery room with her newborn baby. You just can't fake passion like that.

So when it came to funding her product, she obviously got a yes.

SEND ME AN ANGEL

Angel investors are individuals (rather than companies) who have the money to invest in your business in exchange for equity. Sometimes these folks are serial or professional angel investors, as in this is all they do in life. Or sometimes they are wealthy professionals in their field. Some are retired and have the time, energy, and passion to invest their money and advice. Others could be other entrepreneurs who made a killing and now want to let their own money grow in someone else's venture.

So where do you find such an angel? Well, it used to be more difficult to track these god-like creatures down. But now there are angel investing organizations that you can tap into in hopes of a divine intervention of capital:

- AngelList is where most angel investors are listed. You can look through their profiles and locations to see which ones might be the best fit for you and your endeavor.
- Angel Capital Association breaks down regional angel investor groups like Hyde Park Angels or Cornerstone Angels in Chicago.
- ACEnet is an online network started by the Small Business Association that connects entrepreneurs with angel investors.
- FundingPost is a convention of sorts that makes a few stops across the country. You pay to get in, so make sure to have your elevator pitch at the ready.
- Astia is an angel group that funds women-backed ventures.

While angels may sound like a dream come true, they don't write blank checks. Even for angels, the devil is in the details, so make sure you are ready with a lot of careful research into your business plan and strategy before approaching them.

FINDERS, KEEPERS

BITCH TIP

Boss Bitches are collectors. Of people. Over the years, we meet people through work or hobbies or by going out. We know people. A lot of 'em. And if you don't think you do, think harder about the amazing network you've created and how that amazing network has a whole other network that you could tap into. I believe we could all get to anyone if we just mapped out our people chart correctly.

Your collection is valuable—probably the most valuable thing you have in business. So let's say that a friend of yours is trying to raise money for a company or professional endeavor and asks for your help because you've already started a business. And, of course, you want to be helpful, but you don't want to be a sucker. So you say, "Sure, I'll make XYZ introductions, and then I would like a five percent finder's fee for any money you raise as a result of my introductions."

Does saying that skeeve you out? I know I felt a little icky the first time I asked for a finder's fee.* But once I got paid, I got over it fast. And you should, too. Remember, this is not a setup for a date or another helpful introduction, for which, of course, you don't ask for anything in return. But when it comes to a very specific business introduction that will lead to capital being raised, collecting a finder's fee is important to agree to up front. And I promise, it's something people desperate for capital will find well worth it.

Banks charge super-hefty fees for fund-raising for companies. They are opening up important connections that you wouldn't have otherwise, briefing the other party before the introduction, and then following up after the money is raised. That's basically what you are doing, too, when someone asks you to help them to raise money—and, in a lot of cases, you can do it faster and more nimbly than a bank, so what you're doing might be even *more* valuable.

Can you imagine any scenario where an investment bank *wouldn't* expect a company to pay for their fund-raising services? There is no fucking way that an I-bank would do that work for free. After all, it's business, not pro bono work. And if someone wants to get all up in yours, then they have to pay for it, too.

THE ABCS OF VCS

First off, do not confuse the terminology of *angels* with VCs. It's the first sign of an amateur—and investors *will* notice. So here's the difference:

Angel investor: an accredited investor (with at least a million-dollar net worth or an income of at least $200K/year) who invests their own money, usually in the range of tens of thousands to hundreds of thousands of dollars, in a company of their choosing.

VCs: A venture capital fund is made up of other people's money— rich people, insurance companies, university endowments, etc.—who are looking for a return from the success of the fund's investments. Thus, the checks from VCs to entrepreneurs are made up of other people's money—and those checks are usually in the millions.

The saying around the investment community is that if you need to ask if you need VC money, then you don't. That means that smaller start-ups likely aren't ready for the VC world and wouldn't be attractive to venture capitalists anyway. VCs are looking for massive returns of at least ten times their initial investment. They take big swings with big checks, looking for companies with huge growth potential in their market, like the next Facebook or Uber. Otherwise, 99% of companies get rejected.

With that said, we are in a zone where there are no dumb questions. So here are some questions you might have, because I sure did:

Q: Does every VC only write million-dollar checks?
A: Most of them do. But there are mini VCs or early stage VCs that write smaller checks than their goliath counterparts. Take a look at Golden Seeds, which funds female-driven businesses. This VC started as an angel community and is now a full-on investment organization. The "seeds" in their name refers to the first round of funding a company usually goes through.

Q: What's a seed round, and what comes after that?
A: There's no universal model for fund-raising, but here are the typical stages:

Stage one is the "seed capital" round of fund-raising. For early stage funds, you'll likely need about two or three meetings. There are some seed "accelerators," like Y Combinator, that help companies early on with tools (on top of money) to get their ideas to the next level of VC support.

Stage two is often known as the "Series A" round. This is usually when a company is ready to market and advertise their product.

Stage three is often known as "Series B" financing. This is typically the time where a company ups their manufacturing and production game and expands to a wider audience either geographically or through a bigger marketing push.

Stage four is often known as the "Series C" round, where the company is looking to additional markets and a diversification or expansion of products or offerings. This is when a company should have significant revenue and is likely a few years into business already.

Stage five is the "Mezzanine" or "Bridge" round, which is not a stage most companies get to because it's usually done right before funding an "initial public offering" (IPO) or acquiring strategic companies within their space.

Q: Is the value of the company different at each stage?

A. Yes. The company is valued at every stage, but remember, too many "rounds" can dilute a founder's stake in the company because you're giving up more of your stake every time.

HOW THE HELL DO I "VALUE" MY COMPANY?

Calculating the valuation of a company is like tying a shoe: there are a bunch of ways to do it and no one really knows how they did it once it's done.

The different ways to value a company are subjective, too. But the rub is that you're trying not to aim too low so that you're undervaluing your company and your stake in it, while also avoiding going too high so that you don't scare investors off. It's the same concept and psychology as pricing a piece of jewelry. You can list whatever you want on the price tag, but it's only as valuable as what someone will actually pay for it.

There are professional valuation consultants out there for hire, but here are some common valuation approaches:

Asset valuation. This is where you add up everything you own: 1) physical stuff like machinery and office furniture; 2) intellectual property like the trademarks, patents, and copyrights we talked about in the beginning of this step; 3) the value of your employees (in some tech companies, a good engineer can increase the company's valuation by a million dollars); 4) the value of your contracts and regular revenue.

Asset replacement cost valuation. This is basically the same as the above, just accounting for what it would cost now if you had to buy everything all over again.

Market approach. This is similar to looking at the selling price of other homes in your area before you put it on the market. What are other companies in your space valued at or sold for? How do you compare?

Income valuation. This is essentially your current or future profits.

Surprised that valuations aren't an exact science? I was, for sure. Valuing your company is more of an art than a science, despite the term *calculation*. You could say that your doggy day care is worth a million bucks. Great, no one will really argue with you; how could they? But if you are offering 1% of your company for $10,000, an investor will probably pass unless they think they can get a big return, which means you would have to sell it for $10 million for them to see ten times their money. Is that realistic? The only time valuations really truly matter is when there's an "exit" (which we will discuss in the last step of this section) and the valuation isn't just *on* paper but paper *in* your pocket.

Q: How do I find a VC?

A: Look to the National Venture Capital Association or TheFunded.com for a good list and reviews on VCs specializing in your product vertical.

Warning: Don't pay companies that offer you databases and leads. They are bogus, for the most part. Another saying in the investment community to keep in mind is "Money doesn't chase deals; deals chase money." It sounds trite, but if you are really killing it, VCs will beg you to put their money in. Seriously. For example, major investors couldn't put money into Uber or Airbnb now if they tried. *That's* the position every entrepreneur wants to be in.

Q: What do I say to a VC?

A: When you are initially reaching out to the ones that you've targeted from your research, don't send a business plan right away. Instead, send a sentence or two with the catchiest part of your elevator pitch. Oftentimes this is "the [insert buzzy company here] of [insert your industry]." Remember that Rent the Runway pitched itself as the "Netflix of fashion"? Alibaba pitched itself as the "Amazon of China." That formula is one that makes sense to a lot of VCs.

Q: What if they don't respond?

A: Send a short video pitch as a follow-up. Investors invest in people as much as (if not more so than) they do in businesses. An idea is nothing without the right person to execute it. When I invest, I always invest in the entrepreneur. It's a relationship business. If the first product fails, then I want to be there for the next one, because I believe in that person.

Q: How long does this process take?

A: It could take months; it could take longer. Once you do get bites, don't just take any money that comes your way. Seriously. Not all money is created equal. Taking VC money isn't an impersonal thing like borrowing from a bank. Some say you should choose an investor as carefully as you would choose your spouse; after all, your investor will be a partner for the life of the company. Make sure your values align, because you're stuck with them for better or worse, till exit do you part.

FYI

Not every company needs a big check to get a big payday.

Nasty Gal. Sophia Amoruso bootstrapped her company for five years before taking anyone else's money. She started on eBay and grew her business, at its peak, to more than $30 million in revenue.

TechCrunch. One of the most widely read tech sites around, which sold to AOL for $30 million in 2010, was actually bootstrapped five years earlier by Michael Arrington—who still held 85% of the company by the time payday came around. Cha-ching!

GoPro. Founder Nick Woodman moved back in with his parents after coming up with the idea for his mobile camera product. He turned $10K into a company now worth more than $10 billion.

There are growing pains with any businesses—trademark issues, structural screwups, and funding faux pas. If it were comfortable, it wouldn't be growth. And great things never come from comfort zones.

So, Boss Bitch, now's the time to get out of your comfort zone and get into your courage zone. Reality check: this is big, scary stuff. It's okay to have fear. You don't have to be fearless or flawless. You do, however, have to be relentless in chasing your dreams until you are breathless. And even then, you keep running.

BOTTOM LINE

Conventional Wisdom: Name recognition requires paid advertising and marketing.

The Real Deal: Well, sure, both of those things help. But if you choose a name with a high "stickiness" quotient, then word-of-mouth endorsements can often help more than paid advertising or marketing ever can. Don't stress too much over a name. There's a business adage that says, "If you're not embarrassed by your first iteration, you've waited too long." Plus, you can always change it later, like

Google (they started as BackRub ... seriously), BestBuy (they started as Sound of Music), and Pepsi (they started as Brad's Drink).

Conventional Wisdom: If I want my company to be a BFD (big fucking deal), then I need to set up a legit corporation.

The Real Deal: This one is true—mostly. But that corporation doesn't have to be one with a capital C, as in a C corp. Depending on your situation, goals, and timeline, a partnership, an LLC, or an S corp (like my company) might be a better fit for you. While it's always better to choose the best structure at the outset, your growing company might morph through several of these models over its life span. And that's okay, too.

Conventional Wisdom: My start-up needs VC money.

The Real Deal: Maybe. But taking VC money isn't the best route for most start-ups, especially the early stage ones, despite what you watch on *Shark Tank*. A venture capital fund will want a big payout for taking a big risk. If you are looking for money in the five to low six figures, an angel investor is a better option for you. The best funding you can get, though, is your own sweat equity.

STEP

TEAMWORK MAKES THE DREAM WORK

#Winning with an All-Star Team

If someone asks me what my favorite position is, I don't miss a beat: "My favorite position is CEO." This is the tagline I put on the T-shirts I told you I designed earlier in this section. So go ahead, humor me: What's your favorite position?

It could be CEO, like mine, or it could be president or vice president or manager or director or something totally different altogether, depending on your career or field. The important thing is: it should be the role you have at your company now. We're not talking about sexy time. And you would hope that if you asked one of your employees the same question, they would feel the same way. In this step of "Being the Boss of Your Own Business," I will teach you how to love your work, and how to have a work tribe you love and who loves you back.

BUILDING YOUR DREAM TEAM

Now that you've built out a scrappy, can-do team on a shoestring budget and gotten your business off to a rockin' start, you might be ready to invest in hiring people for more substantial roles. Building out a stellar executive team will provide your company with the leadership it needs to grow, but it's also a mega investment. Those roles might be taken by "first in" employees who have been with you from the beginning; however, if the personalities and skill sets required don't align with the people you already have in-house, you might need to hire from the outside.

DROP THE C WORD

BITCH TIP

As in *chief.* Not everyone you hire can be in the "C-suite." Especially when you are running a start-up, it looks weird (and a little cheesy) to have basically everyone in the company have a "chief" title. Instead, opt for titles like president, EVP, SVP, VP, etc. They can still be fun titles, as start-ups are obsessed with, like "VP of happiness" or "president of corporate fun." Try and keep the actual C-suite at max occupancy three roles, like the CEO, CMO, and COO.

Here are the positions you're going to need to fill as you round out your full-time, all-star staff:

1. *CEO.* The CEO is traditionally the founder or cofounder of a business and responsible for strategy, vision, execution, and raising capital. If you are a founder, this could be you, or not—some Boss Bitches don't want the responsibility that comes with the CEO role. It's fine (and actually shows strong self-awareness) to give the title to someone else in the company, or hire someone new, if that's what you think is the best thing to do. (And BTW, if you ever get to a place where you're in over your head, you or your investors might look for a more experienced CEO to take the captain's seat.) It's easy for a team with multiple cofounders to become territorial over the CEO role. It's best to try to choose someone and move on, keeping *cofounder* in everyone's title. If that just doesn't seem feasible, give co-CEO titles (for example, Birchbox has co-CEOs) but understand who is responsible for what. The CEO title might feel like a prize, but make sure you feel the same way about what it means to actually have that responsibility.

2. *Technology.* Whether this person is a cofounder or a developer you bring on from the start, a technical team member is critical to starting your business because they're going to build your website, proprietary software, or app. And yes, no matter what your business is, you need a website or an app. This applies whether you're rolling out a product, which will need a strong online presence to drive sales, or a service, which will also need a good presence online to woo new customers. Without them, you have nothing. Outsourcing development to an individual or a group on Elance may seem like a great and affordable option, but it's easy to get screwed when a stranger on another continent is running the show. . . . Sadly, I've been there, several times. First time, shame on the sketchy developers I found in India. Second time, shame on me.

3. *Creative.* A lot of new companies undervalue the absolute necessity for a creative type to join the team early on. They don't need to be a cofounder or receive as much equity as, say, a technical cofounder, but their role as an artistic visionary for a company is very important. From helping to create editorial content to mapping out the style guide for both your website and photo shoots, this person's aesthetic will be directly reflected in everything that is a consumer-facing part of your company. Sometimes this role can be outsourced to a consultant in year one, but don't overlook it.

4. *Public relations and marketing.* More and more importance is being placed upon hiring a PR person in-house or a firm to represent you and your company out there in the big, bad world. Publicists are expensive (prepare to budget a few thousand dollars per month *at least*), but they can be a critical part of your user acquisition strategy (aka getting more customers, aka making more money). Ideally, press hits = brand awareness = customers = successful companies. There is no harm in interviewing firms to represent you. They might have some good ideas for you on how to market yourself traditionally and digitally (that you can "borrow" even if you can't afford them yet).

5. *Legal.* A killer attorney who has experience with start-ups will most likely be the MVP of your team. If you plan to fund-raise, then an attorney is a must, as you will encounter *a lot* of fine print and regulations that you don't want to mess around with. Even if that isn't in your imminent future, starting with solid contracts and structure will be a (painful but) worthwhile investment. And, I promise, I wouldn't advocate paying big money if it *weren't* worth it.

6. *Advisors.* Every successful company has a team of advisors behind them. Sometimes your advisors are ad hoc, like parents, sig-os, or friends. But most often, you have an "official" board of advisors. These are people from different areas and industries; they might be consultants or retired executives who have the bandwidth to help emerging companies succeed like they did. Ideally, these people have some business clout so you can list them on your website and bolster your level of experience by association with theirs. Official boards sometimes get a very, very tiny piece of your company, like a fraction of a percent (or basis point*). In exchange, they (should) take your calls and help as needed with specific asks. I'm on the advisory board for About.me, a really cool and easy-to-use website that features your contact info and portfolio; it's basically your online business card. I provide advice to their employees and executives on how to present themselves in the media and help them promote new initiatives wherever possible. Think of your advisory board as your super mentors; they've got your back and are (literally) invested in the success of your company.

CONFESSIONS OF A
BOSS BITCH

Don't Get Crushed by the Trust Tree

When I was first starting out with my production company, Nothing But Gold, I hired a friend with whom I had worked for years. We were what business dreams are made of. He was smart, upbeat, and fiercely passionate about the financial markets (swoon). He won me and my team over, handily, and almost immediately we started pulling all-nighters (happily) fueled by coffee, pizza, and our dreams of creating the most badass array of accessible financial content out there.

But there was just one problem: in all of our feverish dreaming and team pow-wows, we failed to put anything down on paper. We got caught up in the feel-good adrenaline and ignored Lapin tenet numero uno: *get it in writing.* Even if it's with your bestie, as I've said before, you need to get every single work/employment-related thing down on paper. Period.

The understanding that we had (or so I thought) was that we'd both keep working gratis (that is, without pay) until our awesome company turned a profit, at which point we'd start collecting salaries like the rest of the team. At this point, I hadn't seen the glory of a salary in about six months, just like most founders of most recently launched companies. That was expected and no big deal. To me.

Apparently, it was a big deal to him—but we had never actually talked about that. So imagine my surprise when he called me up before a speech we were about to give together and dropped the bombshell that he needed to leave NBG to "get a real job." Um, excuse me? WHAT?!

We'd been through a lot of highs and lows at this point: new business ideas, fun parties, even surviving the threat of a potential lawsuit, and he'd never mentioned taking a salary—not once. I just assumed that we'd both wait to make it big . . . and then the cash would come. But I assumed wrong.

That is, until I took a step back and realized that this was 100% my fault. Sure, he could have been more straightforward about not being able to go sans salary. But, ultimately, making those expectations clear and *getting them in writing* was on me as the boss.

As upset as I was that our business love affair fizzled, I only had myself to blame. I assumed. And I got my ass handed to me because of it.

Before you welcome someone into your business tribe, have The Talk in the same way you would in a relationship (okay, maybe minus the "How many kids do we want to have?" part). Get it all down in writing, with a timeline and everything so that you don't have any surprises like I did.

SO YOU THINK YOU NEED AN ASSISTANT?

Well, so does everyone. The first thing you need to think about when potentially bringing on a right-hand woman is: Are you ready to be a manager? Because hiring an assistant automatically means you'll have someone else who is dependent on you: for their livelihood and also for career guidance. If you're not ready to be a manager, or to take the time to train and nurture this person and to assume the responsibility of paying them every month, you might be better off hiring an e-assistant like x.ai or AskSunday, which I mentioned in the previous section. These virtual services can help with scheduling, replying to e-mail, booking travel, and other mundane tasks without the time (and money) suck of managing an actual, living, breathing employee.

If, however, you're ready to have and in need of a real, in-the-flesh assistant, here's where to start:

Where to find one. I'm a big fan of posting on college and university career services bulletins, most of which are now available online to employers. Taking an assistant position is a great job for someone fresh out of college, or even grad school, as it offers exposure to a variety of different tasks and personalities and, hey, even cool stuff like travel and events, so you'll have no shortage of candidates. While you might get someone with less practical experience by going this route, you also get a clean slate; you can teach this person to get things done in exactly the way you want them done. You're also getting someone who's hungry to learn (and likely literally hungry) and will happily take the bus and eat ramen for dinner for the opportunity to hustle for you.

How to narrow down candidates. When I hired my first assistant, I had a stack of résumés from people who were all (overly) qualified. So I narrowed down the search by how they spoke on the phone. I wrote them all back thanking them for their submission and said that I would review it, but if they wanted more information, to call me, and gave out my number. I knew that I would send the unknown callers to voice mail, but I wanted to hear how they left a message.

The way they conducted themselves on a voice mail would be how they represented *me* if they worked for me. So the finalists were the ones who not only took the initiative to call the number but who also left professional, confident-sounding messages. (Yep, all of that schooling and all of that debt, and it might just be how strong your voice-mail game is that gets you a job!)

How to interview. I'd recommend conducting the first interview in your natural work habitat, whether that's a formal office or your local coffee shop. If this is where your recruit is going to be spending the most time, better to see how he or she works within that environment now. So don't pretend to have an office if you don't. How prepared your candidate is for the interview will tell you a lot. Does she show up with notes? Has she done her homework on who you are and what your brand/company stands for and what the work entails? Does this person ask targeted questions that shows she's an eager beaver/future Boss Bitch who wants to take on more? This is where you want to listen more than you talk and feel out your natural chemistry.

How to define the role. You can define it in any way you want as long as you are clear about your expectations, while also offering your candidate opportunities to grow outside of that "admin" job if the person so desires. Trust me: the best candidates will want to. Use a few examples of current projects to walk her through what her support role will look like day-to-day and to make her feel like she's an integral part of the team and the company's overall success. Having skin in the game from the outset is huge for getting anyone working under you to feel motivated.

What to pay. This will vary wildly depending on what part of the country your business is based in, but, in general, you should consider the following:

1. Is she working full- or part-time?
2. Will she be joining you in the office/on the road?
3. What does someone need to earn to live somewhat comfortably in your city?

Let's work backward through those criteria. While the average salary nationally for an assistant is around $35,000, that's not a livable wage in many places (especially major cities like New York and San Francisco, where the latte I say to buy anyway is 5 bucks). And it all depends on which type of business you run (an assistant to an established publicist, for example, will likely make less than an assistant to a budding jewelry designer). Do a little research on sites like Glassdoor to see what other people in your area are paying their assistants, factoring in average apartment rents. A homeless assistant is not a good assistant, so make sure she can afford the going rate for an apartment (with roommates, of course; remember what I said earlier about Boss Bitches paying their dues?). If you plan to have your assistant come into the office (versus working remotely, which may be perfectly acceptable for you, too), you should also factor in commuting costs and build in extra compensation if she'll be expected to hit the road with you. Then look at the total you arrive at. If she'll be with you full-time, offer that amount (plus maybe a little more on top if you can swing it, as an incentive for her to do an awesome job and not take her services elsewhere). If she'll be working part-time, adjust that amount according to whatever percentage of a traditional forty-hour week she'll be working—and maybe look at a basic bonus structure for going above and beyond those part-time hours. I love the incentive of a part-time hourly rate plus bonus structure to start. That way, you can both ease into the new role to make sure it's the right fit, and you'll be able to see whether she takes advantage of the bonus possibilities.

What to call her. Yes, call her by her name (obvi), but I'm talking about her official title. It's easy enough to go with *assistant*, but maybe this person supports your entire team, or perhaps you're grooming this employee for more. In those instances, another title might be 1) more appropriate to describing her true role on the team and 2) a more aspirational one for her to grow into. Let's say your new assistant will be supporting several people on your team, and you work in a creative field. She might be *creative associate* or *project coordinator.* Or will she be supporting the team but also providing operational oversight for your growing workforce, even if it's just interns? Then she might be *chief of staff.* Hoping to move her into a more senior position? Let her try on *creative specialist* or *business development associate* for size. These roles all appear to be fancier than your run-of-the-mill assistant, which looks great on paper for her and could inspire a more motivated employee for you.

*What's your ROI.** You're going to invest in your new wingwoman in very important ways: money, time, and trust. Protect that investment. Is the $35,000 (or $15/hour or whatever you choose) worth it to be more organized and have someone else tackle the day-to-day stuff so you can focus on the bigger picture? Or could that $35,000 be better invested in office space, new equipment or software, or perhaps two part-time hires (like an IT person and a freelance editor) who could make a bigger impact for the price of one? You will also need to hand over your trust wand to this person, because she will likely have access to your e-mail, your calendar, maybe even an expense account—not to mention handling minute details of projects you've previously handled alone. Are you okay with that? No one can judge the return on investment but you. But trust me on this: if you find "the one," the time she will free up for you to focus on other projects will be worth every penny.

JUST IN CASE . . . PLAY IT SAFE

BITCH TIP

Do me a favor and have all of your employees, but especially your assistant, sign a nondisclosure and nondisparagement agreement before they set foot in your office. The former means they won't share any insider secrets of your company after they leave (which is particularly crucial in start-up land), and the latter means they won't run to the press or anyone else and say terrible things about you. Hopefully, you'll never need to rely on either of these agreements. But in case shit goes south, you want to protect your intellectual property and reputation.

YOU BETTA COMPENSATE

As anyone who works with me (I hope) will tell you, I take very good care of my team. In fact, I would rather pay them than pay myself. My thinking: without them I would likely have much less money to offer.

As I mentioned before, it's not uncommon for key members of start-ups not to take a paycheck for a while, putting everything that comes in back into the company. That reinvestment typically helps the start-up get a strong start and creates the best chance for success and profitability later on.

Even if you aren't offering a salary to start, try to pony up some perks and incentives to woo away smart talent from other companies—or ensure that your own smart talent doesn't leave you and head elsewhere.

TAKE CARE OF THEIR HEALTH

Putting together your employee benefits package can feel like a conundrum: Do you offer juicy benefits to attract super-talented employees (and keep the employees you already have happy and healthy?) but forego profit to pay for them? Or do you cut back on the awesomeness of your benefits (and also the expense) but risk losing your best and brightest employees?

Unfortunately, there's no good answer, and as benefits costs (especially health care) continue to escalate, the best you can do is to strike a happy medium: find a benefits package that keeps your employees healthy but also doesn't make your bankroll ill.

Health insurance costs vary depending on company size, industry, and location. A good rule of thumb is to budget around 10–15% of overall payroll costs for health care. You have two main options when it comes to picking your company's plan:

1. *Traditional health insurance.* Plans typically come with super-high premiums but a wide selection of doctors and hospitals.
2. *Managed care.* Plans carry lower premiums but offer a smaller menu of service providers.

Both traditional insurance and managed care plans are sold by names you likely recognize, like Aetna, Blue Cross, Blue Shield, UnitedHealth Group, and Humana—and most states mandate that employers cover at least 50% of the premiums. Most small businesses lean toward the high-deductible plan options, which carry lower premiums but force employees to shoulder more of the treatment costs up front before the insurer kicks in.

HEALTH HACKS

BITCH TIP

You're not the first or the last start-up to try and make your employees happy and healthy without breaking the bank. Here are some resources that might be helpful as you are exploring your options:

Liazon helps start-ups mix and match elements of different health-care plans to find exactly what works for them.

Start-up Insurance acts like a broker to find tailor-made, custom insurance plans geared toward entrepreneurs and business owners.

Oscar offers a ton of different health plans and techie/start-up perks on top of them.

There are tons of different plans out there, so you should shop around and see which one works best for your, well, shop. The nice thing is that a lot of the health insurance providers *want* to get in the door at your place of business early on, hoping to grow their plans with you as you grow. So like anything else in life, you should negotiate the rates they offer; they might hook you up with a good deal if it means locking in some long-term business.

FYI

You should care about Obamacare, because if you fail to comply with the guidelines it lays out for compliant health insurance, you could be out *a lot* of cash. As of 2016, businesses with fifty-one to one hundred employees will face fines of $2,000 to $3,000 per year, *per employee* (!!!) if they don't provide Obamacare-compliant health insurance for their employees. And starting in 2017, those naughty companies who fail to offer the right insurance will be forced into insurance pools that could increase premiums by an average of 18%, which basically means they'd be forced to buy health insurance that's much more expensive than if they had just followed the rules in the first place. It's estimated that these changes will affect more than 150,000 businesses and more than 3 million workers. Boss Bitches don't like to get wrist-slapped by anyone, especially the government. Stay tuned, changes are definitely coming under the new president's administration.

If you aren't financially ready to provide full health insurance to employees, here are a few other options that can make them feel at least partially taken care of, even if they may have to go out and buy additional coverage on their own:

Health savings accounts (or HSAs) or flexible savings accounts (FSAs) allow employees to deposit pretax dollars to cover health-care costs not covered by high-deductible plans, like over-the-counter meds, contact lenses, and even Band-Aids. FSAs are particularly appealing to employers because any money left unspent by the employee goes back to the company (you) at the end of the year.

A *"wellness plan"* at the office can save a lot in the long run by offering your employees things like discounted gym memberships, counseling, and nutrition plans that keep them healthy over time. The thinking is that these preventative health measures, which can cost as little as $100 per employee per year, will mitigate the need for costlier health insurance or sick days down the road.

A *stipend* for employees is another way for small businesses to help off-set the cost of employees having to buy their own health insurance. This is either tacked onto the salary or comes as a separate check and is typically a couple hundred bucks, depending, of course, on the level of the employee and the size of the company.

RETIREMENT EMPOWERMENT

Yes, yes, I know, you're going to work until they bury you (you and me both, sister). Thinking about getting old can feel like a buzzkill for any young start-up. But part of being a strong leader is dealing with less-than-fun stuff, which means taking care of your future and your employees' futures (which is really what retirement is) like a boss.

Retirement options sound like alphabet soup. It's easy to get confused about what they all are, let alone what the letters actually stand for. If you came from the corporate world before starting a business, I'm sure you're familiar with the most popular option given by employers—the 401(k)—and an IRA/Roth IRA, which you (better have) contributed to on your own because these are *individual* retirement accounts.

The awesome thing about having your own business when it comes to retirement is: You have more options! Here are the three most popular ones broken down with pros and cons.

Solo 401(k). If you don't have employees, you can look at a solo 401(k), which is really just a one-woman 401(k) that you control. If you work for yourself and you're killing it, you should look at this as a great retirement vehicle. You control the costs and the investment options, and they are more advantageous than a regular 401(k) because there is a far higher contribution limit. In addition to the $18,000 you can invest annually as an employee—the same limit you'd have in a regular 401(k)—as an employer you can add matching funds up to 25% of your compensation for a total of up to $53,000 in 2016 (so you are basically reaping the benefits of being the employee *and* the employer).

Pros

High contributions. I know $53,000 sounds like a lot to pay toward retirement in a year. But your "future" self will thank you later if you can swing it now. One plus of a solo 401(k) is that you can contribute whatever you want toward that limit, and you don't have to contribute the same amount every year. If you have a good year, throw more in it; if you have a bad year, then throw in less or nada. Since solo 401(k) plans allow you to make contributions as both employer and employee, you may be able to save a larger percentage of your total income than you would through another type of plan.

Tax love. Contributions are tax-deductible as a business expense. But remember, you have to pay taxes when you retire/take the money out (like you would with a traditional 401[k]).

Calendar flexibility. You can set up your 401(k) at any time by the end of the year (even leave it until December 31, if you want); then you can contribute up to tax day for that previous year, once you see how your taxes shake out for that year. If it makes sense for you to contribute more to reduce your tax bill, then you can at that point.

Cons

Can be pricey. You have to pay to set this up (from $100–$300, depending on the maximum plan amount) and maintain it (annual fees of $10–$100/year). There are some plans, however, that don't have account service fees or minimum balance requirements.

Setup can be complicated. You have to find a plan administrator to set yours up; typically a brokerage like Charles Schwab, Fidelity, or Vanguard; or an advisor-sold plan, like Pioneer or ShareBuilder.

Reporting. Once you have $250K in the account, you have to report it using another fun tax form: a 5500.

SEP-IRA. This is a Simplified Employee Pension plan. It's a variation of an IRA just for businesses. The most important difference between a SEP and a 401(k) is that 100% of the contributions are made by you as the employer. The employee contributes nothing. You can allocate up to 25% of employee compensation (i.e., up to $265,000 for a maximum contribution of $53,000 in 2016 [25% of $265K is $53K], just like you can do with a solo 401[k]).

Pros

Easy setup (unlike a solo 401[k]). You fill out a 5305-SEP form and then just let your employees know. Bada bing, bada boom! This requires less paperwork than other plans while providing the flexibility to set aside a different percentage of income each year to put toward it.

Low maintenance. The setup fees and the administrative costs are nominal, and the ones you do have can be written off as a business expense.

Tax-friendly. No need to file annual reports with the IRS as with the solo 401(k). And employer contributions are tax-deductible to you.

Cons

No catch-up contributions (that is, additional money you can put in to "catch up" to the maximum contribution) over the age of 50 or a loan option like a 401(k) offers.

No Roth option, so taxes are owed when the money is taken out, like a 401(k). (And although they are tax-deductible now, you should pay taxes now, too, because by the time you retire you'll be in a higher tax bracket and taxes will be higher in general.)

No contribution variation. Contributions have to be the same for yourself and employees. Yours can't be higher, and all employees must participate.

SIMPLE. While the name makes you believe it's "simple," it isn't. It stands for Savings Incentive Match Plan for Employees, and it's another cousin of an IRA, like the SEP. The employer and employee (if the company has one hundred or fewer employees who earned $5K or more in payroll) can contribute to the plan, unlike a SEP. The limits are lower than the solo 401(k): $12,500 if you're under the age of 50, and $15,500 if you're over the age of 50 (so about $3,000 to $5,000 less than a solo 401[k], depending on how old you are).

Pros

Easy peasy affordable setup and maintenance. You just have to fill out a 5304 and a 5305 tax form and notify employees right after that, like you do with a SEP.

You have catch-up contributions for participants over the age of 50, but they are less than those with a solo 401(k).

No annoying IRS tests and reporting requirements (like a SEP and unlike a 401[k]).

Cons

No Roth option but tax-deductible like a SEP.

Crazy-high fees if you withdraw early. Normally, if you cancel a retirement plan, you pay a 10% penalty fee, but with a SIMPLE, the fees could be as high as 25%. Also, you can't roll your money into a new retirement account for the first two years after cancellation without even more penalties.

Contributions are mandatory. Even if you are having a bad year, you HAVE to make contributions, unlike with a solo 401(k). There are also more stringent calendar restrictions: you only have until October 1 to make contributions.

	SOLO 401(k)	SIMPLE IRA	SEP IRA
Who Can Contribute	Employee; employer optional	Employee & employer	Employer only; must contribute for all eligible employees
Max Employee Contribution	$18K with $6K catch-up if age 50 or older	$12.5K with $3K catch-up if age 50 or older	Not applicable

	SOLO 401(k)	SIMPLE IRA	SEP IRA
Employer Contributions	Optional, up to 100% of an employee's compensation with a $53K cap via match, profit share, or other employer contribution	Required match of 100% on the first 3% of participating employee contributions or 2% of all eligible employee salaries	Up to 25% of an employee's pay with a $53K cap
Vesting* Timing for Employer Contributions	Multiyear options or immediate	Immediate	Immediate
Access to Funds Before Age 59^1/$_2$	Penalty-free loans or 10% penalty for early withdrawal	25% penalty for withdrawing within first two years of participating; 10% thereafter	10% penalty for withdrawal

In addition to retirement options, you should encourage your employees to keep (or start) playing both the traditional and Roth IRA games. They can open both at virtually any bank or brokerage company (like Charles Schwab, Fidelity, TD Ameritrade). The total limit is $5,500/year for both, and you can split it whichever way you want. Here are the main differences between the two IRA types:

Individual Retirement Account (IRA)
- You get a tax deduction on contributions now.
- You pay taxes when you take the money out.

Roth IRA
- You don't get a tax deduction now.
- You don't pay taxes when you take the money out.
- My favorite option because, as I've alluded to in the options above, you are likely going to be in a higher tax bracket when you are older

292 | Nicole Lapin

(because you're going to make so much more money, duh) and taxes are going to go up. No one likes taxes, but you have to pay them one way or another. The better time to do it is *now*.

FYI

Generally, the philosophy is "the more the merrier" when it comes to retirement options. Using only one retirement option is likely going to leave you eating cat food in your old-lady years.

As an employee, it's best to take advantage of all retirement options available: a 401(k) or another plan at work *and* an IRA contribution (Roth or traditional or both!). Same goes for a business owner: pick one main vehicle, like a solo 401(k), SEP, or SIMPLE, max that puppy out, and also keep up your IRA contributions.

SERVING UP THE EQUITY PIE

Instead of paying for employees and contractors at face value with cash, many entrepreneurs pay with equity,* which is essentially giving someone a piece of your company. When you give someone equity in your company, it doesn't just mean you're giving them a slice of the pie as it bakes now; that slice will only continue to have more love and ingredients baked in over time, so what you are really giving them is the chance to enjoy that yumminess later, too.

Let's say you offer an employee 2% of your company that's valued at a big ol' zero now. That 2% is worth nothing today. But let's dream and say that your business grows into a $10 million business. That 2% is 200 grand. Now, that's one fucking delicious piece of pie.

When Facebook was founded by some guys who went to school together at Harvard, Mark Zuckerberg gave equity to his cofounders. One cofounder, Eduardo Saverin, received 2% of the company. That 2% is now worth $2 billion. (On a side note, he originally had 30% of equity in the company before falling out with Mark. If he'd retained that, he would have had $35 billion, putting him among the top ten richest people in the world.)

The reasons to offer equity are 1) it can help attract the best talent and 2) it incentivizes everyone to work harder. After all, the harder equity holders work to make the company as successful and profitable as it can be, the more lucrative *their* stake of it is.

There is no formula for divvying up equity. It's really up to the individual founders and the value of their employees, which only they will know best. The biggest questions founders face when it comes to equity are: "How much?" and "To whom?" How you approach this is up to you, of course, but here are a few general rules of thumb:

A *cofounder.* If you have one who has been a part of the business from day one, consider each other's roles and responsibilities and discuss equity early. You should think about who had the original idea, the skills they bring to the table, and additional elements they have that add value. (Can one of you guarantee press and make a ton of angel investor introductions, for example?) Don't let emotions and your friendship get in the way of this assessment. The equity conversation is a business one and should be as devoid of feelings as possible. There's no one right way. Sometimes it's a fifty–fifty split, but more often than not, it's something unique to the founders.

A *technical cofounder.* If you brought on a person who was integral to the foundation of your technology, it's not unusual to offer them 5% of your company.

Major executives. As I mentioned before, you might be able to get someone you can't afford in an executive role by offering them 1–5% equity.

Members of your board of directors or board of advisors. These people typically get a fraction of 1%, maybe 0.25% or 0.5%. Consultants shouldn't receive equity, but a lot of companies (PR, design/development shops, etc.) will take equity in exchange for payment. If you're super low on cash and must resort to this option to get going, do so carefully, because there is only so much pie to slice up and be eaten.

GET YOUR VEST ON

BITCH TIP

In the business world, *vesting* means that equity percentages or shares of stock don't come to you all at once. Instead, the stock "vests"—which is kind of like a waiting period—over a certain amount of time. Let's say you are giving out 10% of a company. You want that percentage to vest over some time, typically four or five years. That means that person doesn't get the 10% right away, because if they peace out in six months, they'll take that equity and the company is screwed. Only after those four or five years are up are they entitled to that full percentage. Having a vesting schedule protects you as a founder to make sure your equity holders don't just pick up and run with it.

CALLING BOGUS ON BONUSES

Don't give cash bonuses. No, I'm not being a grinch here, I'm just giving it to you straight up, no chaser. For a start-up, cash bonuses don't make sense for the following reasons:

1. *It's not about the money.* Contrary to traditional theories of economics, people don't want money when they join start-ups. I mean, they do, but generally they are in it more for the mission and the potential for future glory, which is something no cash bonus can buy. Employees of start-ups are a special breed. They want to build something significant, and because of that, equity options will incentivize them more than any one-time check will. Perks like bigger retirement and health-care options, in addition to equity, go much further for start-up employees than a quick hit of cash.

2. *Beware of "take the money and run."* Because equity should "vest" over time like I suggested above, it's a better retention tool than a cash bonus. Cash can also incentivize employees in the wrong way. Microsoft and Google, for example, are famous for having a flurry of employees stick around for their bonuses then leave the company soon thereafter. And while those employees have

their eye on the door until they get their bonuses, how do you think they perform? Do they go above and beyond? I. think. not.

3. *Don't shoot your wad.* Cash bonuses are not good for start-ups financially. As a fast-growing company, you are likely cash constrained. You should try and limit cash expenditures as much as possible. The only exception here is commission for sales reps.

You want your employees drinking your passion punch. Any compensation offered should act to incentivize them to feel invested in the company, its growth, and its success for the long run.

RUNNING THE OFFICE

You've heard stories of all the cool things companies might have: a Ping-Pong table, a pop-a-shot machine, or free gourmet food. When I was at Bloomberg, they had free freshly ground peanut butter. (I definitely took advantage of that, like, every day.)

These perks sound super awesome, but which of them really matters when you're trying to run a fun but efficient office? The short answer is: the more substantive ones. Run the kind of office that people are excited to show up at every morning—but also the kind of office where work actually gets done.

NO MORE POINTLESS MEETINGS

Meetings can be really useful and effective, but they can also be a total waste of time. The myth of the meeting is that it's a place where people get work done. That *can* be right; that is, until there are twelve meetings on your calendar a day and you are just running from one meeting to another with no time to follow up on any of the steps discussed in that meeting, never mind getting the rest of your work done like you should.

That's when meetings can be a total time suck—and even a money suck. There has been research estimating that $37 billion worth of productivity is wasted at companies during meetings held just for the sake of meetings. Imagine for a second if you could take just a small sliver of that amount back. Well . . . you can.

The first thing you should do is implement one meeting-free day per week. That's right—a full day, one each week, where no one is allowed to schedule meetings, just good ol'-fashioned work and talking to people on an as-needed basis for said work.

The second thing you should do is to have smarter (read: smaller) meetings. Jeff Bezos, the founder of Amazon, famously said if two boxes of pizza doesn't feed all the people in your meeting, then there are too many people. Aside from limiting the number of people invited to the meeting to only the most relevant ones, here are some other things to keep in mind when you plan your "meetings of the minds":

> *Have a leader.* Yes, I know, leaderless meetings are all the rage these days, but the truth is, to get the most out of a meeting you need one clear person in charge to set a specific desired outcome and an agenda, and to make sure that agenda is followed. Sheryl Sandberg, COO of Facebook, creates an agenda for what needs to be done in every meeting, and then she drives the conversation from one point to the next.
>
> *Take only the time you need.* Sandberg says if the time allotted for a meeting is thirty minutes, and it takes five minutes for all the points to be covered, then the meeting is over and she sends everyone back to work.
>
> *Stand and deliver.* Research has shown that meetings where people stand up are much more efficient, usually concluding within one-third of the time of a traditional meeting. So if it makes sense for your work environment, try it. Or take a walk. President Obama, Steve Jobs, and Mark Zuckerberg have been said to have done the biggest deals of their careers while walking and talking. Mark finalized his deal to buy WhatsApp while taking a long stroll with the messaging app's cofounder Jan Koum.
>
> *Rethink "weekly" anything.* The "weekly marketing meeting" . . . really? What usually happens in those meetings? You bullshit about things you did or want to do with no clear direction? You should never hold meetings that have no purpose other than the

fact that they're "on the calendar." Period. If that habit is hard to break, cut the meetings to half the time of what they used to be. Trimming the time from a meeting means bulking up productivity outside of the meeting.

CONFESSIONS OF A
BOSS BITCH

Do a Meeting Boot Camp

When I first started my business, I fell into the trap of holding meetings for the sake of meetings, thinking, "Oh, this person would be interesting to talk to" or "I think I could do *something* with this person" or "There's definitely '*there*, there.'"

I started taking so many meetings that I found I wasn't able to adequately follow up with the deliverables of the meeting I just took—because, yup, there I was, on to the next one.

Here was my solution: if I don't have a specific reason for meeting a person with a clear goal before going into that meeting, I pass on it.

Also, to whatever extent I can, I now try to schedule all of my meetings for the week in one day. Most of my meetings are out of the office (if I need to meet with one of my employees, I just do; we don't need a calendar invite for that), so scheduling them all back-to-back helps me with commute time. It also means that I get a blowout and put eyeliner on for that day but don't waste time on that the rest of the days when dry shampoo will do. Just keepin' it real!

Americans spend an average of thirty-one hours per month in meetings. That's almost four full workdays! While meetings have become an unavoidable (and often an annoying) staple of corporate life, you can at least make sure you're making them count now that you're in charge. There are actually online meeting calculators and an app called MMP Cost that help companies compute the actual cost of the meeting. You can enter the number of attendees and their average salary and then compute the total dollar value of those employees' time to assess whether that sit-down (or stand-up) is worth it.

MAKE THE OFFICE OPTIONAL
(OR AT LEAST PARTIALLY OPTIONAL)

Who said that work needs to be done in the office? Who said you need to be in the office five days a week? Well, unfortunately (outside Silicon Valley at least), a lot of companies.

If you take nothing else away from this book, remember that I want you to rethink conventional wisdom at every turn. Simply because it's "just the way it's always been done" doesn't mean that's the way it always needs to be done. You went into business so you can start thinking for yourself, right? So do that.

WORKING OUTSIDE? WHY NOT?

Who likes sitting in one place for a long time? Not it! People tend to get frustrated and antsy. To nip the restlessness in the bud, uproot your employees. Take the meeting outside, go to a café, go exercise . . . just do something to get employees out of their cramped workspaces and into the open air. There's really nothing like a breath of fresh air to get your people's creative juices flowing.

WORK FOUR DAYS A WEEK? WHY NOT?

Back in 2010, Utah ordered all of the state's 20,000-ish employees to work four days per week, ten hours a day, and take Friday off. The positive results were overwhelming. More than 75% of employees reported that they were happier, more focused, and more productive. There were fewer sick days, reduced overtime costs, and utility savings (if no one is there, you don't need to turn on the lights!). Think about taking a page from Utah's new employee handbook and making the four-day workweek work for you:

1. *Divvy up differently.* If you want your employees to work a strict forty hours a week (instead of, um, just working for as long as it takes for things to get done?), then think of the "4/10" rule that Utah came up with. Or, some companies have tried the "9/80" plan, where employees work eighty hours over nine business days, which gives them an extra day off every two weeks.

2. *Baby steps.* You don't need to make a sweeping change. Start with one four-day week per month and see how employees respond and how productivity fares.

Much has been written about how a shorter amount of concentrated time is more impactful and productive than a lot of unfocused time spent procrastinating or falling down Internet K-holes (yeah, you know, where you start shopping for shoes and end up on Wikipedia reading an article about the history of Jimmy Choo). If a four-day workweek isn't right for you, then it isn't right for you. Maybe a five-day workweek is, and that's fine. Just don't take it as a given and poo-poo anything that strays too far from it. Ultimately, don't forget: it's your company, your rules.

HAVE THE COOLEST OFFICE AROUND

From beanbags to nap pods, start-up offices have some pretty sick swag. And, yes, a good chevron print and a yellow accent wall *do* go a long way to brighten things up. But you know what goes even further? Things that make your employees' lives easier and better—not just more colorful. Here are some of my favorites, if and when you can afford them:

On-site dry cleaning. Some companies provide their employees with free laundry and dry-cleaning services at the office. If you don't want to pay for your employees' laundering, a nice perk is just to arrange with local cleaners for in-office pickups and drop-offs. For bulk deliveries like that, most cleaners will deliver for free.

Make it a family affair. Some companies offer fun classes on nights and weekends for their employees *and* their families. Offering people a chance to introduce their sig-o or their kids to their colleagues brings your team closer together. It also allows employees to kill a personal and professional bird with one stone, so to speak: there's so much pressure about "balance" that it's nice to check off something from both categories at one time sans guilt.

Walk their dog. Send a daily dog-walking service to take their pooch for a spin around the block so your employee doesn't have to worry about rushing home immediately after work to let them out. You might eke out another hour of productivity, and they'll appreciate you treating their fur baby as the legitimate member of their family that they are.

I've seen companies mow their employees lawn or even send a housekeeper to their home. The secret to these perks is that they are not only awesome for your employees, but, more important, they are helpful to you as their boss. Why? Because your employees are not spending their own time doing errands that would be a distraction or time suck when they could be doing, well, work.

WHO'S IN A BOSS BITCH'S ENTOURAGE?

If you want to grow your brand and your business, it's going to take an entourage to help you. But despite the name, you can still be scrappy and afford an entourage. These can be freelancers or consultants in addition to your staff that you don't need to hire full-time—but they still need to be thoughtful hires.

ACCOUNTANT

Given how complicated the paperwork is for setting up a business, whether you incorporate or not and whether you have employees or not, it's probably a good idea to get some professional help right from the start. A certified public accountant (CPA) can help you:

- File the incorporation papers with the state and apply for an employer identification number (EIN), which you'll need so you can file taxes or do business with other businesses.
- Review bookkeeping.
- File your monthly payroll taxes and arrange to have the money sent electronically directly from your business bank account.
- File your annual (or quarterly) business tax returns. (I'll decode some of this below.)
- Advise you on ways to mitigate your tax burden with deductions.

- Help you obtain workers' compensation, unemployment, and any other types of insurance you may need.

What's it gonna cost? Depending on where you operate your business and how large and complex it is, this might run you a few hundred to a few thousand dollars a year—but given how much time accounting can take every month, this might be money well spent. And it's tax-deductible money to boot.

HR, PAYROLL, AND BENEFITS FOLKS

More than 85% of companies now outsource this type of stuff. A professional employer organization (PEO) will take care of your payroll tax, HR, benefits (like retirement plans), and health insurance for you. In fact, since these companies work with lots of employers, they are able to pool all of those employees to get better rates on health care and workers' compensation insurance—which is great for both the company and the employees. ADP, XcelHR, Best Employment Solutions Team (BEST), TriNet, and Paychex are all highly rated PEOs that will assume the responsibility of vacation time, workers' comp, and insurance while freeing up your management time for actual content and projects. But keep in mind that what you're getting is an (admittedly fancy) call center; there is only so much customization you can provide with these off-campus resources, and as you grow and your biz becomes more complicated, it might be better to invest in actual humans to take care of, well, your actual humans.

What's it gonna cost? It's not cheap. Most PEOs charge based on the average salary of your employees and the number of employees you have. On average, this typically ranges from $1,000–$2,000 per employee per year (or around $60,000/year for a small company).

SOCIAL MEDIA COORDINATOR

These days, having a rock-star online footprint is key to any successful business. Remember, your online presence is an extension of your brand, and one that many potential customers and clients will see before anything else.

I can't tell you how many cool new start-ups I've "discovered" from their Instagram or Twitter accounts. The thing is, though, in order to run successful social campaigns, you need to "feed the machine," basically 24/7. This doesn't have to be a full-time position in the beginning (although it could be), but finding a freelance social media guru is a great way to go. Again, you're investing some major trust here, as you'll be handing her the keys to your social media kingdom: not just the usernames and passwords, but also the trust that she'll churn out content that's high quality and on brand.

What's it gonna cost? Depending on the size of your business, a good social media coordinator will run you $1,500/month; a great one will cost $3,000 but also run e-newsletter campaigns and manage your SEO and analytics. You should also budget in some advertising and bot dollars, even just a couple hundred bucks or so, so she can boost posts on social media and reply to your doting fans with clever emojis. And if you plan to use Google AdWords to boost your company in search (which I definitely recommend), figure in about $1,000 per month for ten or so keywords.

BLOGGER/CONTENT PROVIDER

Hopefully, you've taken my advice and hired a solid tech person right from the start, because in today's digital-first landscape you're going to need one. Where you can afford to go the freelance route is with someone to populate content across all of your platforms, whether it's to provide editorial direction across your blog or to ghostwrite for other forums and blogs. Finding a smart journalism student or young magazine reporter to work for you as a side hustle can be a great way to keep up with your content obligations and keep your work (and your face!) "out there" without breaking the bank.

What's it gonna cost? Five hundred per month is the going rate for this type of work, if you want someone keeping an eye on your editorial profile on the regular. If you go the per-project route, work out a deal where your freelancer is paid based on traffic or number of clicks to incentivize her to share the content on social and get the word out. After all, as badass as the content might be, it sucks ass if no one sees it.

SPEAKING AND EVENTS COORDINATOR

If public appearances and events are part of your job, it can be a huge help to find someone to arrange and "produce" these for you. Whether it's negotiating contracts for speaking engagements on your behalf; conducting research and preparing talking points for the speech; or dealing with logistics like venue rental and ground transportation, an events pro can take some of these logistical nightmares off your plate.

What's it gonna cost? A good events coordinator will work part-time for $20,000 or so per year, which could be a great option if you have regular events. Otherwise, if you just need a little extra help for one-off engagements, hire on a per-project basis for $1,000–$5,000/pop, depending on the size of the event. Some will also charge a percentage commission based on how much you're getting paid to be there.

CONFESSIONS OF A
BOSS BITCH

My Boss Bitch Entourage

People ask me all the time what my entourage of agents, PR folks, and business people costs—and let me tell you, face-to-face, that they are not cheap. In the same way that we need to start being more open with how much we make, we could also stand to be more open about how much we pay for the support we need. So here's my breakdown:

WHO THEY ARE	HOW MUCH THEY COST
Manager	10% of all earnings
Agent	10% of all earnings
Speakers bureau	10% of speaking fee
Literary agent	15% of book advance
Entertainment lawyer	5% of all deals
Corporate lawyer	$300/hour
Public relations	$2,500/month

Accountant	$750/month retainer
Digital/social media producer	$1,600/month
Assistant	$5,000/month

What I hope you can see here is how quickly all of that great money you have coming in goes right back out. After everyone in your entourage takes their cut of a $100K deal, for example, that deal quickly withers to less than half of the original amount (not counting taxes). And that's okay: a Boss Bitch understands that one of the best investments she will ever make in herself and her brand is in her team. The more you make, the more *they* make, and in turn the more they help *you* make—just make sure the value they add is worth it to the overall financial health of your operation. Otherwise, it's time to cut some spending calories and trim the fat so you can be a leaner, meaner business overall.

The costs above are specific to me, and might be similar for those who work in the media world. Boss Bitches in other fields or industries might need a totally different "support system." Maybe you run an online clothing site and need an additional freelance IT person on hand (in addition to the in-house techie you hopefully hired to help with web-related emergencies, like if the site crashes or the servers go down). That could be $500–$2,000/month, depending on the scope and technicality of the project. Or maybe you need a designated distribution person to handle shipping products; this might cost you $500–$1,000, depending on their hours. Every industry has their own "people"—who are yours, Boss Bitch?

TAXES ISN'T A FOUR-LETTER WORD (BUT IT SHOULD BE)

They say that the only two things certain in life are death and taxes. Well, in business, there are two certainties: failure and taxes. But do yourself a favor and keep those two things separate. Because while it's okay to fail in other aspects of your business, you do NOT want to fail with your taxes.

In the last step, we went over taxes in the context of the structure of your business; now let's discuss how they relate to your employees. Even if you hire an accountant, you need to know how to talk the talk yourself. The IRS talk might not be fun, bitches. But neither is getting audited.

PAYROLL TAX

Past-due payroll taxes can cause you huge penalties. And not to scare you, but fucking them up can also lead to a federal criminal investigation and/or losing your business. Sadly for us, the IRS has found that small businesses are the biggest tax evaders in the system, so there's much more scrutiny on them. So, as much as taxes make you want to break out in hives, listen up: here are some payroll tax dos and don'ts.

DO make sure you are withholding money from employees' salaries for Social Security, Medicare, and FICA taxes. (Yes, yes, I know. . . . No one is banking on Social Security and Medicare, but you still have to pay it.)

DON'T spend the money you withheld from their salaries or use it for something else. Some businesses get in big trouble if they "borrow" from payroll taxes for their business's operating expenses. The money taken out of paychecks is for the government, not you.

DO make sure you make a federal tax deposit (by phone or at the bank or via a tax filing service) three days after the date the payroll checks are issued. Otherwise, you face late penalties, which start around $60 and can snowball into the hundreds.

DON'T assume that just because you failed to file but didn't fail to pay means you're off the hook. There are three major payroll tax penalties: failure to file, failure to deposit, and failure to pay. They can add up crazy fast—up to 33% plus interest—if you don't pay within sixteen days after you file your 941 (payroll tax return).

DO know that all business owners, whether you have a corporation or an LLC, need to make sure that they are on top of payroll taxes, if they have employees. The IRS is the only creditor that can go after individuals no matter the structure of the business. They have something called the Trust Fund Recovery Penalty (TFRP) that penalizes individual owners and shareholders.

DON'T bury your head in the sand if you get audited. Just like it's a bad idea to represent yourself in court, it's a bad idea to take this on alone. Since this particular area can have criminal ramifications, you need to get a tax attorney and/or a certified tax resolution specialist. Besides, if you took my entourage advice, you already have an accountant. So turn the process over to them. That's why you hired them in the first place.

FREELANCERS

Does your business employ freelancers? As you probably know by now, because you've been one or worked with one (they're increasingly common in our postrecession workforce), freelance employees can be wildly helpful to a budding business. They bring valuable skills and perspectives to the table for short-term projects or help out as you need them without the hassle of hiring a full-time employee. But you are still tax beholden to these temp hires. If your freelancers make $600 or more from you during a single year, you don't have to pay payroll taxes, but you *are* required to create and file a 1099 form at the end of the year for each freelancer.

If your freelancers incur any expenses while working for you, you'll also need them to save the receipts for reimbursement and file those as business expenses as you would any other employee. Pro tip: My team and I have a "close-out" period with our freelancers in which we allow for a nice runway of time to clean up our affairs on both ends before the project is officially over. During this time, we collect their W9s and gather any expenses. Why? Because it can be a bitch (the *bad* kind) trying to track down a freelancer months after you've stopped working together, especially to ask them to fill out tax paperwork and provide receipts they've likely lost in the meantime. Do it now and save yourself the hassle later.

TAX DEDUCTIONS

It's this simple: the more tax deductions you take (the more *legit* ones, anyway . . .), the lower your overall taxable profit—which means mo' money in your company's pockets at the end of the year. You can write off some pretty surprising things, and even get creative with mixing a little business and pleasure (i.e., tacking a personal vacation on to the end of a business trip so you can write off the flight . . . but not the hotel nights "for pleasure").

As long as you have ample and organized receipts, you can make a claim for the following things as a business:

Auto expenses. If you use your car for business, you can deduct some of the costs of keeping it on the road, including gas and mainte-nance. You can either keep track of these expenses the same way you would any other (i.e., saving receipts, using software, or high-lighting your credit card statements) or use the IRS's standard mile-age rate (you can find the current rate on their website) to deduct a certain amount for each mile driven, plus tolls and parking fees.

Travel. If you travel for business, you can deduct airfare, taxis, hotels, meals, shipping business materials, cleaning clothes, telephone calls, and even tips. And what about combining business and plea-sure, as I mentioned before? Totally kosher, as long as business is the *primary* purpose of the trip. (And, if you take your spouse or family along, you only get to deduct *your* own expenses.)

Entertaining. When you pick up the tab for taking out present or pro-spective customers, say, to dinner, you can deduct 50% of the cost IF (and only if) it's directly related to the business *and* business is discussed there (not just gossip and small talk, no matter how well you hit it off), or if the dinner takes place immediately before or after a business discussion. So, a catered lunch in the office for clients? Totally fine. Meeting a friend who happens to work for one of your clients for tapas and no business was discussed? Nope, sorry.

The cost of getting off the ground. The costs of getting a business started are called capital expenses*—and you can deduct $5,000 worth of them during the first year you're in business. Make the most of that first year, because any remainder must be deducted in equal amounts over the next fifteen years.

Books and legal and professional fees. Yes, you can deduct the cost of textbooks, including those that help you DIY legal and tax stuff (woot!). Fees that you pay to lawyers, accountants, or consultants can also be deducted during the year you use 'em. However, if the work clearly relates to future years, you have to deduct them over the life of the service you get from the lawyer or other professional.

Educational expenses. If they are related to your current business, trade, or occupation, you can deduct educational expenses as long as they are for maintaining or improving skills required in your present job. (No, sadly, that kickboxing class is not deductible and neither is the cost of classes that qualify you for a *new* job.)

Moving expenses. If you move because of your business or job, you can likely deduct some of those relocation costs, like boxes, tape, and a moving truck, which normally would fall into the category of nondeductible personal living expenses. To qualify, you must have moved in connection with your business (or job, if you go back to being an employee of someone else's business), and your new place of work must be at least fifty miles farther from your old home than your old workplace was (so upgrading into a sweet new pad in the same 'hood doesn't qualify).

Advertising and promotion. Getting the word out about your biz can have huge tax benefits (in addition to the other obvious ones). For real: If you're ordering business cards, Facebook ads, etc., you can deduct these costs as a current expense. Promotional costs that are also good for business, like sponsoring your local girls' recreational basketball team, are also deductible as long as there's a clear connection between the sponsorship and your business (like putting your company's name on their uniforms . . . adorbs!).

Charitable contributions. If you've structured your company as a partnership, an LLC, or an S corp, your business can make a donation to charity and pass the deduction through to you to claim on your individual tax return. C corps can deduct charitable donations outright. If you've got some old computer equipment or office furniture lying around, donating it to a school or nonprofit can give you a great tax benefit (plus, just be a good person, thanks).

While you should always, always, always try and save receipts for any business expense (and, better yet, jot down a few notes of "evidence" on each one, including how it was used, who you met with, where the expense led from a business standpoint, etc.), remember that you can still deduct expenses if you've lost the receipt. No expense is too small. But in the event that you're audited,* you want to make sure that you have some backup documentation for the IRS to prove you were spending responsibly, not just making it rain.

BITCH TIP

EMPLOYEE EXPENSE TRACKING

Come up with a system for tracking expenses for you and your employees so that come tax time you'll have all your ducks in a row (and you can keep tabs on your team during the year to make sure no one's getting crazy with the rental cars and client lunches).

Some of my favorite apps for this are:

- BizXpenseTracker
- Concur
- Expensify

They will make your life easier by helping you track your expenses and allowing you to connect your company credit card for easy automatic payments at the end of each month. If your peeps are traveling a lot, try Mileage Log+; it tracks your employees' gas miles and IRS rates so you know exactly how much to reimburse them.

When you first started a business, I'm sure some people told you that you were crazy. I know some people certainly called *me* crazy (okay, a lot of them still do). Those people are my biggest motivators. And the biggest victory in business for me is when the people who called me crazy call me for favors. So, keep hustling, girl, until your haters ask if you're hiring.

BOTTOM LINE

Conventional Wisdom: I need to hire a team ASAP; after all, I can't crush it alone!

The Real Deal: Yes—and no. You will certainly need help in these early stages, but don't go bananas on adding dozens of costly employees at a time to your ever-growing payroll. That will come. Instead, see what you can creatively outsource on a freelance or part-time basis, especially where a specialist is required so that you can focus your time and resources on managing your core crew.

Conventional Wisdom: I can skimp on benefits as long as I offer competitive salaries.

The Real Deal: Just like this mattered to you when you were looking for a new job, it matters to prospective hires. In today's insanely competitive world, you're gonna need a solid benefits package to attract top talent. It's high time you start thinking of your employees' benefits packages as one and the same with their salaries. But don't offer perks just to offer perks; offer the right perks to keep your employees motivated and focused, regardless of what's going on outside the office.

Conventional Wisdom: Look at me, I'm working soooo hard. I have soooo many meetings.

The Real Deal: Well, mazel tov if your job is as a professional meeting taker or maker, but I doubt it is ('cause that's not even a thing). Sorry, but meetings for the sake of meetings are not productive. In fact, they are often counterproductive because they take away from the work you are actually supposed to be doing. So instead of working "so hard" that you're hardly working, get your meeting situation under control. Your productivity will thank you.

GIRLS JUST WANNA HAVE FUNDS

*Making Money and Losing Money
(Without Losing Yourself)*

When it comes to bars, Boss Bitches don't hop them—we raise them. There's no such thing as having "arrived." The key to success is to keep striving, to keep getting better and better. Once you've reached one goal, make another, bigger one. Whenever I feel stuck or spent or burned out (and I do), I think: "I haven't come this far to *only* come this far." And neither have you, bitch. So let's keep going.

In the last step of "Being the Boss of Your Own Business," I'm going to teach you how to keep raising that bar—then raising it some more—until you start dancing on it because you've turned your business into bank.

STEP IT UP

By now, your business is officially out of "beta" and on its way to the big-time. There was a time for scraping by on a bootstrap budget and sacrificing everything (resources, sleep, sanity) to turn your side hustle into a legit business. But that was then. This is now—and *now* is when it starts getting interesting. Now is the time to go big or go home.

In the lead-up to this fifth and final step, you defined your passions, structured your business, and built out your team. All of that hard work has given you a solid foundation upon which to build the business of your dreams. But don't go hiring the interior decorator just yet; there is still a lot of work to be done. You've gotta work until your bank account looks like your phone number (lots of digits!)—and know how to pivot if it doesn't.

Working your ass off has been a given. Remember, working like that for something you don't care about is called *stress*. But working for something you *love* is called *passion*. And while you can get paid without having passion, if you have passion, you should also be paid. So let's get paid, bitches!

DON'T FORGET THE GHOSTS OF BUSINESSES PAST

I'm not here to give you a history lesson, but I do want you to be well versed in the recent history and trends of start-ups. Some of it isn't so cute, but in order to avoid the missteps of those who came before you, you need to know what they were so you can walk your own way in style.

Let's go back to how tech companies partied like it was 1999 back in, well, 1999—a time otherwise known as the "dot-com bubble." Wall Street invested lavishly, as did angel investors, and it seemed like there was a new IPO every week. But there wasn't much substance to most of these enterprises, or at least not enough to warrant all the money they were getting. It was what the Street called "irrational exuberance." And, just like how it sounds, it meant that tech companies were getting and taking ridiculous (irrational) amounts of cash, and that cash was changing hands fast and furious (exuberantly). Companies would lease huge office spaces and then fill them with staff and more staff, as though square footage and head count were in and of themselves signs of success. But the go-go days would soon come to an end. In most cases, waves of layoffs followed, and companies found themselves collapsing under the weight of their broken dreams. And just as quickly as it had started, the dot-com bubble burst—and it all came crashing down.

I tell you this cautionary tale to remind you that even when things feel like they are rockin' for you, keep yourself grounded and don't get too big for your britches. Watch your back at all times because you never know who or what is coming after you. A lot of people achieve success quickly,

Not a lot sustain that success. One of the surefire ways to go the way of all those failed late-'90s companies is to try to grow too big too fast. Just like on the slopes, in order to keep sustained momentum, you can't go too fast too quickly or you'll tumble over your skis.

Despite all the hyped-up instant-success stories you heard in the press, in reality, most of those successful entrepreneurs worked at building their "instant" successes for *a while.* It took a long time for the greatest companies of our time to become . . . the greatest companies of our time. For example, when Microsoft went public in 1986, founder Bill Gates made $350 million "overnight." But he'd been at it for more than ten years, hustling day in and day out to land a contract with IBM to create the operating system for their new PC computers—a contract that would seal their fate as a computer goliath for decades to come.

Most great entrepreneurs have stories like this. To quote one of my favorite movies of all time, *A League of Their Own,* "It's supposed to be hard. If it wasn't hard, everyone would do it. The hard . . . is what makes it great."

ARE YOU GROWING OR ARE YOU JUST GAINING TRACTION?

Of course, the most important factor to stepping it up a notch is growth. Don't get me wrong, Boss Bitches got nothing against gaining traction. But I'm talking about *real* growth here. It sounds so obvious, but you have to ask yourself: Is your baby really growing, or is it just putting on some pounds that *look* like growth?

1. While growth rates vary from week to week, are your sales year over year seeing positive growth?
2. Is that growth more than 1–3%?
3. Are your customers reliable, repeat, loyal customers?
4. Do you have money not only to keep the doors open but also cash reserves in case something breaks or if you have to replace or upgrade equipment or systems?
5. Do you have a trusted team in place to help you make decisions? If you left for a couple of days, would everything still run smoothly?

If you answered YES to all of the questions above, then you are likely experiencing a good amount of growth. If not, you're likely just gaining traction, which is fine, but it's not enough momentum for a sustainable growth wave that successful start-ups ride.

To get a little economics-y on you, when businesses start out, they likely experience a "survival period" where they are treading water to see if there's something "*there*, there." If there is, the next stage is growth, followed by takeoff—the most significant part of a business cycle. Imagine an S curve from your high school math class days (sorry to bring you back there). The slope up to the top of the S is the takeoff phase that comes after the curve up from the bottom growth phase. So in order to achieve liftoff, you need that growth to launch you into another business stratosphere.

BE THE BEST, NBD

If you watch *The Office*, you might remember this line: "Always think one step ahead, like a carpenter who makes stairs."

Foresight is the most important start-up success strategy. Regardless of the type of business you have, your efforts toward supersonic growth should have one goal: to be the best at something. And by that I mean to be superior in *one* thing, not a list of things. Too many companies fail to ride that one big wave as far as possible because they are too distracted trying to catch every single wave that comes their way. So go ahead, answer this question: "I want my company to be the best at _____."

This answer is what you want to be known for, in one or two words. It's such a simple question, but often founders don't ask it—or, more unfortunately, don't communicate the answer to their team. Yet that seemingly basic question is the cornerstone upon which any good strategy is going to rest. What is the one thing you are going to be the best at? Even if you are good at a lot of things, what are you going to be *known* for? Then reverse engineer to figure out how to get there.

Let's look at Mrs. Field's. That brand is known for their cookies. They do other things, but if you ask anyone, they will likely say that the company bakes and sells cookies. Same thing goes for Tony Roma's restaurant. Their employees and customers would all agree that they are the best at making ribs even though they obviously serve more than that. Figuring out what *you* are the best at not only helps employees focus on a clear mission for the company but attracts better talent, because potential employees can easily understand and believe in that mission. Just as important, figuring out the answer to that question also helps your customers understand who you are and what you're about, and thus should be the driving force and inspiration behind your marketing messaging. The greatest business leaders design the company's entire strategy around making money off of what the company is best at—but you can't make money off of something until you know what that something is.

WHAT'S YOUR MONEY MODEL?

Don't get intimidated by models and charts that illustrate how to grow your business's moneymaking potential. Most of these are unnecessarily complicated and confusing. IMHO, the most useful business model you can come up with is one that simply connects the dots between the major touch points of your business. Start with a common, well-known structure, like this one:

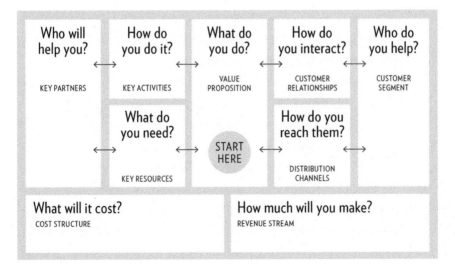

316 | Nicole Lapin

This structure is super easy to re-create on a whiteboard. (Pro tip: Write your answers on sticky notes so that you can move them around as you are "painting" a picture of your business story.) Okay, so how to attack this? I would start on the top right, with customers. *Who are they?* The answer to that goes in the "customer" box. *What do they want?* The answer to that goes in the "value proposition" box. *What are the ways in which you give customers value?* That answer goes in the "channels" box. *And how do you make money from that transaction?* That goes in the "revenue" box. Now you are starting to understand how your business generates revenue, what works, and what needs to be reconfigured. Getting to the bottom of your financial model will help you articulate how and why you make money, which is essentially what a business model aims to do. See if your business fits into one or more of these common types:

> *Cut prices and gain a large audience.* This is Amazon's model. They slashed prices across every sector in order to gain market share, then figured out how to profit later. For as large of a company as it is ($75 billion), their net profits (remember, Richard Branson taught us what that means) are actually tiny, although their customer base is, well, Amazonian, and their stock price is through the roof.
>
> *Create aggregate demand.** This is the eBay business model. They hook up both sides of the equation. The sellers get the largest swath of buyers in one place, and the buyers get a wide selection of products to choose from. By bringing the buyers and sellers together, they make the biggest bang for their buck.
>
> *Franchise.** Yes, this is the Golden Arches model. If you create good systems like we talked about above, you can consider finding other like-minded entrepreneurs to open up and manage independent locations and operations. Just be sure you've given them a clear playbook for how to do it—not to mention the recipe for that special sauce you have.
>
> *Hold a reverse auction.** What do you have and how much will someone pay for it? This is Priceline's model. If you add a share economy segment to this, that's Airbnb's model.

Your model can look like any of these, a derivative (or portion) of them, or a combination. But, in a business landscape that's changing as rapidly as ours is today—with new companies and new products and new ways of doing business surfacing like crazy—what was profitable yesterday might not be profitable tomorrow. So always be ready to iterate.

FYI

When you are selling an actual product, the business models are relatively the same: make more stuff more cheaply and sell it to more people. But in tech land, where you're selling something intangible, this model goes out the window. If you're running a tech start-up or a company that has a big web presence, here are the three major revenue models you can choose from:

1. *Free product.* If you are giving your product away for free, like Facebook, the most obvious revenue stream comes from ads.
2. *Freemium.* This model is used by LinkedIn. You give away a "basic" product for free, but premium versions come with extra bells and whistles (like souped-up job search features) and cost more.
3. *Subscription.* If you are a subscription model, you are relying on monthly or yearly recurring payments in exchange for a service, like BarkBox (basically Birchbox for dogs).

Check back and rejigger your model at least once per year, or after major milestones like closing out a round of fund-raising or launching a big new product. Is there a new opportunity to create a do-it-yourself variation of your product for those who can't afford it? That not only gives you a different customer base but a different source of revenue, too. As you fine-tune and hone, here are some dos and don'ts to make your ever-changing business model keep showing you the money:

DO create your own luck. Luck is just being ready for every opportunity. Plan out what's ahead and be ready, well-versed, and studied when the time comes.

DON'T delegate the important stuff. When it comes to major moves and decisions, that's all you, baby. Even if you are juggling a lot of moving business parts, you shouldn't assume that anyone can do what you've done to get there. Yahoo! CEO Marissa Mayer works ninety hours a week, making it known that she isn't CEO in name only.

DO keep testing every step of the way. A trick some entrepreneurs use to figure out their pricing models (which continually change) is to keep buying and selling their own product on eBay or Craigslist. What's the highest price you can get for it? How did you get that price? What changed? Was it the headline? Was it posting a different picture? This is what I mean when I talk about getting your MBA at the school of hard knocks.

DON'T assume that just because it *looks* easy for the winners in business that it is. Don't sit back with your CEO business card just following the footsteps of successful Boss Bitches who came before you. Pave your own way instead.

DO live like you're poor. Two-thirds of America's millionaires are self-employed, and a vast majority live below their means. Remember, the rich stay rich by acting like they are poor, and the poor stay poor by acting like they are rich.

DON'T sit on a mountain of cash and get lazy. You might be saying, "Who, me?! Never." But it's tempting to play the "we will worry about that later" game that comes from the comfort of having money or funding. That mentality kills the hustle that got you the money in the first place.

INTRODUCE YOURSELF LIKE A BOSS

Now that you are growing like a boss, you need to start introducing yourself like a boss, too.

So instead of saying, "I'm Avery, and I own a small boutique that aims to reach Charlotte's growing young female population," say this: "I'm Avery, and I own the only clothing franchise that provides 3-D fit imaging for custom tailoring. We are the go-to destination for Charlotte's young female shoppers and will soon expand into the rest of North Carolina and beyond."

Cut out "small business" from your vocabulary altogether. No business owner I know has ever wanted to be called "small." In our minds, we are a big business for whatever we are doing and whichever market we reach. Project that feeling to the world by framing all introductions of your business around your confidence in the brand, potential for growth, and being awesome at that one thing.

CREATE A MINI-ME ARMY

As your company grows, so will your staff. And as your staff grows, so will the challenges of keeping everyone on track, organized, and aligned toward the company's larger goals. This is why big businesses have complicated "systems" (think software like Salesforce and Basecamp) for coordinating and managing work among their employees. While they might spend millions of dollars a year on a method to streamline and organize work flow, division of labor, and daily tasks, there's no reason you can't do the same thing on the cheap.

It might be frustrating at first to come up with a system for how to do regular tasks. In fact, it will likely take you longer to explain to others how to do normal operational stuff than to just do it yourself. But now that you have hired an army of people, many of whom will be performing at least some of the same duties, you'll save yourself a whole lot of time if you have a uniform checklist in place explaining to those new hires how to get done what needs to get done—the way you want it done. The more you streamline and "routine-ize" the more mundane aspects of your work, the more you can focus on driving the strategy and business development that will result in even more growth. Don't waste your sweat (equity) on the small stuff.

CELEBRATE GOOD TIMES, COME ON!

Taking a quick beat to celebrate your successes is not just good for the soul; it's good for morale. Offering small rewards and shout-outs for your staff when they crush it makes them feel appreciated and incentivizes them to continue to do a good job. It could be something as big as a product launch or something as small as adding another room to your WeWork office, but these business milestones warrant a brief hurrah.

Here are a few ways to pump up the jam before moving on to the next big thing:

Give out a small, spontaneous bonus to everyone in the office. Whether it's a crisp $50 or a $25 gift card to Starbucks, bonuses don't have to be of the four-figure variety to make an impact (and you know by now how I feel about major cash bonuses).

Hire a masseuse to come to the office for a day. Treat your employees to free fifteen-minute neck massages.

Free food. Those two little words go a long way in *any* office. Call a local food truck for curbside munchies or order in the fixings for a sundae bar.

A few little pick-me-ups like these will keep your team motivated—and keep them from moving on to someplace else, too. Human capital can be just as (if not more) valuable than financial capital. If you celebrate your smaller successes (and they might be quite small in the early days), then you'll be more likely to build bigger ones together.

THE LITTLE GROWTH ENGINE THAT COULD

You've reached a point where "I think I can, I think I can" has turned into "I know I can, I know I can." Here are some strategies to help you rev your growth engine in a way that doesn't just take you from 0 to 60 mph but keeps you accelerating toward your goals even after you've reached your stride:

Find partners. Strategic partners outside of your particular industry can help recruit new users or customers by tapping into other companies with a similar target but different product base. An example would be Uber's 2013 partnership with the NFL. The NFL was able to encourage their fans to take safe rides, and Uber was able to reach a more mainstream audience, which it needed to grow exponentially back then.

Joint ventures. This is a simple agreement with another business that reaches your target demographic. Perhaps it's cohosting an event or sharing like-minded services. In the past, I've teamed up with women's charities like Step Up or professional groups like Levo League to cobrand events where I teach women about business and finance. In turn, I promote the work of these organizations to my mailing list and in the media.

Say yes to saying no. As your company and its reputation grows, so will the opportunities that come a-knockin'. I know, I know, high-class problems. But here's the thing: many of these opportunities won't make sense to your mission—they won't get you closer to your answer to the question "What do you want to be best at?" that we talked about earlier. Remember our "hell yes" litmus test from Section 2? Use that here. If it's not a hell yes, then it's a no.

Embrace market segmentation. How do you differentiate yourself from your main competitor? Find your niche and own it. You'll never win trying to be all things to all customers.

Go shopping for competitors. You might think I'm crazy, but big business does this all the time. They buy competitors to increase market share. You might be thinking, "Are you joking, Lapin?! How the hell am I going to buy a whole other business?!" The truth is, you can if it's the right business or right product. It doesn't need to be a large acquisition as long as it's a strategic one. If you own a vegan bakery and there is a young, scrappy vegan chef who has been gaining traction selling her vegan brownies all over town, you might consider buying her business. Chances are it wouldn't be expensive in the scheme of things to bring your competition on board, even at the early stages, and capitalize on their clientele and possibly their expertise if they stay on and work for your company.

Develop new products and services. Think about how you can expand your product or service offerings. Start brainstorming new products that can generate sales with your current customer base. Choose carefully and test your patootie off. Once you come up with the expansion you want to take on, map out a long-term plan for strategic execution. Don't blabber too much about it to anyone but your team before you are ready. Remember, you are the best at one thing. If you have a consumer product, you should be known for your "(s)hero" product before doing anything else. The UGG brand was well known for boots, for example, before expanding into slippers and such. Don't muddle your brand until you are 100% sure it's additive and something you can actually accomplish. Until then, shut your mouth, mamacita, and keep a fucking secret—at least for now.

CONFESSIONS OF A
BOSS BITCH

The Tooth Fairy Tale

On one recent episode of my show *Hatched*, a woman named Kristin walked into the pitch room to "hatch" her idea into retail. She had long Rapunzel hair, glitter all over her body, and jewels in her hair, atop of which rested a tiara. Needless to say, she wasn't the *typical* entrepreneur who comes on the show.

"Hi! I'm the tooth fairy," she said, smiling so hard that I had to, too.

It's not a line you hear every day. I said, "Okay, Kristin, how are you the tooth fairy?"

Still smiling, she said, "I created a line of Tooth Fairy products, from a book where parents can keep their kids' teeth, to a doll, and, ultimately, a store and an entire tooth fairy tale revolution!"

I meet hundreds of entrepreneurs each year, and none of them have looked the part like she did (if I had to imagine what the tooth fairy looked like, it would be Kristin). And few of them have her energy. But many do fall into the same trap: pitching too much too soon.

I said, "Kristin, I actually love the idea of a keepsake book for saving teeth; most parents just put them in a bag. Studies have shown that there is actually important DNA in there, as well. So this works not only from a posterity standpoint but a health one."

She was tickled as pink as her dress to hear that.

"However," I said, raising a brow and about to throw down a can of whoop ass, "*that's* the thing I want you to grow first. You have no competition here now. And it's a high-margin product. Own that market! Go to all the kids' dentists in America. Make that product great *before* you go and spin your tooth fairy wheels with other stuff."

This made her a little blue, but she was still smiling. She had grown her business out of her home so that she could care for her disabled daughter. She had taken her product as far as she could go and now needed a brutally honest outside perspective to get to the next level.

I had her back. I said, "Madame Tooth Fairy, get rid of all those other prototypes for stuff. Just get that book to become *the* thing all moms want when their kids start losing their teeth."

Kristin took my advice, and today she has her book in major retail distribution. Her ideas for more products related to her Tooth Fairy Tales brand will come, but in the meantime, the sales from her first product are stuff business dreams are made of.

TALK A BIG GAME

I've worked with dozens of publicists over the years. Some great. Some . . . meh. Regardless of how much or how little they did for me and my brand, I was *always* the chief publicist. Just because you're paying someone doesn't mean they will care more about your business than you do. In fact, they won't, so don't be delusional. I don't care how much you are paying someone; no one, and I mean no one, is going to care more about the success of your business than you. And if they don't work to get your name out there, then you have to. After all, it's *your* name at the end of the day, not theirs. And the press you get can make or break the fate of your company.

Yes, you've got what it takes, but it will take everything you've got to get the word out about your business. Remember, you don't want to *just* get the word out, because you aren't in it for vanity, after all. You want your customers to do more than window shop: you want them to actually buy what you're selling. Reaching—and then retaining—new customers will be one of the numero uno most difficult things you'll do as a Boss Bitch. And if you want your business to have staying power (which, of course, you do!), it's a process you'll have to repeat over and over and over again.

Now, as a business on the upswing but not yet on the coasting area of the S curve (i.e., at the top), you probably don't have a ten-figure marketing budget, or maybe even a five-figure marketing budget—and that's okay. There are a ton of low-cost ways to promote your brand without gouging valuable resources from the rest of your coffers. Here are three things you can basically do fo' free:

1. *Hit the streets.* Creative street marketing campaigns can be really effective for gaining intrigue and free media coverage. Successful guerrilla marketing campaigns have been as simple as handing out fliers or offering free hugs in the park to more elaborate (and expensive) stuff like hiring the Goodyear blimp or the Oscar Mayer Wienermobile.
2. *Spread the word . . . of mouth.* At the end of the day, there is just no better marketing tool than a glowing review from a happy customer. Offer incentives for your customers to review you, like 10% off their next order for writing about you on Yelp or a review site appropriate for your business. No, you can't reward only good reviews; that's unethical. But they'll appreciate your transparency

and the ability to offer feedback, both of which are great for your reputation. Referral programs are also great because they incentivize happy customers to get their friends to join. Perhaps you take $25 off your customer's order when a friend she refers signs up for your service or purchases something at your store—now you've got *two* loyal fans whose purchases will pay that $25 off many times over.

3. *Get social.* Depending on the nature of your business, you may not need to be on *all* social media platforms. Go for quality over quantity. Instead of wasting precious resources setting up all kinds of channels, which you will then need to populate with an endless stream of content, choose a few to focus on that make the most sense for your brand. For example, clothing boutiques and restaurants tend to outperform their peers on Snapchat, Pinterest, and Instagram because they are so visual (who doesn't love a good #OOTD shot or a delish-looking slice o' pie?). Tech- and service-based companies, in contrast, tend to do better on Twitter and LinkedIn, where they can establish themselves as an authority in their area by offering quick tidbits and additional reading. No matter the platform, the goal is to give your followers something that's useful, interesting, and shareable. Start small, posting a few times per week, until you learn who your audience is and what they want. Then start ramping up efforts with giveaways and other fun promos.

FYI

"Liking" or commenting on other people's photos on Instagram and other sites increases the chance that they will follow you—or at least know who you are. Find strategic influencers in your industry who have clout, but not a crazy number of followers, and make an extra effort to engage with them. But be realistic. I don't care if you're a budding musician, Taylor Swift is not going to notice if you comment on her photo. However, an up-and-comer or, better yet, a music producer or an agent might.

Ever notice that when someone likes or comments on your photos or posts on social media, you remember them? Sometimes you remember them fondly (or unfondly) in a personal way, but sometimes you think, "Oh, yeah, so-and-so! She would be great for the XYZ project I have coming up. I should reach out about that opportunity." Well, the same happens in reverse. And *that* is something to like for sure.

TALK ISN'T CHEAP

As you start to get more press coverage, you need to be on point with messaging and presentation. Once you get an opportunity on TV, in print, to present on panels, or to give speeches, you can't just wing it. You're in the big leagues now, bitch! And getting the right outcome for your business means creating the right image.

MEDIA TRAINING

Yes, even though I'm a professional TV person, I have had media training. *Everyone* can use a little help when it comes to being interviewed on camera (which, by the way, is just as hard as it looks when done well). Media training will teach you how to come up with quick sound bites to get your ideas across and how to present yourself like a pro. A good media coach will videotape mock interviews so you can see how you come across and help you fix any weird tics or habits. They'll teach you how to field any question like a good politician: that is, answer the question quickly so you don't seem like you're avoiding something, then quickly transition into your talking points. Even if you never encounter the media in promoting your work, this kind of training can be invaluable in teaching you how to speak and stay on message in front of a crowd, even if that crowd is your own team.

SPEECHES AND CONFERENCES

The pen may be mightier than the sword, but the voice is just as mighty as the pen. As your business grows and you begin to be recognized as the leading Boss Bitch that you are, you will likely start being invited to speaking engagements. If you aren't asked outright, you just have to identify the ones that make the most sense for you (there's a convention or group for *every* industry) and pitch yourself. There's no shame in that game. It might be best to have someone else on your team, like your publicist, assistant, or even your "fake assistant" (yes, I fully admit I did this), do the initial outreach. Don't worry, we've all done it, and if you do it right, you won't need to do it for long.

BITCH TIP

HOW TO SPEAK UP, NOW

Confused about how to start booking speaking engagements? The truth is: everyone is. There's no exact formula, but follow these steps to set yourself up for stump success:

1. *Get listed.* There are a ton of speakers bureaus out there that will put you on their website and proactively (but often reactively) deal with inbound requests for speakers within a particular space. A few of the big ones are Washington Speakers Bureau, APB, and Executive Speakers Bureau. If you're nonexclusive to an agency (which you should be), then the more of these you can sign up for the better. And remember: they won't all actively pitch you, at least not at first while your star is still rising. So don't expect hand-holding. Instead, use their name and platform to leverage your own bookings, then loop them back in to handle the business side after you've booked a gig. The more "gets" they see you getting organically, the more likely they'll be to start hustling for you directly.

2. *Build a résumé.* It's a catch-22: you need the speaking experience to book the speech, but you need the speech for the speaking experience. We are all in the same boat here. This means you should document every little speech you give. And videotape it! If you really need video of yourself but haven't done an official one yet or didn't tape it, just record yourself giving a faux speech in your living room until you do.

3. *Make a menu.* Come up with a list of topics for speeches you would like to give, then set a starting fee for various types of engagements. I like to think of this as a Chinese takeout menu: list a bunch of different offerings à la carte, then some special combination deals. . . . You get the idea. And be sure to build in language about them covering travel, accommodations, and ground transportation—you don't want your entire earnings being eaten up by those costs.

Many places won't pay at the outset until you have a good number of speeches under your belt or have a high profile in a particular field, so you should expect to do some free talking to build up that résumé first.

TELL YOUR STORY

It's cool to talk about your company and all its awesome goings-on. But what's better is to tell *your story*. Why did you want to start your own thing? How did you come up with the idea? People are generally interested in the *people* behind the brands. We remember the stories more than we remember the details of a product. So get comfy in your own skin, be human, and tell *your* story. You can take a page from my "Confessions of a Boss Bitch" and even go so far as talking about your failures and embarrassing adventures and misadventures. Chances are, your authenticity will resonate and be more relatable to your audience than if you were spending time talking about a product or service.

Take Blake Mycoskie, the founder of TOMS (yep, those super-comfy slip-ons that you probably have in several colors and styles; I know I do). He founded the company after he and his sister spent time running (yes, *running*) through Argentina as one of the teams of contestants on *The Amazing Race* back in 2006. But more than the pangs of losing the race by a mere four minutes, Blake felt the pangs of poverty he'd witnessed throughout *his* travels. So *his* story is all about his dedication to helping children in poverty, which is a story that resonates authentically in the brand: for every pair of shoes you buy, Blake and his team send a pair to a child in need. This one-for-one model has resulted in more than 60 million pairs of shoes for kids all over the world. It's an easy company to get on board with, not just because it's doing good, but because we connect to Blake *himself.* TOMS is now worth an estimated $600 million. Be your most authentic self and own it. The fame and fortune really can follow.

CONFESSIONS OF A
BOSS BITCH

SHOW ME THE MONEY

Your money might come from one gigundo check (lucky Boss Bitch!). But, more likely, it will come from several different places. In fact, the average millionaire has about *seven* different sources of income—their salary, and then six additional ways of making cash. And that's a statistic I'm proud to be. I told you what some of my salaries have been in Section 1, now here are some of my other streams of cash:

- My appearances on talk shows: at least SAG/AFTRA (my TV union) "scale," which is around $1K/pop with extra checks each time it airs
- My speeches: range from $10–$25K/pop depending on the time, travel, and work involved
- My books: my advance for *Rich Bitch* was $110K and my advance for *Boss Bitch* was $225K

Of course, not all these things will make sense for everyone and every business. But I'm listing them to show you that when it comes to making money as an entrepreneur, there's no need to sit around and wait for your big zillion-dollar "exit" to make bank.

Because you've made it all the way to the end of this book, I know three important things about you: 1) you're a hustler, 2) you know how to multitask, and 3) you're a straight-up Renaissance woman who has more than one skill and passion. Boss Bitches use those three things to show *ourselves* the money whether or not the Googles of the world come calling.

THE BIG PAYDAY

It might be rare, but it can happen, and in some cases it can be big enough to be worth the wait. But don't start mentally spending the cash in your bank account before the check is even written. Be careful about talking too openly about your big "exit strategy" at the wrong time and to the wrong people because it could make the wait even longer.

If I were looking to invest in you, I would be the "wrong people" to talk exit with. I mean, since when is it a good idea to sell someone getting in on your business with the notion that you are going to peace out?! I've seen and heard it time and again when a company comes in to pitch me, and I ask, "What's your goal?" If they're a digital media company and they say something like "to sell it to AOL" or a food product and they say "to sell it to General Mills," then I'm out. Why should I give you my check if you are already ready to check out? That doesn't work for me or any other investor.

If I am your employee looking to you for guidance, I would also be the "wrong people" to talk exit with. I would rather hear something like, "I am going to grow this business into the best digital media company there is, not stopping until every eyeball is on our content" or "I aim to grow this food product into something every household knows about and enjoys."

Now, as a Boss Bitch who has been on both sides of this equation—as an entrepreneur and as an investor—I can tell you that just because you shouldn't be *telling* an investor or your team about your ultimate plans of being acquired* by another company (aka your big payday) doesn't mean you shouldn't be *thinking* about it—constantly, in fact—and adjusting that exit plan as your business grows in the same way that you adjust other business goals.

What might that exit look like? Here are a few scenarios:

Exit Option 1: Selling to a Friend or Friendly Company

What this is: You don't have to sell your company to a monster corporation like Google to get the payday you want. In fact, most sales happen between a company and a true believer—a customer, a family member, an employee—in your company. This is the Willy Wonka story of exits, where the chocolate company goes to a true fan of the brand.

Pros: You know the person or company, so there's less due diligence involved, and they will likely stay true to your founding mission.

Cons: Emotions might cloud your judgment, and you risk undervaluing yourself and your business by "being nice." Alternatively, getting into business with family or friends can wreak personal havoc on relationships. You can also overvalue your company because you are so tied to it emotionally.

Exit Option 2: Acquisition

What this is: This is the Google type of getaway. You find another business that wants to buy yours, negotiate a price, and sell. Acquisitions are the type of exits that get all the buzz, because normally it's a bigger company with a fatty checkbook writing a check to a smaller company that contains more zeros than they've ever seen. The best way to get acquired is to find a strategic fit, a company that needs whatever you're the best at doing to offer their customers.

Pros: If you find the right company that sees undeniable value in what you've built, they will likely pay you more of a premium than what you're valued at on the open market.

Cons: Acquisitions, especially big ones, often come with non-competes,* which means you're on the bench for a while. You might be rich, but you could get bored. Also, if the acquirer is the wrong fit, they could run your baby into the ground, and to any good entrepreneur, that hurts more than fewer zeros in your bank account.

Exit Option 3: IPO

What this is: IPOs are sexy and all the rage if you read business press. But, to keep it real, statistically you have the same chance of winning the lottery as going IPO: only about seven thousand out of *millions* of companies in the US make it to IPO territory. So know that while it is possible, it's about as likely as your becoming the next Gisele.

Pros: If you are funded by serious professional investors with a long, strong track record of taking companies public, you might be invited to the IPO party. But let's just say they generally aren't fun parties, nor are they always worth the amount of time and effort and legal fees you'll spend to attend.

Cons: Usually, IPOs go to companies backed by a ton of VC funding, which, as you read in the last step, is not always how Boss Bitches roll. Very few bootstrapped businesses are IPO material, and those founders who eventually do go IPO will have spent years busting their asses to sell their company, only to dilute their role and their stake in the business once the company goes public.

FYI

When you hear about private companies* with big valuations,* like Twitter, who boasted a $20 billion valuation *before* they even went public,* you must think the founder has at least a couple billion in the bank, right? Not necessarily. "On paper," you can really have any valuation, as we discussed in the last step. Remember, a valuation isn't necessarily an objective value that a company is worth but rather what someone is willing to pay for it at any given point in time. Which means that you don't actually make money until that company has exited, either by raising money and selling shares, selling the whole shebang to another company, or going public.

When you *are* ready to sell your company or otherwise "exit," you'll likely deserve every penny you'll cash out (not to mention any time you take off for the hard work you've done over the years). Being "ready" means having your business ducks in a row:

- current financial statements
- last three years of financial statements
- last three years of tax returns
- list of all inventory (product, equipment, furniture, etc.)
- property appraisal or lease agreements

THE NOT-SO-BIG PAYDAY

Even if you don't end up with the big payday you dreamed of and you want to call it a day, you can still recoup some of the money you invested in your business, fire-sale style. This is basically where you sell off the company piece by piece (like you might do with your belongings after a fire rips through your home). This is not the fun kind of sale in which you are acquired by a larger and/or more established business, make gobs of money, buy your yacht, and sail off into the sunset. This is the kind of sale in which your business has run its course, i.e., failed, and you're doing everything you can to recoup some of your losses, pay off employees and creditors, and make it back to port. No, it's not ideal, but it happens, so let's make the most of it.

There may be several components to your business. Are you selling inventory? Are you selling assets such as equipment or real estate? What about licenses, trademarks, and copyrights? It may be that you sell different parts of your business to different entities. Are you selling the brand and all it stands for? When Bethenny Frankel sold her Skinnygirl alcohol line, it was estimated that the brand alone was worth $8 million of the $39 million price tag. You have to decide before you sell whether you hope to sell to a like-minded individual or company that will keep your brand or product running with your existing staff, or if you're okay with the buyer dismantling your company and laying people off.

FYI

Schmuck is a Yiddish word that people use to mean *idiot*. *Schmuck insurance* in business prevents you from looking like one. It's not the actual insurance you buy, it's just the act of not selling 100% of a company. Let's say you sell your company for peanuts thinking you are washing your hands of it, but the new owner brings it back from the dead and makes it a huge success. D'oh. Schmuck insurance would be keeping 10 or 20% of the company so that, in the event it really takes off under the new ownership, you aren't left with nada.

Until you are totally ready to drop the mic with confidence, let's keep our plans for world domination between us girls. Would you tell a potential romantic partner about your desire to have five kids together or what your contingency plan is for a breakup—on your first date? I didn't think so. Of course, a Boss Bitch has a contingency plan (and another contingency plan for that contingency plan) for basically every aspect of her life, but she keeps it to herself. After all, if plan A doesn't work, there are twenty-five more letters in the alphabet.

E-COMMERCE FOR YOUR BUSINESS

BITCH TIP

Yes, yes, I know you "sell" your business sizzle online. That's a given for a strong business. But you can actually sell your entire business online. There are sites that specialize in selling certain types of businesses—from restaurants to franchises to Internet properties. The two biggies are: BizBuySell.com and BizQuest.com.

Some of these sites have a monthly subscription fee to list your business for sale. You'll also have to prepare a one-page document that offers highlights of your business. You can and should set this up as a "blind profile" so that potential buyers can see the specifics only after they have signed a confidentiality agreement.

BOSS BITCH, OUT

The view from the top might be a-mazing, but it takes a lot of guts and balance to stay there. It also takes a lot of guts (and planning!) to make the call to shoulder your pack and descend. Your business journey might come to an end for many different reasons: maybe it doesn't work out or you get tired of trying. Or maybe it does so well that you can walk away from the table and cash in your winnings. Whatever the path, there's a way to have a graceful exit—on *your* terms.

FIVE SIGNS THAT IT'S TIME TO WALK AWAY

When is it time to pull a Cher Horowitz and say, "I'm outty"? The answer is different for every Boss Bitch and every business. Making an exit—whether by selling the company or simply calling it quits—is a tough decision, but if you read the signs and get out at the right time, you can save yourself a lot of money and heartache.

1. *You're no longer hitting your financial targets.* During the first two to three years of your business, projections are all over the place; as you work to get off the ground and hone your product, it's perfectly understandable that you may miss a few targets. But three to four years out, those initial investments should start paying off—and you should start seeing results. If you're still not turning a profit *and* you're out of money, you've got a problem. And no, this does not mean that it's time to take out more loans that put you further into debt. It's time to cut your losses and save financial face for both yourself and the company. Remember when you incorporated your business way back when? The whole purpose of doing that was to keep your business and personal finances separate. The last situation you want to be in is on the hook for personally repaying a business loan that you can't afford.

2. *Your mission is unclear.* If you're starting to ask yourself that existential question, "Why did I start this thing in the first place?" then it's time to get out. This line of questioning is bad for two reasons. 1) You no longer have a clear mission, which is bad for your employees, who are working away to hit a moving target, and bad for your customers, who no longer know what they're even getting from you. Until you know what your objectives are and who you're trying to reach, you're going to keep treading water—while drowning in unnecessary spending. 2) You might just have lost the fire in your belly. Hey, it happens. But without your passion for your business, who the hell else is going to drive the business forward?

3. *You heart your product more than your customers do.* Ask yourself, are you truly providing value? Does your business do something that your customers actually need? Or is your company centered on something you care about and really, really want others to care about, too? Trust me, if your customers care, you'll know, because they'll show you with actual dollars. If you're missing this positive feedback, it's not that they're cheap; it's that your product isn't valuable to them. In this case, it's not them—it's *you*.

4. *Your key employees are bailing.* You rely on your key employees not just for their skill sets and work ethic, but for their drive in moving the company forward. Other than yourself, those employees should be the biggest cheerleaders of your company and your product. So if they're ditching, you're in real trouble—and it's time to listen to what their leaving says about the state of your business. The resulting brain drain will spell out doom for your company, while mass exodus lowers morale (and encourages job hunting) for those who remain. It's a toxic environment for anyone to work in, and unless you can turn it around quickly, it will not end well.

5. *Your personal health has suffered.* I get it, as a Boss Bitch you probably work more and sleep less than anyone you know. But there's a difference between being mildly sleep deprived and legitimately unhealthy. Have you stopped taking care of yourself (working out, properly grooming, eating a balanced diet) in favor of all work all the time? Are you starting to get flus, colds, migraines, and other recurring illnesses more often than ever before? Have you lost or gained a ton of weight? Are you constantly fighting with your partner and ignoring your family? Are you anxious all. the. time? If you answered yes to even one of these questions, it's time to take a long hard look at whether or not it's worth it to sacrifice your physical and mental health to save a sinking ship. You started this business because it made you happy, and it's pretty hard to be happy when you're over- or underweight and sick all the time. You started

this thing to be the Boss Bitch, not to let your business become a bitch.

SWOT IT OUT

The first time I heard about SWOT analysis, I was confused. "Swat?" I thought, "Like 'SWAT team'? What the heck is that?" Well, it's just an acronym for *strengths, weaknesses, opportunities,* and *threats.* It's the formal tool for self-analysis that you should be doing throughout your Boss Bitch career journey, but especially when you find yourself at a crossroads.

If you're at said turning point, list out all of your internal strengths and weaknesses and external opportunities and threats. List them side by side with the strengths and opportunities on the left as your "positive" column and your weaknesses and threats on the right as your "negative" column. Which list is longer? If the negatives outweigh the positives, that might be a sign that it's time to take a bow and drop the curtain on this show. SWOT isn't a science, but it will help you decide what's the best path to follow. And yes, only you can decide.

POSITIVE	NEGATIVE
Strengths:	Weaknesses:
Opportunities:	Threats:

I'M OUTTY

"Boss Bitch, out" can mean different things for the future of your company. If you don't sell the company through one of the methods described above, you have a couple of options: you could peace out but keep the company alive in the competent (manicured) hands of a successor, or you could just want to be totally done and close it down altogether. There's no shame in either, if handled in the Boss Bitch way.

FINDING A SUCCESSOR

If you're spent and want to be out of the company yourself but not put the company on the outs, then it's in everyone's best interest to find a rock-star successor. After all, it's the company you started, so even if you're not interested in making money (or losing money) from it anymore, it's in your (and your reputation's) best interest that it succeed.

A lot of founders deal with this. Even founders of big multinational conglomerates struggle to find replacements. The most smoothly executed transitions come from within, when the head of a company can groom a second in command who learns the ins and outs of the company, as well as the founder's vision, but then offers a unique skill set of their own to move the company forward. A good example is Tim Cook, who carried the mantle left by Steve Jobs. Cook had worked at Apple for nearly a decade before Jobs made him COO in 2007, four years before Jobs died in 2011.

Naming and grooming a successor is important even if you're not involved in the day-in-and-day-out operations anymore. Why should you care who takes over when you're gone? Because it's your baby, with your name all over it. Don't you want to leave a legacy, bitch? Well, this is your chance!

CLOSING UP SHOP

It might be a sad day, but closing up shop is easy to do. Here are the five things you will need to take care of before you call it quits:

1. *File your final tax return.* You have to file an annual tax return for your last year in business, even if you were only in business for part of the year. All S corp, C corp, and LLC tax return documents have what's known as a denotation (more like "detonation," if you

ask me) that this is your "final tax return." Check that box and then contact the IRS to close your EIN account.

2. *File your final employment tax return.* If you have employees (or have had them in the last year), you also need to file a final employment tax return. This includes submitting final federal tax returns on behalf of your employees as well. (No, the IRS won't just let you lie down and die.)

3. *File for dissolution.* Skip this step if you want to keep racking up taxes and fees on a business that isn't even running. Oh wait, that doesn't sound like fun? Then you have to formally dissolve your business with the state you're in, which means more than just saying it's over. The government needs to know what the deal is so it can strike your business from listings and leave you alone. Filing dissolution papers is especially important if you have partners or other owners in the business, as it prevents future confusion about ownership and liability.

4. *See what you can sell.* Take inventory of what you have and see what you can sell, including licensed projects and templates as well as software, office equipment, and even furniture. Be sure to report all business assets using IRS Form 8594 (the asset acquisition statement), since you might be able to recoup some of your business losses by selling your stuff. Can't sell it? Donate and get the tax deduction instead. It's still something!

5. *Cancel the paperwork.* This includes licenses, permits, and insurance policies. Contact your city, town, or state's licensing office and cancel the licenses you took out. Then contact your insurance broker to cancel your team's health insurance plan. Don't forget to cancel business liability and compensation insurance, too; no need to get that bill every month.

Selling your beloved company can be hard, but, as they say, better to have loved and lost than never to have loved at all. Perk up, Boss Bitch! There's more out there for you. Get out and grab the next great opportunity by the balls.

FYI

CHANGE YOUR PERSPECTIVE

Stats about how many new businesses fail are enough to make you sick to your stomach. Here's how to puff your entrepreneurial chest back up: don't focus on the percentage that fails. Instead, look at the percentage that *doesn't* fail! Lori Greiner, *Shark Tank* judge and serial entrepreneur, says, "Dear optimist, pessimist, and realist: while you guys were busy arguing about the glass of wine, I drank it! Sincerely, the opportunist!"

- 50% of all new businesses fail within five years. That means 50% succeed!
- 60% of new companies don't turn a profit. That means 40% do!
- Less than 1% of entrepreneurs come from a super-rich upbringing. That means 99% of us have had to make our lives happen ourselves and depend on our- selves for our futures. So instead of looking at your own personal struggles as impediments, view them as assets. If you've gone through trauma, you're more likely to look at business challenges with a different perspective, thinking that they are more easily manageable compared to the past trauma you've dealt with. Studies have shown that "post-traumatic growth" can be equally as com- mon as "post-traumatic stress," and I'm happy to say that more of us, myself included, are falling into the first category.

By now, you know that Boss Bitches value being in control of all the aspects of their lives more than anything else. Don't forget: your life is your story. You decide how it's written, what gets edited out, and what gets added in. And at any point in time you have the power to say, "Wait, this is not how my story is going to end."

I don't know how my story is going to end just yet, either, but here it is so far, as honestly as I could tell it. It's not a fairy tale in the tradi- tional sense and it never will be. But I will have my "happily ever after" because I define what *happy* means. And you can, too. So, what's *your* story, bitch?

BOTTOM LINE

Conventional Wisdom: If you have new customers, you have growth.

The Real Deal: Maybe. If you are gaining customers, building a loyal fan base, *and* generating the minimum amount of money needed to keep your doors open, then you could be experiencing growth, which can lead to the all-important "takeoff" phase of your business. But if not, you're likely just gaining traction *disguised* as growth.

Conventional Wisdom: The best marketing is paid advertising because you can control the message.

The Real Deal: Not necessarily. If you can afford it, paid advertising works, no doubt. But if you can't, some legwork in courting journalists and bloggers will go a long way. Also, smart guerrilla and street marketing stunts can sometimes generate more meaningful, organic buzz.

Conventional Wisdom: Never, ever give up.

The Real Deal: Decent advice, generally speaking. But in business, knowing when to fold them and knowing when to walk away aren't weaknesses—they are virtues.

Conventional Wisdom: You need to grow some balls to start a business.

The Real Deal: First of all, having a vagina doesn't stop me from believing my balls are bigger than yours. Second, as Boss Bitch Betty White said, "Why do people say 'grow some balls'? Balls are weak and sensitive. If you wanna be tough, grow a vagina. Those things can take a pounding."

Conventional Wisdom: Fairy tales *are* possible.

The Real Deal: No, girl—if you lose your shoe at midnight, it probably just means you're drunk. However, I do like the line from "Cinderella": "Live like there's no midnight." I take that to mean: "Hustle like there's no tomorrow." Don't wait for someone else to come sweep you off your (bare) feet. You don't need a prince. You're a queen Boss Bitch, and you decide what "happily ever after" means. "And the princess lived happily ever after in her own big castle and with all her own money and she took care of herself—the end."

THE BUSINESS DICTIONARY
(THAT YOU DON'T NEED A DICTIONARY TO UNDERSTAND)

401(k): A retirement plan offered by an employer. The coolest thing about it is that you can put money in tax-free. That means you can add income straight into it before payroll or other taxes are taken out. (Right?) The IRS hooks you up with that incentive to encourage you to save now and have that money available when you're old—because you're not supposed to use it until then (at which point you pay the taxes). As a business owner, you have a solo 401(k) option.

A

Accounts receivable: Money that's owed to you for a good or service that's already been used by your customer but for which you have not yet been paid.

Acquire: What happens when you buy a company that's for sale (as opposed to taking over a company that isn't for sale, as in the case of a hostile takeover).

Aggregate demand: How much everyone wants something, like everyone in the world.

Amortization: This is spreading a loss out over a fixed period. It has two meanings: 1) the breakdown of your payment between interest and the amount you owe when you have a mortgage. 2) For Boss Bitches, this comes into play when you talk about depreciating something in your business that's intangible (copyrights, patents, intellectual property, franchise rights) on your taxes evenly over the time you expected to use it for but didn't (because it wasn't as valuable as you thought). For example, "In order to pay off the enormous debt she incurred securing a patent for making dresses for alpacas (for which she realized there was zero market), Nicole will amortize her loss over the next few years." This means she'll pay off those losses piece by piece, a little bit each month, instead of covering the loss all at once—way less painful to her bottom line. You will hear it used as part of the acronym EBITDA (it's the A). (*See also*: EBITDA)

Angel investor: An individual who invests in a start-up, often a friend or family member of the founder(s). Angel investors are so named because they're typically more interested in helping an entrepreneur get her business off the ground than in earning a big payout for themselves, like most investors would be. (*See also*: VC)

APR: Don't let the acronym confuse you, it's just the interest rate on your credit card.

Audit/Audited: A look at a company's financials under a microscope. Usually this happens by the IRS if something looks sketchy.

B

B2B: "Business to business"—this applies to businesses that do business with other businesses, like a photocopier company that services machines for corporations or a developer that creates software for businesses to run more efficiently.

B2C: "Business to consumer"—this applies to businesses that offer products or services to the public rather than to businesses. Most of your favorite clothing, electronic, and food brands are B2C because you're the end user, not a business.

Balance sheet: This is a snapshot of your financial health as a company. The name comes from the idea that both sides of it—assets (the stuff you have) and liabilities (the stuff you own)—"balance out." (*See also*: Bottom line)

Bandwidth: Technically, this is the amount of data a network can successfully handle before it crashes. Slow Internet connection? You might not have enough bandwidth. In business, the term has also become synonymous with how busy people are. If you don't have time to take someone's call, you might tell them you don't have enough bandwidth—aka current capacity—to do so at the moment.

Bankruptcy: When your debt is more than the money you are bringing in and it gets to a point where you or your company are no longer able to make even minimum payments on your bills. Filing for bankruptcy can be voluntary or involuntary. The former is called Chapter 11 and can provide a safety net while the person or company regroups. The latter is called Chapter 7, where a company's creditors force it into bankruptcy with an eye toward selling the business off piece by piece to repay the debt.

Basis point: A business way to explain a fraction of a percent: 0.02% = 2 basis points, 0.20% = 20 basis points, and 2% = 200 basis points. It's tidier than reading out the mouthful of decimals that you learned in elementary school.

Bearish: Just like you have to get the animals straight in politics (Democrats are donkeys and Republicans are elephants), in business the bulls are positive and the bears are negative. If someone says they are "bearish," they mean they are not particularly enthusiastic about something, while if they say they're "bullish," then they're all in for it. (*See also:* Bullish)

Beta: This is the test version of a product or service before it's distributed to the masses. Tech companies often release a beta version of a program to a limited number of users for free in exchange for their feedback about what works and what may still need fixing so that by the time they bring it to market they have better chances of success.

Beta test: A trial run of software or other product by an outside party before that product is made available to the public. Like a dress rehearsal, it should be as close to the "real deal" as possible to uncover any surprises or setbacks before the product is fully launched.

Black swan: An unexpected and nearly impossible-to-predict event, like a terrorist attack or the housing crisis, that can have unexpected consequences for a product, an industry, or even an entire market.

Bond: When a company or government needs to raise money for, say, a shiny new machine or fancy bridge, it borrows money by selling bonds. Bonds have durations of ten years or more (durations of one to ten years are technically called "notes"). There are different kinds of bonds—typically government or corporate bonds—but generally speaking, if you invest in a bond, you'll get paid back the full value (or *principal*) at the end of the bond's duration (*maturity date*) plus interest payments (called the *coupon*). You can now buy bonds directly from the government through TreasuryDirect.gov, thereby bypassing using a broker, which can be pricey. Or, as a business owner, you can finance your debt by selling bonds, and pay those who bought them a little extra for having loaned you the money.

Book value: The value of a company based on the numbers they show on paper. It's the estimated worth of a company if the business were shut down and everything sold. Book value is the opposite of market value, where companies feel more valuable than their books would suggest. Buzzy tech companies like Apple experience a higher market value than what the underlying business is doing. The concept is analogous to valuing your car by Kelley Blue Book. There's a value based on stats of age and mileage. But if, for some reason, Brad Pitt was seen in your car, what you could get for the car would go way up.

Bottom line: Refers to the last line on a balance sheet, which reflects—and is synonymous with—an individual or company's profit or gain. This is the money left over after all expenses have been accounted for. That's why colloquially (and at the end of all the steps in the book) it's just like saying "at the end of the day" or "when all is said and done."

Brand: That magical way in which a company describes itself and differentiates itself from the rest of the market. (Tissues are a product; Kleenex is a brand.) Your personal brand is how you set yourself apart from the rest of the herd, as well as the compass used to point your personal, career and business goals in the right direction.

Broker: A company or person who carries out a financial transaction for you. Regular folks aren't allowed to actually buy, sell, or trade assets like stocks and bonds. You can place orders for them, but then you need a broker to actually execute those orders for you. For that, they will charge you either a fee per transaction or a fee based on a percentage of your assets. There was a time when only the rich could have a broker. These aren't those times anymore. Today, there's no lack of options for discount brokers who charge very small fees, allowing everyone the option to trade.

Buffett, Warren: I wouldn't say that you have to know about many people in the finance world, but Warren Buffett is a must. He is one of the greatest investors of all time. Oh, and one of the richest men in the world, too. His nickname is the "Oracle of Omaha," which speaks to his ability to pick great value investments, whether choosing stocks or buying companies (from his home in Omaha).

Bullish: Markets have feelings, too! And when they're feeling "bullish," it means that stock prices are rising. Similarly, when investors are bullish, they're feeling confident about a particular stock, a company, or the market. (*See also:* Bearish)

Business development: You'll usually hear this referred to as "biz dev." Typically, it will refer to forming relationships and making deals with the goal of getting more business.

Business plan: Remember that course prospectus you got on the first day of class that explained what you were going to learn (and what your homework would be) for the entire semester? Your business plan is like a course prospectus for your business. A typical business plan starts with an executive summary or mission statement, aka a somewhat more detailed version of an elevator pitch. It should also include information about the market the business is in or planning to enter and how you plan to stand out in this field, along with information on past growth and future strategies. It should include information about your management team, financial metrics, and projections. If you are asking for money, that should be in there as well.

Buy-in: An endorsement from someone, be it your boss, your work team, or an investor, when you have successfully persuaded them to accept an idea or a proposal. Used in a sentence: "Nicole is excited that she got 'buy-in' from the committee to move forward with her event, after she presented projected earnings based on last year's. Their support means the event has a better chance of crushing it."

C

Capital expenses: When a company spends money on big stuff—like machinery, equipment, a building, or land.

Capital "cap" gains: It's exactly what it sounds like—you are gaining on capital (money). So when you buy something (a stock, a mutual fund, a house) and then sell it for a profit, you have a capital gain. (BTW, if you sell it at a loss, you have a capital loss.) If you sell before one year after the purchase, it's called a short-term capital gain, and you usually don't get any tax love. Investors want to be taxed at the long-term capital gains level (more than a year) for money they make because it's way better from a tax perspective since capital gains are taxed at a lower rate than ordinary income. The highest personal tax rate is 35%, whereas the highest cap gains tax bracket is 20%—so by getting as much of their profits into the lower capital gains tax category bracket as possible, they get to keep more of their money.

Capital investment: Funds invested into a company to help it be successful, such as for building a new website, making a big hire, or expanding into a new market.

Carve out: An exception to an area of a contract. If an employment contract has demands that you work exclusively for your employer, you can "carve out" something that you might already be doing so that it will not be deemed to be in violation of that clause. For example, "Annie is asking to carve out her side hustle of selling jewelry in her new employer contract; otherwise she will have to stop her side hustle or she will be deemed in breach of her contract." In this case, her employer will probably allow a carve-out to the exclusivity clause because they realize that if it's important to her they might risk losing her altogether if they don't make that exception.

Cash flow: You probably already know that money can flow out of your hands like water. Cash flow measures how much cash you do—or don't—have on hand. You can measure a company's cash flow, or you can measure your own, with cash inflows being things like your salary or side-hustle income, and cash outflows being things like your living expenses and credit card bills.

Cash flow positive: When you have more cash coming in than going out. Think of it as that moment when you or your business has "arrived."

Cash reserves: Your emergency fund, or cash you put away and can easily access for known near-term costs and also (perhaps more important) unforeseen problems and expenses. You should *always* have six to nine months' worth of expenses in a place you have ready access to when you need it—typically in a savings account. Companies should have cash reserves, too—and if they don't, just like you, they can face bankruptcy.

C corp: Most major companies, especially the public ones, are C corps. The company itself is the one on the hook for any legal action or debt incurred by its employees, because a C corp is essentially an entity on its own that can sue and be sued. With a C corp, the money going into the company is taxed *and* the money you get from it as income is taxed. (*See also:* S corp)

CEO: The chief executive officer runs the whole show, no matter the size of the business; all of the other C-level executives report to her.

CFO: The chief financial officer manages all of the company's finances.

CMO: The chief marketing officer is in charge of the company's communications and marketing efforts.

CPM: This acronym stands for "cost per thousand." I know it's confusing, but the *M* is actually the roman numeral for *thousand*. Let's say a website you want to have your ad seen on charges $1.00 CPM. That means you have to pay a buck for each thousand times that ad was clicked on.

CRO: The chief revenue officer is responsible for business development, or bringing in the deals that bring in the money so that the CFO can manage it.

CTO: The chief technology officer is your business's tech guru, overseeing everything from IT to web development.

Click-through rate (CTR): The percentage of users who visit a web page with your ad on it and actually click on that ad. The higher the CTR, the more successful the ad—and the more dollars (you hope) in your company's pockets.

Closeouts: Inventory that is sold off at a reduced price. This tends to happen right before a new model of a product, like a car, comes out, and the dealer needs to make room on the lot. Companies like Ross or Marshalls are filled with closeout apparel from other brands, and flash sale sites like Gilt and Bluefly operate similarly online.

Cloud computing: Using Internet-based computing rather than local networks or your computer's own storage. Many companies like Amazon, Dropbox, iCloud, and Google offer cloud computing options, which allow multiple users access to the same files and applications over the Internet.

Compensation: The overall package of pay and benefits that you get from your employer in exchange for the work that you do, including not just salary but also health benefits and any additional perks (which hopefully you've negotiated for), like transportation reimbursement.

Compound interest: A "snowball effect" for your money. This is the money you make off the interest on the money you are investing. That means it's really "interest on interest," which will snowball over time and make an investment or loan grow at a much faster rate than regular ol' interest.

Concentration: This is how much of your business is dependent on a particular client or partner. It's expressed as a percentage, and you want to keep it as low as possible so you don't depend on too few clients or partners in order for your business to stay afloat.

Consumer acquisition: What happens when you successfully persuade a consumer to purchase your company's products or services.

Contract, at-will: If two parties sign an agreement that lays out certain terms, such as an employment contract, it is understood that the company can't force you to work; that you are doing so "at will," regardless of the terms of the contract. It also means they can fire you "at will," even if the contract is for a set period of time.

Contract, implied: Even without a signed agreement, two parties can enter into an implied contract by their behavior. For example, when you go to the dentist, it is implied that the dentist will use her best knowledge to fill your cavity, even though she didn't promise to do so in writing.

Copyright: This is a law that protects intellectual property, giving creators of books, music, and films the exclusive right to publish, sell, reproduce, or otherwise use the material for a set amount of time. (Fun fact: All works published in the United States before 1923 are in the public domain, aka not subject to copyright. Works published after 1923, but before 1978, are protected for ninety-five years from the date of publication. For works created, but not published, before 1978, the copyright lasts for the life of the author or artist plus seventy years.) Anyone else who wants to use the material must pay a licensing fee to the owner of the copyright. When that set amount of time is up, the work is considered in the public domain, which means anyone can use it fo' free.

Corporation: If you're starting a business, you can do so without incorporating. But as your business grows, you don't want to be held personally responsible should the you-know-what hit the fan. So you form a corporation (or "incorporate") so that it's your company—not you, as an individual—that is held responsible. A corporation is its own living, breathing thing: it can enter into contracts, hire employees, borrow and loan money, and pay taxes—all of that fun stuff you can do, but without dragging your personal name and assets along (that's a good thing especially if it gets dragged through the mud).

Corporate entrepreneur: An innovator who develops new businesses, products, services, or processes within a company that create value for the company while still operating within its existing structure.

Cost-benefit analysis: A method for making a sound business decision. First you determine what the benefit of an action—say, a software purchase—is, and then you subtract the cost to see if it's worth it.

CPA (certified public accountant): This numbers pro who will help you do your taxes and may assist in other areas of your financial life, like investing and retirement. If you're an individual or a smaller shop, you can likely handle these yourself (perhaps with assistance from software like TurboTax). But as soon as you grow large enough to have payroll, it's a good idea to meet with a specialist and make sure you're doing it right to avoid getting slapped with fines from Uncle Sam down the road. When looking for an accountant, make sure they have this designation.

Crowdsourcing: Getting info or news from a group of people, usually on the interwebs, e.g., asking your Facebook friends for recommendations for a small-business accountant.

Crowdfunding: Raising money from people online on sites like Kickstarter.

C-suite: The top executives (C = *chief*) of a company, which can include the CEO, CFO, CMO, CRO, CTO, and others.

D

Debt: Also known as borrowed money, whether for yourself—as in credit card debt, student debt, or a mortgage—or for your business. Not all debt is created equal. You can take on debt for legitimate reasons—in the case of business, to build your company's beta website, to purchase necessary office equipment, to get a license that's essential to open your particular venture. If you are responsible with your debt and make your payments on time, it can be a great way to grow your business. But if you are irresponsible with it and make late payments (or don't pay at all, aka default), you can end up with interest payments, scare off potential investors, and worse yet, end up in bankruptcy.

Deck: A presentation that you create, typically in PowerPoint or PDF, to present or pitch your idea or business to colleagues or investors in a cohesive, organized way.

Default: Failure to make payments on a loan. You'll likely get charged big penalties, and if the loan was for a particular item, like a car or a piece of office equipment or even the actual office space, you could lose it—hello, repo man. Seriously. Those loans are secured loans, where the item is collateral that the bank takes if you don't pay up. Defaulting on unsecured loans (like credit cards) can lead to wage garnishment, which is when money is forcibly deducted from your paycheck to pay the loan.

Deficit finance: Financing an endeavor or a business by borrowing money (from investors, friends and family, or your own bank account).

Deliverable: The product or service that is the result of a specific project. For instance, if you promise a client that you will deliver six new widgets by the end of the month, those widgets are the deliverable.

Demographic: A particular sector of the population, such as millennials or suburban housewives or female business owners. For our purposes, this will be your business's target consumer.

Depreciation: When something loses value over time. Something that depreciates is typically an actual item, like a car or computer—they lose value/ relevance soon after you purchase them. For example, used cars depreciate by 15–20% of their value the second you drive them off the lot. This is the D in EBITDA. (*See also:* EBITDA)

Dilute: Just like you'd weaken a strong drink, when you weaken your ownership position by giving away too much equity to investors, you are diluting the power and control you ultimately have over the company.

Direct reports: The staff who report directly to you. Your direct reports may have people junior to them who report directly to them, and so on.

Disrupt: When you are so innovative that you shake up the status quo. It's a good thing, as opposed to being disruptive, which is just annoying.

Dividend: One of the things a company can do with its profits is give them to the shareholders in the form of cash; this is called a dividend. Getting cash is nice, and thus so are dividends. Even better, as earnings grow, companies can give out more dividends, which is even nicer. I often say that investing in yourself will pay dividends later on. You'll hear it used in that context, and it means that the work you put into something now will allow you to reap the rewards later.

Double taxation: In a C corp, both the business and the employees are taxed (double taxed). In an S corp or a partnership, only the employees are taxed (not double taxed).

Drop ship: Instead of keeping inventory, a retailer will take a customer's order and pass it along to a manufacturer who will then ship the product directly to the customer.

Duck: Unlike an eagle, who is set to soar, a duck will complain about how much work sucks without making an effort to change anything, because "that's how it's always been done." (*See also*: Eagle)

E

Eagle: An eagle flies over the crowd and finds solutions to problems rather than merely complaining about them, like a duck would. (*See also*: Duck)

Earned income: Income that comes from wages, salaries, tips—in other words, money that you've earned and that is taxable.

Earnings: Not to be confused with revenue, this is the amount of profit that a company takes in over a given period of time *after* taxes, expenses, etc. So it's effectively the amount of money the company actually makes (bottom line) versus revenue (top line), which is everything the company brings in. (*See also*: Bottom line, Revenue)

EBITDA (Earnings Before Interest, Taxes, Depreciation, and Amortization): EBITDA is another way to look at profits. It's a term you'll hear a lot if you are starting a business, so know what it stands for (there are different versions, like EBIT and EBITA, depending on the business). The better this number is, the better the company is doing.

EIN (Employee Identification Number): It's like a Social Security number for corporations in that it ties together a company's taxes, debts, contracts, etc.—and keeps a record of them over time. When you form a corporation, the federal government issues you one.

Elevator pitch: Your thirty-second description of your business, concept, or brand—something short and sweet that you can explain in the time it takes to ride the elevator. Whether you're starting a business or carving out your niche at work, you must have one of these.

E-mail marketing service: An online company, like MailChimp or Constant Contact, that helps businesses to create e-mail marketing campaigns targeted to users who are most likely to purchase a particular product or service.

EQ: Emotional intelligence, as opposed to IQ, or intellectual intelligence. EQ is all about understanding other people, reading their signals, and reacting appropriately. A high EQ is a must for any Boss Bitch, whether she's born with it or proactively develops it over time.

Equity: Also known as having "skin in the game." You invested money in the company in exchange for shares in that company, so you now have a stake in it (and how it performs over time). You can have equity in a public or private company.

Estimated taxes: If you are a sole proprietorship, your clients will pay you in pretax dollars, which mean you'll be on the hook to pay Uncle Sam quarterly estimated taxes. *Estimated* is the key word here; it's tough to predict how accurate these taxes are, especially during the first year or two of your business, so it's a good idea to set aside 25% or so of each check you receive for the purpose of taxes. That way, if you end up with a larger-than-expected tax bill at the end of the year, you'll have the funds to cover it.

Exit strategy: Your script for the final act of your business. This is the means by which you will cash out of your investment in your business, for instance, by selling to or merging with another company. This strategy can and will change over time as your business grows and objectives change, but Boss Bitches always have a plan for when it's time to take a bow.

F

Financial planner: Someone who gives you financial advice and guidance to help you meet your long-term monetary goals. They may be certified or just have been at it a long time. A good financial planner should be knowledgeable in all of the different aspects of your financial life including taxes, estate planning, and retirement, but remember, they aren't experts in those areas. Think of them as a manager of a band and you're the rock star. They outsource to people who focus in those specific areas (e.g., accountant, investment manager), which means you have to pay them but also the specialists they might bring on.

Finder's fee: A fee paid to someone who makes introductions between an investor and a business owner, resulting in an investment in the company or other financial benefit (like a matchmaker for entrepreneurs and investors).

Fire sale: The type of sale you might have to undertake to sell off your company and all of its assets if it's damaged, i.e., in major financial distress. The idea is to sell off all of the parts of the business that you can, piece by piece and often at heavily discounted prices, in order to recoup some of your losses, pay off your creditors, and close up shop. (*See also*: Exit strategy)

Fiscal year (FY): It's the special twelve-month calendar that a company uses for preparing financial statements and drawing up their accounting. Whereas the calendar year runs the same year in and year out (January 1 to December 31, obvi), the fiscal year in the US typically runs from October 1 to September 30 of the following year. The fiscal year is written as the year in which it ends, so FY2017 will begin on October 1, 2016, and end on September 30, 2017, and is broken down by quarters, written Q1, Q2, Q3, Q4.

Fixed costs: These are costs that don't change over time, such as your rent or mortgage. It's the same payment every month. (*See also:* Variable costs)

FOMO: Stands for "fear of missing out." Seeing all of your friends' vacation pics on social media can give you a wicked sense of FOMO. Seeing other Boss Bitches get ahead at work while you're just spinning your tires should also give you FOMO.

Form 1040: The standard federal (IRS) tax return form for individuals.

Founder: The person who starts a business or company.

Franchise: A type of license that allows a business owner to have access to a larger business's secret sauce (processes, trademarks, and marketing) in order to carry out a subsidiary product or provide a service under the business's name. The best example here is fast food: if you open a Pinkberry franchise, you are getting a license to run your Pinkberry with the larger company's support in exchange for paying initial start-up and annual licensing fees (and agreeing to play by their rules).

FSA (flexible spending account): You can put money in an FSA on a pretax basis to cover medical expenses not covered by your insurance, such as copays and contact lenses, as well as child-care expenses. The downside is that any money you don't use on qualified expenses is lost, so you have to estimate carefully what you think your health-care expenses will be throughout the year—and then make sure to use it all up before the year is out so you don't forfeit your tax break. (*See also:* Health savings account)

Funding round: A start-up company gets its initial capital funding in rounds. If you're lucky, you'll get all you need to get up and running with a single round of financing, but many companies have to go back to investors for additional rounds as they grow and their objectives change. (*See also:* Capital)

G

Going public: What happens when a privately held company has an Initial Public Offering (IPO), where it sells shares to outside investors for the first time.

Golden parachute: A contractual guarantee that an executive at a company will get hooked up with stock options and other perks even if they get fired.

Goodwill: The value of an organization's reputation. Like your own, it's priceless.

Google AdWords: Google's online advertising program, which features tutorials about targeted online marketing and tools for creating ads and tracking traffic. Kind of like your analytics dashboard, only for advertising (and making money!).

Gross income: How much money you make before taxes. The salary you agreed to in your company's offer letter is typically in gross income, so before accepting a job offer, you should factor in taxes to get the amount you will actually be taking home each paycheck.

Gross margin: Subtract the cost of making something (manufacturing, etc.) from the revenue you get from that product, aka the markup, and voilà! Gross margin.

H

Headhunter: Not some guy with a spear who wants to make soup out of you; this is a recruiter who has been hired to fill a position at a company.

Hedge: To act in such a way so as to reduce risk.

Hostile takeover: When one company acquires another one by force, typically by bypassing management (or replacing management altogether) and going directly to that company's shareholders. This can happen when they buy substantial amounts of stock, thus buying the company from the bottom up. The key characteristic here is that the company being taken over (also called the *target*) doesn't want the deal to go through, while the company doing the taking over (also known as the *acquirer*) is doing everything it can to make the deal happen.

HSA (health savings account): An account into which employees can choose to put pretax money from their paychecks to cover high health insurance deductibles and other noncovered medical expenses, like copays and contacts. Unlike an FSA (flexible spending account), any unused money in the account rolls over to the next year and earns interest that is also tax-free. If you've got money left in your HSA when you turn 65, you get to spend it on anything you want. (*See also:* Flexible spending account)

I

Influencer: A person with clout in a particular industry (e.g., Mark Zuckerberg in tech or Diane von Furstenberg in fashion).

Initial Public Offering (IPO): An IPO occurs when a company sells stock to the public for the first time. It's essentially the debutante ball for a private company announcing that it will now let anyone buy into it. The buzzy IPOs tend to be well-known consumer platforms (B2C, which is business-to-consumer) like Facebook, but all sorts of companies go public that you haven't heard of (including B2B, where businesses sell to other businesses). It's also a time when founders make actual cash and not "paper money," or equity that hasn't been liquidated. (*See also:* B2B, B2C)

Innovation lab: A smaller start-up-type department within an existing company. This could be a department that is spearheading a brand-new product or taking the company in a new direction, but still reporting to the same executive team (like Google's department for Google Glass), or it could be an actual company under an existing company that has its own leadership, product, or software (like Current at General Electric, which is the company's clean technology subsidiary).

Instrument: No, not that thing you played in the fifth-grade band. In this case we're talking about a financial product, like stocks. Think of it as an "instrument" for making more moolah! (*See also:* Stock)

Interest: It's what you pay when you borrow and what you receive when you lend. Interest rates are determined by market conditions and the condition of the borrower (aka you or your company). The better the condition of the borrower, the lower the interest rate—which is why your credit score is vitally important when you want to do something like take out a mortgage or a business loan.

Intern: A trainee, often a college student, who works for job experience in exchange for a minimal salary or hourly rate or for school credit. Internships provide a way for businesses to hire help at no or low cost, and for young people to get some experience under their belts in an industry in which they're interested: a win/win. Note: If school credit is not available for the intern, you must pay them at least the state minimum wage. Interns cannot work for free. This is against the law.

Internship: A short-term job, often during the summer, that allows students and recent graduates a chance to learn the ropes at a company for pay or college credit.

In the black: Means your company is profitable—congrats! This term brings us to Black Friday, because it's typically the day that retailers hit their target sales numbers, bringing them out of the red (negative earnings) and into the black (positive earnings = hooray!).

In the red: A term for when your company is in the negative earnings zone—not good, but also not necessarily bad as long as you don't stay there too long. Sometimes companies need to go "in the red" to invest in longer-term growth, so they can kill it "in the black" later on.

IQ: Intellectual intelligence (aka book smarts) as opposed to EQ, which is emotional intelligence (aka people smarts). (*See also:* EQ)

IRA: Stands for "individual retirement account." The money you put in is tax-deductible now, but you will have to pay income tax on it when you make a withdrawal. Unlike a 401(k), which is offered through your employer, an IRA is yours and yours alone.

IRS (Internal Revenue Service): Your favorite guy: the tax man/Uncle Sam. The IRS is the government agency charged with collecting and enforcing taxes and coming up with all of those crazy rules and regulations.

Itemized deductions: This is why you save all those receipts during the year, *especially* if you're in business for yourself. If your expenses amount to more than the standard deduction, then you'll want to "itemize" your taxes (you can only do one or the other). Eligible expenses include mortgage interest; state, local, and property taxes; medical expenses; business travel and entertainment; home office equipment and supplies; and charity donations (this all appears on Schedule A on your federal Form 1040).

Iterate: What you should always be doing, in business and elsewhere. It means that you are continually repeating a process, tweaking it slightly each time depending on what you learned from it the time before, with the purpose of meeting a desired goal, target, or result. You might iterate on an idea, honing the concept until you get it "just right," or you might iterate on an entire business model, repeatedly improving upon it until you get to the most successful version.

J

Joint venture: When two or more parties join forces to achieve a particular goal, or when two existing businesses contribute equity toward a new business. Like "going halfsies" in the business world. If you go into a joint venture with a friend or other individual, what you're forming is called a *general partnership*. Just know that in this case, if your partner makes a bad financial decision, you'll be on the hook just as much as she is.

K

Key (wo)man insurance: A life insurance policy taken out by a company on the life of the founder or CEO or other person without whom the company could no longer function. The policy is meant to pay off the company's debts and provide severance to employees in the event that, God forbid, something happens to that essential or "key" person.

Keywords: The most relevant and descriptive words to describe your business that will help steer search engine users to your website or advertisement.

L

Leverage: A tool that gives you extra weight in a negotiation, like using a job offer from another company to get your boss to give you a raise or promotion at your current job.

Liability: Something you're on the hook for. You might think of liabilities as obligations that will need to be settled at some point. Spent 100 bucks on your credit card? Well, you know you've got to pay it someday. That's now a $100 liability. Take out a business loan? That's a liability, too. (Office space and equipment you bought with it are "assets," even if they might not feel that way.) (*See also*: Balance sheet)

Liquidity: Your ability to pay now; having liquidity means you have cash. Note that even the wealthy can sometimes be illiquid if they own an illiquid asset (for example, real estate, sports team, land) that can't be turned into ready cash the moment they need it; after all, it takes a while to sell big stuff like a house!

LLC: A limited liability company is a business structure that is set up to shift the liability from you as an individual to your new business. Laws vary by state, but in general, LLCs can be formed by any business or group of people. Members are not protected from the liability of another member. (*See also*: C corp, S corp)

LLP: A limited liability partnership. This type of business setup is generally restricted to professionally licensed individuals, such as lawyers and accountants. Members are protected from the liability of another member.

Loan-out corporation: A popular way for actors, musicians, writers, and the like to get paid. It's an arrangement where the person is technically an employee of their own business (it can be an LLC, S corp, or C corp), and the company or person writing the check is doing business with that structure in exchange for "loaning out" your acting or performing services.

M

Margin: The difference between the cost of making something and the price it's sold for. In other words, it's the markup.

Market share: The percentage of a market a business holds, such as iTunes's 64% market share of digital music downloads.

Mass e-mail senders: There are two kinds: Free software allows you to send bulk e-mail and track which recipients opened it so you know who's read your note. Paid services also allow you to track people who unsubscribe and/or click through any links inside the e-mail, which is a good way of telling if your e-mail was persuasive in getting recipients to do what you wanted them to do.

Mentor: Someone you know or just someone whose path or career or work ethic or vision you admire and who inspires you to follow a similar path to achieve your own goals.

Minimum viable product: A product that has just enough features to gather valuable insights from customers while still in development, aka while in the beta version of that product. You often see this with the initial launch of a smartphone app: the simpler version comes out first, then once the company has seen how it does and has worked out the kinks, a fancier (and often more expensive) version of the app follows. Also known as MVP (not the most valuable player . . . because that, of course, is *you*.)

Mission statement: A statement that defines your or your company's goals.

Mompreneur: A Boss Bitch mom who runs a business from home while raising her family.

N

Net income: An individual's or a company's total income after deductions, credits, and taxes are factored in. In a few words: it's the amount of dough you're actually bringing home.

Net margin: This is how much of our revenue you have left after expenses (interest and taxes, too) have been factored out. It's a percentage. If you have low expenses, you'll have a higher percent net margin because you'll be keeping a bigger piece of the margin pie when all is said and done.

Network: As they say, "Behind every strong woman is a group of other strong women who have her back." Your network is this group of women (and men) with whom you have formed a connection to work and conspire, and help each other in a professional (but also sometimes personal) capacity.

Networking: Getting out there and meeting other people who can help you achieve your business goals. Remain open-minded and you never know who you might meet—or the impact they might have on your career.

Noncompete: This is a clause an employer may put in an employment contract to prevent you from working for a competitor for a fixed period of time after you leave (whether voluntarily or because you were fired), such as six months or a year after leaving the company.

Nondisclosure agreement (NDA): Also known as a *confidentiality agreement*, this legal document tells an employee that they shouldn't talk about confidential work stuff outside the office—and outlines the consequences for doing so.

Nonsolicitation: This is a clause built into an employment contract that prevents you from poaching the company's clients and employees after you leave.

O

On brand: Making sure everything you do in your business—marketing, sales, talking to customers, even the colors you use—is relevant to the company's goals or message.

Operating costs: The day-to-day expenses of running a business, including things like rent, payroll, software and equipment needs, and utilities.

Outsourcing: Hiring people to do tasks for you so you can focus on your core business and make the most of your precious time.

P

P&L statement: *P&L* stands for "profit and loss." We like the *P* but hate the *L*. It's also called an "income statement." Companies have P&Ls to show how much money they've made and how much money they've spent. Your online bank statement is like your very own P&L. Sometimes it can be very good or very bad. PS: Sometimes people will confuse the abbreviation and say *PNL*. That doesn't exist (I would know. . . .), so don't be that person.

Partnership, limited: This is a slightly more protective option than a pure partnership. One of you is the general partner, responsible for running the business and also handling any liabilities that might come your way; the limited partner does not have a say in running the business but does share in the company's profits (as well as shouldering potential losses).

Patent: A government license issued by the US Patent and Trademark Office that gives an inventor or other patent holder exclusive rights to a new design or product or process for a specific length of time (twenty years in the US).

Phoner: A phone interview. That is, one in which you won't have the advantage of using your body language to convey your ideas, so you need to make sure you're on point and on message (and have strong cell reception!).

Pivot: Sometimes the best strategy is to change direction on a dime, or pivot, to a more successful approach or idea.

Pretax earnings: A company's earnings after expenses have been deducted from revenue but before taxes have been taken out. (*See also*: EBITDA)

Principal: Not the person whose office you might have been sent to for passing notes in class, but the total amount borrowed on a loan, and/or the amount you still owe on that loan, separate from interest. So if you took out $10,000 in student loans at an interest rate of 4.66%, your principal for that loan is $10,000. A few years down the road, when you have paid off some of the loan and have $6,000 remaining, then $6,000 is your new principal.

Privately held business: A company that is owned by one or more individuals rather than publicly traded on a stock exchange.

Profit: Repeat after me: profit = total revenue − total expenses. Once you have overcome the expenses, costs, and taxes needed to sustain your business, the rest of the money coming in is profit.

Pro forma: Think of it as looking toward the future. In investing, it's a way of figuring out financial results based on current or projected earnings.

Pro rata: Giving something out proportionately. For example, let's say you own 75% of your company, your friend owns 20%, and your sister owns 5%. You guys get 100 bucks and decide to give it out "pro rata": you would get $75, your friend would get $20, and your sister would get $5.

Proof of concept: Showing that your idea or business is viable and likely profitable over the long term, especially to investors. You want to do your homework ahead of time and go into any meeting armed and ready with proof.

Publicly traded company, aka public company: A company that anyone can buy into (i.e., buy shares of on a stock exchange). This company has already had its "coming-out party" by joining the stock market via an initial public offering (IPO). The biggest advantage to going public is the ability to sell stock (which can make the company, its employees, and its shareholders a lot of money). But the downside is that it opens the door to increased regulations and less control for the company's founders and majority owners. (*See also*: IPO)

Purchase order: Also known as a "PO." If you have an actual product, this is the amount of your product that gets ordered from a company who wants to sell your stuff. While a big PO is usually a cause for celebration, start-ups often struggle trying to finance or fulfill a large order that could help them "make it big"—so don't break out the bubbly too early. You've gotta fulfill the order first!

Q

QA: Quality assurance, i.e., the measures you take to make sure that the product or service you're offering is the way it's supposed to be.

Qualitative: Measuring something by its qualities—characteristics, behaviors, overall performance—rather than how much of it is on the market.

Quantitative: Measuring something by its quantity—volume, frequency, market saturation—rather than how it behaves or how well it performs.

R

Registration: Getting a company name or brand name trademarked so that you can use it exclusively, which gives you an advantage over the others in your market and legally prevents competitors from using your name or brand without permission.

Revenue: The total amount of money a business receives before expenses are deducted. Because a profit and loss statement (also known as a P&L) starts with revenue, revenue is sometimes called the *top line*. (*See also:* P&L)

Reverse auction: A type of auction in which sellers bid for the prices at which they are willing to sell their goods and services. So let's say you're a whiz at photo editing. You might go on a site like Upwork and bid on the listings from people looking for freelance photo editing services by offering the amount you are willing to be paid for doing the work. At the end of the auction, the person who's willing to do the same work for the lowest amount typically wins.

ROI (return on investment): This is the money you make back after investing in something. It's a good indicator for whether or not the initial investment makes good business sense. You want this number to be as high as possible, because that means you're getting the maximum bang for your investment buck. But the "return" part doesn't always have to be tangible. If you invest in a kick-ass web developer who creates a site that helps to successfully launch your business, you can consider the investment in that person a great ROI (even if there isn't an exact value to assign to the website just yet). Your favorite LBD (little black dress, duh) might also have a good ROI; if you wear it once per week and it makes you feel like a boss, then you're likely getting a pretty solid return on that $150 you shelled out for it.

Roth IRA: Like a regular IRA, it stands for "individual retirement account." The Roth part is one whose contributions are not tax-deductible, but you can take the money out tax-free (because you pay taxes now). Unlike the regular IRA, you don't have an age cutoff to stop investing, and you don't actually have to withdraw money like you do with a regular IRA. The catch is that if you are lucky enough to make $133K if you're single, or $184K if you're married, you earn too much to play the Roth game.

Royalties: Money for your brainchild: if you write a book or an article or a piece of music, you will get a royalty for every purchase or download of your product for a set amount of time (depending on the way your contract is set up). So those car commercials featuring catchy tunes? Yep—they're shelling out beaucoup bucks to those performers and the songwriters every time they air.

S

Schedule C: It's the page on your IRS Form 1040 on which you can list and deduct your business expenses—aka, the first place you hit up to brain-dump those receipts you've been saving all year (ahem!).

Schmuck insurance: Not actually insurance, this is a way to structure the sales of a product or line of business while keeping your hand in the financial cookie jar by, say, keeping 10% or 20% ownership of that product in case the new owners do really well with it.

Schtick: Your signature thing that makes you memorable and stand out within a crowd or industry.

S corp: The full name is Subchapter S corporation, named for the part of the IRS code that defines it. This is a way to incorporate your business (and shift the liability away from you and onto the business) without being double taxed as you would be in a regular corporation, in which business tax comes out of the company and personal tax comes out of your income. Instead, profits and losses pass down to you as the shareholder, so you report them on your personal tax return. In other words, you pay taxes on every dollar the corporation earns (after all deductions have been calculated). An S corp must have no more than one hundred employees and must also be owned in the US of A; no foreign ownership.

Seed money: Aka *seed funding,* or the money you use to help you get your small business off the ground. You'll likely get your seed money from friends and family who believe in you and your dream (that's why your first round of fund-raising is often called the *friends-and-family round*). If you're not lucky enough to have a supportive community around you, you'll probably turn to your savings or your credit cards for money to make your company grow, baby, grow.

SEO: This acronym stands for "search engine optimization," and it's how you can get your website presence seen by more eyeballs.

SEP IRA: Stands for Simplified Employee Pension plan. It's a variation of an IRA just for businesses. The most important difference between a SEP and a 401(k) is that 100% of the contributions are made by you as the employer, not your employee. As of 2016, you could contribute up to 25% of an employee's compensation up to $265,000 for a maximum contribution of $53,000 (25% of $265K is $53K, so that's the max you can put in).

Series A: The first round of funding for a start-up after the initial seed funding, or friends-and-family round. (*See also:* Seed money)

Severance: Compensation a company pays employees who are laid off or leave the company for reasons other than "for cause," aka you didn't fuck up but you had to go anyway due to a company reorganization or simply not being the best fit for the job.

Share: The amount, or "stake," that you have in a company in which you own stock; also the unit used to measure stocks. For example, if you own 50% of a company that has one hundred shares in circulation, you own fifty shares.

Share economy: An economic model in which people share something they own with people who need it and charge money for that transaction, such as renting out your home on Airbnb or offering the use of your vehicle on Lyft.

Shareholder: The owner of stock in a company. If the company does well, they stand to make moolah—and sometimes big moolah. But if the company does poorly, then shareholders have the potential to lose money, too. Your stake in the company as a shareholder depends on how many shares in that company you own—the more shares you own, the greater your stake. The person who owns the majority of the shares is called the *principal shareholder.*

Side hustle: An additional job or passion project that you take on to make extra money on the side of your day job.

SIMPLE: While the name makes you believe it's "simple," it's not. It stands for Savings Incentive Match Plan for Employees. It's another cousin of an IRA, like the SEP. Unlike with a SEP, however, the employer and employee (if you have one hundred or fewer employees who earned at least $5K or more in salary) both contribute. The contribution limits are lower than with a 401(k): $12,500 if you're under the age of 50, and $15,500 if you're over the age of 50 (so about $3,000 to $5,000 less than a 401[k] depending on how old you are). (*See also:* SEP)

Small Business Administration (SBA): The US government agency set up to help entrepreneurs with loans, grants, and other forms of support.

Solo 401(k): If you don't have any employees, you can look at investing in a solo 401(k), which is really just a one-woman 401(k), but one that you control. If you work for yourself and you're killing it, you should look at this as a great retirement vehicle for yourself. You control the costs and the investment options. But they are more advantageous than a regular 401(k) because there is a far higher contribution limit. In addition to the $18,000 you can invest annually as an employee—the same limit you'd have in a regular 401(k)—as an employer you can add matching funds up to 25% of your compensation for a total of up to $53,000 in 2016. So you're reaping both the employee and employer benefits for yourself (and your spouse, if you have one).

Stickiness: A measure of how memorable a product or company name is to a consumer. You want your name and idea to be as sticky as possible!

Stock: A share, or stake, in a company. As a shareholder, you own part of the corporation's assets and earnings—so you're (technically) a part owner! Your stake in the company depends on the number of shares you own relative to the total number of shares (so, sadly, your one hundred shares of Apple probably won't get you into the next shareholders' meeting). Stocks are also the "meat and potatoes" of most investment portfolios and have outperformed most other investments historically. Publicly traded stocks have a ticker symbol to identify them and trade on—you guessed it—the stock exchange. (*See also:* Share, Shareholder)

Stock, common: The lowest priority stock in a company. You may or may not see dividends (aka get money back) depending on what the company's board chooses to do. If a company's assets are liquidated, common stockholders are the last ones to get paid. (*See also*: Dividend, Liquidity)

Stock, preferred: The highest priority stock in a company. If you have this type of stock, you get dividends paid out regularly, and they are usually of a fixed amount, as well as being guaranteed. (And yes, in this case you might actually be invited to that shareholder's meeting). (*See also*: Dividend, Shareholder)

Sweat equity: It's the best advice you'll ever get in business: outwork everyone. *Sweat equity* is a measure of how much you and only you invest in your company by working at it, not just taking cash from the outside and looking pretty. It's said that your sweat equity will pay off most in the long run. It's kinda like if you own a home, and you decide to go to Home Depot and redo your kitchen yourself before selling the house for a profit. You've upped the value of your home by working at it yourself instead of paying someone else to do it.

Sweatworking: A new trend that involves networking and exercise at the same time! Instead of grabbing a drink or scheduling a lunch date, meet your colleague for a run. You can talk biz and get your workout in—everyone wins.

Synergy: When the combination of two ideas or companies results in great value and performance is better than the sum of the individuals or companies. This can apply to two departments or even two people working together for a better result, too—basically a fancy word for the old adage "Two heads are better than one."

T

Tax deduction: Expenses like health insurance and contributions to tax-deductible retirement plans like an IRA or a 401(k) that are not subject to taxation. If you deduct those payments from your taxes, you are essentially lowering your total tax liability, or amount of money for which you are on the hook to pay taxes. (*See also*: IRA, 401[k], Liability)

TFRP (Trust Fund Recovery Penalty): This is what the IRS slaps you with if you, as an employee, willfully fail to withhold or pay employment taxes. The amount of the penalty is equal to the unpaid income taxes plus the employee's portion of the withheld FICA taxes. Aka you'll pay way more than if you had just withheld taxes properly in the first place.

Tombstone: The basic info interested people (i.e., investors, potential shareholders) get about a company before it goes public. (*See also*: IPO, Shareholder)

Trademark: A symbol or phrase that is recognizable as belonging to a specific brand, like the Golden Arches belong to McDonald's. You have to research and register for one, and it can be very expensive—but also very valuable should others try to enter your same market with a similar brand or idea. While your trademark is pending, you can use the ™ symbol next to your idea. Once that registration is approved and finalized, you can start using the ® mark. (*See also:* Registration)

Turnover: Another way of saying net or total sales.

U

Underwater: This is what happens when the amount of an outstanding loan is more than the thing you borrowed it for is worth. For instance, if you take out a $300,000 loan to start up your business, but your idea flops and the value of your assets (including office space, equipment, and software) now has a market value of only $250,000, your company is considered underwater (by $50,000—eek).

Unicorn: A start-up with no track record that is valued at more than a billion bucks. Think Facebook before it went public.

V

Valuation: Measures how much something is worth, now or in the future. There are different ways to value companies: some are tied to profits, while some are tied to other metrics like how many users the product or service has. In the tech world, you often see companies like Facebook or Twitter valued in the billions of dollars with no profits because their "valuation" is based on a strong user base.

Variable costs: These are the costs that change over time, like the price of gas or your monthly utility bill. (*See also:* Fixed costs)

Venture attorney: A lawyer who specializes in the ins and outs of getting a new business, or "venture," off the ground. This person will help your budding business with things like incorporating and fund-raising.

Venture capital: This round of fund-raising comes after you've sought the seed money to get your business off the ground. And if you need it, you will have to give up some control of your idea and company to the venture capitalist or a venture capital firm giving you the, well, capital. The VC will give you the money you need only if they think you have potential (i.e., ability to make *them* money).

Vertical: Refers to a category of business. On my show, *Hatched,* each episode is a different product "vertical": one week it's pet food, one week it's cosmetics, one week it's food products, etc.

Vesting: A schedule that a company gives you for stock or matching funds in your 401(k) that you don't see the benefits of all at once but rather accumulate over a period of time. If you leave the company before that period, say five years, is up, you may get only a *portion* of the money you would have gotten if you'd stayed the whole five years and become fully "vested."

W

White knight: A company or person that swoops in during a hostile takeover to buy a company and does so on terms that are favorable to that company (like letting the management stay in place) when another company attempts a buyout. (*See also:* Hostile takeover)

White space: Borrowing from the idea of a printed page—white space is where there is no print—in business, it's the space in an industry or a market for a new business to enter. If the market is saturated, there is no white space. If there's no one else doing what you're proposing to do, then that white space is yours for the taking!

Work groups: Smaller groups or teams within your workplace.

Y

Year on year: Measuring the current value of something, such as a business, against its value exactly a year earlier to see how (and ultimately why) the business has performed as it has.

Z

Zombie company: This ill-fated company needs to be put out of its misery: it keeps trudging along and draining resources, even when it's basically done-zo and looks like death.

ACKNOWLEDGMENTS

Behind every successful woman is a tribe of (mostly) other women who have her back. I'm one lucky bitch to have such an incredible tribe behind me, without whom *Boss Bitch* would not be possible.

So, first, the tribe: Lo Bosworth, Kara Council, Michelle Edgar, Megan Fong, Michelle Ghent, Mike Giordano, Jessica Gordon, Mindy Grossman, Paige Kearin, David Madden, Daphne Oz, Lisa Oz, Michelle Pulfrey, Shachar Scott, Andrew Siegel, Steve Seigel, Elizabeth Stephen, Paula Sutter, Nigel Travis, Jaclyn Trop, Lauren Wallack, Randi Zucker-berg. And my badass agents Courtny Catzel . . . and a couple of guys who don't mind being called Boss Bitches, Tyler Kroos and Andy Stabile.

And a special shout-out to:

Steve Troha, the flyest book agent in all of the land who has proudly been the only male Rich Bitch and Boss Bitch in every room. Here's to many Bitch books to come!

Talia Krohn, my (extremely) patient superstar of an editor. It's an (extremely) hard job to manage me and edit my work, but you took the challenge and crushed it. To you and the entire (mostly female!) Crown Business team: I bow down to your greatness and am so grateful that you believe in me and the Boss Bitch mission.

Nicole Wool, my ride-or-die Golden Girl. If we go down, we go down together—when we said *best friends*, we meant forever.

Ellen London, my wifey, my soul sister, my better (at everything) half. To never giving up. ("And if you do give up, fuck you.")

INDEX

ALSO BY NICOLE LAPIN

RICH BITCH
A Simple 12-Step Plan for Getting
Your Financial Life Together...Finally

Available in Paperback and E-book

"Let Nicole be the doctor for your financial health and
you will feel better in more ways than you'd think."

—Dr. Oz, host of *The Dr. Oz Show*

Rich Bitch rehabs whatever bad money habits you might have and
provides a plan you can not only sustain, but also thrive on. You won't
feel deprived but rather inspired to go after the rich life you deserve,
and confident enough to call yourself a Rich Bitch.